INTERSECTIONS OF AGEING, GENDER AND SEXUALITIES

Multidisciplinary international perspectives

Edited by
Andrew King, Kathryn Almack and Rebecca L. Jones

First published in Great Britain in 2019 by

Policy Press
University of Bristol
1-9 Old Park Hill
Bristol
BS2 8BB
UK
t: +44 (0)117 954 5940
pp-info@bristol.ac.uk
www.policypress.co.uk

North America office:
Policy Press
c/o The University of Chicago Press
1427 East 60th Street
Chicago, IL 60637, USA
t: +1 773 702 7700
f: +1 773-702-9756
sales@press.uchicago.edu
www.press.uchicago.edu

© Policy Press 2019

British Library Cataloguing in Publication Data
A catalogue record for this book is available from the British Library

Library of Congress Cataloging-in-Publication Data
A catalog record for this book has been requested

978-1-4473-3302-9 hardback
978-1-4473-3303-6 ePdf
978-1-4473-3529-0 ePub
978-1-4473-3530-6 Mobi

Cover design by Policy Press
Front cover image: istock
Printed and bound in Great Britain by CPI Group (UK) Ltd, Croydon, CR0 4YY
Policy Press uses environmentally responsible print partners

Contents

Acknowledgements

As editors of this book we would like to acknowledge and thank a number of people. First, we would like to thank all those individuals who attended and/or presented at the conference Intersections of Ageing, Gender and Sexualities (IAGES), which was held at the University of Surrey, UK, 6–7 July 2015. This conference, which was supported by funding from the Institute of Advanced Studies, University of Surrey, formed the basis of this book and many of its chapters were initially presented there. Many thanks must go to all the authors who have contributed to this collection and been understanding and responsive throughout the process. Much thanks also goes to Laura Vickers-Rendall at Policy Press, who has always been helpful, encouraging and patient during the process of the writing, editing and producing this book. Finally, we would also like to acknowledge the important contribution of Sue Westwood, who was central to the organisation of the IAGES conference and the initial stages of this book.

Acknowledgements

Notes on contributors

Kathryn Almack is Professor of Health and Family Lives in the School of Health and Social Work, University of Hertfordshire, UK. She is a sociologist whose research addresses family lives, health and well-being across the life course. In the past decade her work has had a substantial focus on lesbian, gay, bisexual and trans (LGBT) older people, ageing and end of life care. She has completed a number of funded projects and published widely in this area. Findings from her research have been used to develop new resources for practitioners and policy makers. She is co-editor of *Older Lesbian, Gay, Bisexual and Trans People: Minding the Knowledge Gaps* (with Andrew King, Yiu-Tung Suen and Sue Westwood, 2018) and on the editorial board for the British Sociological Association journal *Sociology*. She is currently researching lesbian parenthood as part of a longitudinal qualitative research project.

Elham Amini completed her PhD in sociology of health and gender at Durham University, UK, in 2017. She has a BSc degree (midwifery) from Tehran University of Medical Sciences, Iran, and two Master's degrees: one in women's studies from Alzahra University, Iran, and the other in sociology and social research methods from Durham University. Her work focuses on the gendered and sexual experiences of Iranian Muslim menopausal women through a life history biographical narrative approach and by highlighting menopause, ageing, notions of the body, and medicalisation in relation to sexuality and gender, articulates women's understanding of and from their menopausal bodies.

Elizabeth Barry is Associate Professor in English at the University of Warwick, UK. She is the author of *Beckett and Authority* (2006), and has edited issues of *International Journal of Cultural Studies* (2008), *Journal of Beckett Studies* (2008), and *Journal of Medical Humanities* (2016). Her interests lie in and between modernist narrative, performance, medicine and ageing. She has held two Arts and Humanities Research Council grants to work with doctors and healthcare providers, using literature and performance to investigate ageing, illness and mental health.

Toni Calasanti is Professor of Sociology at Virginia Tech, USA, where she is also a faculty affiliate of both the Center for Gerontology and Women's and Gender Studies. Her research on the intersections of age, gender and social inequalities has appeared in several journals in aging and sociology as well as in the books *Gender, Social Inequalities, and Aging* (co-edited with Kathleen F. Slevin, 2001), *Age Matters: Re-Aligning Feminist Thinking* (co-edited with Kathleen F. Slevin, 2006) and *Nobody's Burden: Lessons from the Great Depression on the Struggle for Old-Age Security* (co-edited with Ruth. E. Ray, 2011). Recent explorations of the intersectional approach and of age, gender and sexuality appear in the *Handbook of Theories of Aging* (2009, 2nd ed) and the *Routledge Handbook of Cultural Gerontology* (2015), which lay the foundation for her present research on same-sex partner caregiving.

Raffaella Ferrero Camoletto is Associate Professor in Sociology of Culture at the Department of Cultures, Politics and Society, University of Turin, Italy. Her research focuses on two main areas: body, gender and space in emerging urban sports and critical perspectives on masculinities and (hetero)sexualities, with a specific focus on the social impact of Viagra. She is currently working on the research project 'Ageless sexuality? Intersecting "positive/active ageing" and the medicalization of sexuality'. Among her recent publications: (with C. Barrett and E. Wentzell) 'Challenging the "viagratization" of heterosexuality and ageing', in C. Barrett, S. Hinchliff (eds), *Addressing the Sexual Rights of Older People: Theory, Policy and Practice* (2017); (with C.Bertone), 'Medicalized virilism under scrutiny: expert knowledge on male sexual health in Italy', in King A., Santos A.C., Crowhurst I. (eds), *Sexualities Research: Critical Interjections, Diverse Methodologies and Practical Applications* (2017).

Vanessa Fabbre is Assistant Professor at the Brown School at Washington University in St. Louis, USA, where she also holds an affiliated faculty appointment in the Department of Women, Gender, and Sexuality Studies and is a faculty scholar at the Institute for Public Health. She received her PhD from the University of Chicago and is a licensed clinical social worker. Her research explores the conditions under which gender and sexual minorities age well and what this means in the context of social forces such as heteronormativity, heterosexism, and transphobia. She is also interested in critical perspectives on social work practice and interpretive methodology in the social sciences.

Julie Fish is Director of the Centre for Lesbian, Gay, Bisexual and Trans Research at De Montfort University, Leicester, UK. She has conducted research and published in the areas of lesbian, gay and bisexual health and health inequalities for 20 years. She has been a member of several Department of Health advisory groups on sexual orientation and gender identity. Her collection, edited with Kate Karban, was published in 2015 by the Policy Press, *Lesbian, Gay, Bisexual and Trans Health Inequalities: International Perspectives in Social Work*. She has recently completed a study, funded by Macmillan Cancer Support, and conducted in five British hospitals: Fish, J., Williamson, I., Brown, J., Padley, W., Bell, K. and Long, J. (2018) *'More than a Diagnosis': Promoting Good Outcomes in Lesbian, Gay and Bisexual Cancer Care: A Qualitative Study of Patients' Experiences in Clinical Oncology*.

Mark Hughes is Professor of Social Work and Chair of Academic Board, Southern Cross University, Australia. He has worked as a social worker in community health, aged care and mental health settings in Australia and the UK, and has previously worked as a social work academic at the University of Queensland, the University of New South Wales and Goldsmiths College London. He is a former editor of *Australian Social Work*. Mark's research interests focus on the organisational dimensions of social work, social work practice with older people, and the ageing experiences of lesbian, gay, bisexual, transgender and intersex (LGBTI) older people. He is currently involved in research on the health disparities faced by LGBTI older people, as well as strategies to reduce gay and bisexual men's experience of loneliness.

Karen Hvidtfeldt is Associate Professor at the University of Southern Denmark. She works in the border area between critical cultural studies, gender studies and health sciences, and applies cultural analytical methods to issues related to health, illness, reproduction, sexuality, gender and the body. Her research examines literature, film, digital and social media, and includes independent and collaborative studies on transnational surrogacy, motherhood, family and age. She heads the research project 'Medicine Man: Media Assemblages of Medicalized Masculinities' funded by Independent Research Fund Denmark from 2018–2021.

Rebecca L. Jones is Senior Lecturer in Health at The Open University, UK. She researches in the areas of ageing, sexuality and, especially sexuality in later life. She has published widely on topics including ageism and age discrimination, imagining personal ageing, older women's talk about sex, bisexuality, LGBT issues in health and social care and LGBT ageing. She chaired the Centre for Ageing and Biographical Studies at The Open University for 10 years, overseeing its long-running seminar and publication series with the Centre for Policy on Ageing. She is a founder member of BiUK, the UK national organisation for bisexual research and activism (www.biuk.org), is one of the authors of *The Bisexuality Report* (2012) and is best known for her work on ageing and bisexuality.

Jamil Khan holds a Master's degree in critical diversity studies and is a PhD candidate at University of the Witwatersrand, Johannesburg, and has completed an Honours degree in psychology at Stellenbosch University. Previously, he has worked as a content writer and journalist for various publications and corporate entities. His research interests include race and power dynamics between oppressed groups in South Africa.

Andrew King is a Professor of Sociology in the Department of Sociology, University of Surrey, UK, where he is also Co-Director of the Centre for Research on Ageing and Gender. Andrew has published widely in the field of LGBT ageing. His monograph, *Older Lesbian, Gay, Bisexual Adults: Identities, Intersections, Institutions* was published by Routledge in 2016. He is co-editor (with Kathryn Almack, Yiu-Tung Suen and Sue Westwood) of the ground-breaking collection *Older Lesbian, Gay, Bisexual and Trans People: Minding the Knowledge Gaps* (2018) and has published in a wide range of journals. Andrew's research projects cover different aspects of LGBT ageing including housing and social care. His current project, funded by the Norface consortium of European Research Councils is examining intersectional life course inequalities among LGBTIQI+ people.

Kinneret Lahad is Senior Lecturer at the NCJW Women and Gender Studies Program at Tel Aviv University, Israel. She had been involved in various prestigious research projects, which merited international attention and publication in leading journals. Her research interests are interdisciplinary and span the fields of gender studies, sociology and cultural studies. Her book *A Table for One: A Critical Reading of Singlehood, Gender and Time* was published in 2017. Her current projects include independent and collaborative studies on aunthood, friendships, feminism and emotions, feminist age studies, egg freezing, solo dining and belonging.

Maricel Oró Piqueras is Associate Professor at the Department of English and Linguistics, University of Lleida, Spain. She has been a member of research group Dedal-Lit since 2002, when it started work on the representation of fictional images of ageing and old age. Currently she is conducting research on British contemporary writers such as Kazuo Ishiguro, Julian Barnes and Deborah Moggach, and on the portrayal of ageing and old age in TV series. She has published in journals such as *Journal of Aging Studies* and *Journal of English Studies*.

Finn Reygan is Chief Research Specialist at the Human Sciences Research Council (HSRC), Extraordinary Associate Professor in Educational Psychology at the University of the Western Cape, and Visiting Senior Research Fellow at the Wits Centre for Diversity Studies, University of the Witwatersrand, Johannesburg. Previously he has held posts as deputy director (seconded) in the Department of Basic Education of the South African government; principal investigator on a two-year, Southern Africa study on homophobic bullying in schools; and research manager at GALA (Gay and Lesbian Memory in Action), an LGBTI civil society organization. His work engages issues of power, privilege and difference especially in Southern Africa and education systems and he publishes widely in the field.

Anna Siverskog has a postdoctoral position at Jönköping university, Sweden, and a PhD in Ageing and later life, from Linköping University. Anna's research focuses LGBTQ ageing through a framework of critical gerontology and feminist and queer theory. It explores how notions of gender, age and sexuality intersects and ties in to life course expectations.

Yvette Taylor is Professor of Education at University of Strathclyde, UK. She received a Fulbright Scholarship, Rutgers University (2010–11) and formerly held a senior lecturer post at Newcastle University. Yvette has published four sole-authored books based on funded research: *Working-Class Lesbian Life* (2007); *Lesbian and Gay Parenting* (2009); *Fitting Into Place? Class and Gender Geographies and Temporalities* (2012) and *Making Space for Queer Identifying Religious Youth* (2015). Edited titles include: *Educational Diversity* (2012) and *The Entrepreneurial*

University (2014). Yvette edits the Palgrave Gender and Education series and co-edits the Routledge Advances in Critical Diversities series.

Feliciano Villar is Professor in the Department of Cognition, Development and Educational Psychology, University of Barcelona, Spain, where he coordinates a research group and directs the Master's degree in psychogerontology. His research interests lie in two main areas: the study of the determinants and social and personal consequences of older people's participation in family and community contexts; and the policies and practices of long-term residential settings with regard to providing residents with opportunities for participation and guaranteeing their rights, including sexual rights. He has authored more than 80 papers in peer-reviewed journals and has been visiting scholar in more than 10 international higher education institutions, including the University of Oxford (UK), Wilfred Laurier University (Canada), University of Twente (Netherlands) and the National Autonomous University of Mexico.

Jill Wilkens achieved her PhD at London South Bank University in January 2017. Her PhD research continued to explore the experience of habitus dislocation and the importance of affinity groups for older lesbians and bisexual women. Jill is currently a tutor at the Northern College in South Yorkshire, UK, where she teaches on the PGCE and BA courses within the teacher-education department.

Foreword

Sara Arber
Centre for Research on Ageing and Gender,
University of Surrey

Over the past decade there have been profound societal changes in attitudes towards and institutional practices regarding sexualities and gender identity. The legalisation of same-sex marriage is just one example, but others include increasing public discussion about trans individuals. Within the field of ageing, the lives of lesbian, gay, bisexual and trans (LGBT) individuals, the analyses of sexualities and of trans ageing have been largely neglected. This insightful and timely edited collection successfully redresses this imbalance, while also offering new insights into the dynamic interrelationship of ageing, gender and sexualities.

A novel aspect of the book is that it critically examines not only the intersections of ageing and sexualities, but also the interconnections of gender and sexualities in later life. The chapters provide a nuanced illumination of the intersections of ageing, gender and sexuality, while also considering the importance of intersections with other sources of social division, including race, ethnicity, social class and disability. These are not only discussed as representing sources of social division, but also representing relations of power, privilege and oppression.

A particular feature of ageing is the impact of the cohort in which individuals were born, and the ways that institutional changes throughout their life courses have influenced their early lives and later life experiences. For LGBT elders, feelings of dislocation and 'unbelonging' may have accompanied them throughout their lives and continue to influence their later years. Key concerns are how normative expectations may have been disrupted and reformulated.

This edited collection clearly shows there can be no single understanding of ageing, but a need to understand the various contours shaping diversity among older people. It is equally important not to homogenise the 'category' of older people, but seek to understand their unique experiences that may be patterned by gender, sexuality, social class and ethnicity, as well as historical and societal contexts. The book highlights the ways that intersections of ageing, gender and sexualities are influenced by societal context, in particular through the international nature of the collection with chapters from a wide range of countries, including Australia, Iran, Italy, South Africa and Spain.

By taking a multi-disciplinary approach, *Intersections of Ageing, Gender and Sexualities* highlights how various disciplines provide depths of insights into a range of inequalities associated with gender and sexualities in later life. Multi-disciplinarity is fundamental to the book's organisation around four key themes. Chapters in the first theme focus on ways of theorising gender and sexualities in later life, including intersectionality theory and queer theory. The second theme explores the impact of culturally dominant representations of ageing and how these affect and are resisted by different groups of elders. The third theme illuminates how the alterative and often unexpected ways that power, privilege and oppression influence experiences of ageing according to gender and sexuality. The final theme focuses on the important area of health and well-being, including how dominant ideas of sexual health and well-being are gendered and heteronormative.

This thought-provoking collection questions existing ideas and perspectives relating to ageing, gender and sexuality. It offers novel insights of central relevance for researchers, policy makers and practitioners within the field of ageing and also within gender and sexuality studies. An important empirical and theoretical collection, it provides insights and exemplars that will have a lasting influence on scholars and practitioners in the field of ageing.

Series editors' preface

Chris Phillipson (University of Manchester, UK)
Toni Calasanti (Virginia Tech, USA)
Thomas Scharf (Newcastle University, UK)

As the proportion of elders worldwide continues to expand, new issues and concerns for scholars, policy makers, and health and social care professionals emerge. Ageing in a Global Context is a book series, published by Policy Press in association with the British Society of Gerontology, which aims to influence and transform debates in what has become a fast-moving field in research and policy. The series seeks to achieve this in three main ways. First, by publishing books which rethink the key questions shaping debates in the study of ageing. This has become especially important given the restructuring of welfare states alongside the complex nature of population change, with both elements opening up the need to explore themes that go beyond traditional perspectives in social gerontology. Second, the series represents a response to the impact of globalisation and related processes, which have contributed to the erosion of the national boundaries that originally framed the study of ageing. From this has come the emergence of issues explored in various contributions to the series: for example, the impact of transnational migration, cultural diversity, new types of inequality and contrasting themes relating to ageing in rural and urban areas. Third, a key concern of the series is to explore interdisciplinary connections in gerontology. Contributions provide critical assessments of the disciplinary boundaries and territories influencing the study of ageing, creating in the process new perspectives and approaches relevant to the 21st century.

Given this context of increasing complexity that accompanies global ageing, we are pleased to be able to include in the series a book, one of the first of its kind, which takes a serious, interdisciplinary look at the intersections of power relations based on age, gender and sexualities. Editors Andrew King, Kathryn Almack and Rebecca L. Jones have brought together chapters that explore these intersections (as well as those related to other marginalised positions, such as race and ethnicity) from multiple disciplines, including sociology, social work, health, gerontology, policy studies, psychology, gender and sexualities studies, and socio-legal studies. The chapters employ various lenses to illuminate different concerns relating to ageing, gender and sexualities, thereby foregrounding the issues and perspectives of marginalised and often invisible populations. The different theoretical approaches, the explorations of power, privilege and oppression, the examinations of representations and the focus on health and wellbeing all serve to expand knowledge of the ways that age, gender and sexuality influence elders, regardless of their particular social location. In so doing, the book affords us some guideposts through which we can examine the complex kaleidoscope of elders' experiences. As such, this volume comprises essential reading for scholars, policy makers and practitioners interested in understanding and intervening to improve the quality of life of elders too often homogenised by the moniker of 'old'.

ONE

Introduction: intersections of ageing, gender and sexualities

Andrew King, Kathryn Almack and Rebecca L. Jones

Introduction

This book aims to encourage thinking about ageing as it relates to (at least) two other key aspects of people's lives: their gender and their sexuality, or more precisely how ageing, gender and sexuality co-construct one another. This first chapter explains how this book emerged and developed, its key themes and structure. In so doing, the chapter will discuss intersectionality, multi-disciplinarity and why, as editors, we think this is a timely and important collection.

There have been suggestions that ageing societies will entrench social divisions and inequalities, thereby exacerbating social tensions, while others see ageing societies as having considerable potential to promote and increase social inclusion and integration. Considerable research has been conducted on the interrelationship of ageing and gender (Arber and Ginn, 1991; Calasanti and Slevin, 2001; Cook-Daniels, 2006), as well as gender and sexuality (Jackson, 2006; Taylor et al., 2010) and, more recently ageing and sexualities (Cronin and King, 2010; Almack et al., 2010; Jones, 2011). However, there has so far been little interrogation of the interconnections of ageing, gender and sexualities, or more precisely their intersectionality. There is a need to fully address the complexity of intersections among and between these forms of social division, identity, (in)equality, power and privilege, and how they produce uneven outcomes in later life for different people and in different contexts. This also necessitates exploring how the intersections of ageing, gender and sexualities are informed by intersections with other social divisions, such as, but not limited to, race, culture, ethnicity, dis/ability, social class and geographical location.

Taking intersectionality and multi-disciplinarity seriously

Since its inception in black feminist scholarship in the late 1980s, intersectionality has been influential across, and been explored beyond, disciplinary boundaries. It has been described as a 'threshold concept' (Launius and Hassel, 2015), since it helps us to understand interlocking forms of oppression and privilege and how these are manifested at both structural and everyday levels. At its simplest, intersectionality points to how categories of identity and social division co-construct one another, such that an understanding of one is incomplete without a thorough assessment of how it is lived in relation to others: for instance, how an understanding of gendered and racial oppressions and discriminations are incomplete without an analysis of both (Crenshaw, 1993; Hill-Collins, 2000).

Intersectionality is not used in this book to look specifically at the oppressions that come from gender and race alone, although we recognise the importance of this interlocking axis. Instead, we are following important work that has utilised intersectionality and made important contributions to exploring the relationship between class and sexuality (Taylor et al., 2010) and to the exploration of ageing sexualities (Calasanti, 2009; King, 2016). By drawing on intersectionality and its important insights, the book demonstrates that thinking about ageing is incomplete without a concomitant focus on other forms of social division, such as gender and sexualities, among others. Intersectionality maybe a threshold concept but it is also a multifaceted one, especially how it is employed methodologically. In this book a number of authors utilise intersectionality or approaches which point towards it in a variety of ways. Indeed, taking intersectionality seriously means exploring these interconnections across a range of contexts/settings; in short, it emphasises the importance of taking both a multi-disciplinary and international perspective.

A number of the chapters in this book utilise an intersectional lens to explore the connections between ageing, gender and sexualities, but not all. Indeed, we believe it is a strength of this collection that a range of different theoretical approaches are utilised. What does unite them all, however, is a desire to move beyond simplistic notions of ageing and to take a critical, interrogative approach to the relationship between ageing, gender and sexualities. Furthermore, as May (2015) has indicated, any attempt to advance knowledge about the intersection of ageing, gender and sexualities must be multidisciplinary too. This book certainly does that, with contributors emanating from sociology, gerontology, social work, social policy, politics, psychology, gender and sexualities studies, socio-legal studies, and health, social care and social policy. The book is therefore multidisciplinary in its organisation, range and scope, and target readership. It brings together scholars from a range of disciplines in the social sciences and humanities and speaks to a range of concerns relating to ageing, gendered, sexualities across and between those disciplines. We believe a strength of this book is the way that readers can explore the relationship between ageing, gender and sexualities from different disciplinary angles, while thinking how those differences can be transcended by reading beyond one's discipline.

Similarly, it is important to understand ageing, gender and sexualities from an international perspective; in other words, not to prioritise voices or perspectives from the global north, at the expense of others (Connell, 2007). We are therefore particularly pleased to include in this collection a chapter based on fieldwork undertaken in Iran and another discussing the South African context. These chapters expand our understanding of the intersections of ageing, gender and sexualities by making clear the significance of global and national politics in framing discursive and cultural resources, providing useful contrasts to more Western-centred chapters. Moreover, we are also very pleased to be able to move beyond the Anglophone focus of much ageing, gender and sexuality research by including work from such countries as Denmark, Israel, Sweden and Italy, thereby adding to cultural and regional intersectionality of Western-centred studies too. Readers should also keep in mind when reading all these chapters: where does this knowledge come from, in whose name is it written, whose voices are heard and whose are not?

This book is primarily aimed at academics, providing thought-provoking interjections into existing ideas about intersectionality, ageing, gender and sexualities. It will also be a useful teaching resource to illustrate the transdisciplinary nature of intersections and how ageing, gender and sexualities are interconnected and mutually constituted. The book will also be of considerable interest to social policy makers who are concerned with the changing dynamics and needs of ageing societies, as well as those concerned with gender dynamics/inequalities and with those associated with sexualities.

Key themes of the book

There are four broad themes in this book and we have consequently sectioned it according to those themes. The first theme concerns the way that theory can illuminate our understandings of the relationship between ageing, gender and sexualities. We have already explained why intersectionality theory is important, but other theories and theoretical perspectives are drawn on throughout this book. Some of these theories, such as queer theory, are more associated with the deconstruction of gender and sexualities and have been applied less often to ageing. Others, such as the practice theory of Pierre Bourdieu, are often more associated with social class. However, in this book, authors demonstrate how Bourdieu's ideas can usefully be applied to the embodied ways that ageing, gender and sexuality intersect with class, status and power. De Beauvoir's feminist scholarship is revisited and revised, especially as it applies to ageing and a number of chapters re-emphasise the importance of taking a life-course perspective, to look back and forward, noting (dis)connections and points of difference.

A second theme involves the significance of representations of ageing, gender and sexualities. This is principally and explicitly explored through the (re)analysis of literary texts, as well as the textual analysis of online web columns and magazine articles. Close reading of these texts demonstrates the ways in which people both draw on and resist culturally dominant representations of ageing, gender and sexuality. They also suggest possibilities for new imaginings. However, many of the chapters across the book deal in one way or another in how ageing, gender and sexualities are re-presented in different forms and ways – whether that be through statistics, texts, visual images or broader cultural imaginaries.

The third theme of the book relates to power, privilege and oppression. As one would expect with a book that has intersections in the title and which emphasises the importance of taking the relationship between ageing, gender and sexualities seriously, the ways that these categories of identity and social division are shaped by power is a key theme across many of the chapters in the collection. Power is constituted here in many guises – whether in the form of patriarchy, the choreography of the interview, how some older people's voices are silenced in institutional settings and how normativity related to ageing, gender and sexualities functions to empower some people and to oppress others.

The final theme relates to issues of health and well-being. Both representations and debates about ageing are often dominated by concerns with the health and well-being of older people. Similarly, sexual health and well-being are gendered and subject to normative constraints. A number of the chapters explore how older people's lives are shaped by dominant notions of good health and positive well-being and also how these are both gendered and subject to ideas about good and bad sexuality.

Structure of the book

The book is structured around the themes identified above and how they exemplify intersections between ageing, gender and sexualities. Part 1, 'Theoretical interpolations', has three chapters which have a strong theoretical focus. Chapter Two, 'On the intersections of age, gender and sexualities in research on ageing' by Tony Calasanti, provides an important discussion of intersectionality and how it can be useful in gerontology. Calasanti develops this with reference to spousal/partner caregiving. Yvette Taylor's chapter is next and is titled 'The queer subject of "getting on"'. Taylor demonstrates the significance of queer theory and challenges ideas about a normative life course and time, using examples from her own research projects and biography. Chapter Four, by Vanessa Fabbre and Anna Siverskog titled 'Transgender ageing: community resistance and well-being in the life course', also adopts a queer theoretical perspective, combining this with a life-course approach. Fabbre and Siverskog summarise the empirical landscape concerning the well-being of trans older adults, present the theoretical perspectives they are using, and then present insights from two social science projects carried out in Sweden and the US.

Part 2, 'Representations', is composed of three chapters, each exploring the way that texts or other media represent the intersections of ageing, gender and sexualities. In Chapter Five, 'Endogenous misery: menopause in medicine, literature and culture', Elizabeth Barry uses a literary source, Virginia Woolf's *Mrs Dalloway*, as a lens to think about cultural representations of the menopause. Barry argues that major feminist writers on the menopause, such as Simone de Beauvoir and Germaine Greer, continue to employ pathologising understandings of the menopause and of the sexuality of older women. Barry argues that Woolf's *Mrs Dalloway* offers scope for a more nuanced and complicated understanding of this underrepresented aspect of older women's lives. The following chapter by Maricel Oró Piqueras is titled 'Representations of female ageing and sexuality in Penelope Lively's *Moon Tiger*, Angela Carter's *Wise Children* and Doris Lessing's "The grandmothers"'. This interdisciplinary chapter takes social scientific findings about common discourses for talking about sex in later life and uses them to explore three contemporary British texts featuring women's later life heterosexual relationships. Oró Piqueras demonstrates that this literature offers new and less binary ways of thinking about women's sexuality in later life. Chapter Seven, the final chapter in Part 2, is by Kinneret Lahad and Karen Hvidtfeldt; '"Last-minute mothers": the construction of age and midlife motherhood in Denmark and Israel' explores the ways in which older 'midlife' mothers employ 'ageing capital' to negotiate around normative expectations about the proper time to become a mother and resist the stigma of being 'too old'. Despite the very different political and cultural contexts of Denmark and Israel, the authors find that similar discourses around good mothering and its relationship to age, gender and sexuality are found in both settings.

In Part 3, 'Dis/empowerments', there are four chapters, which, in differing ways, explore the dynamics of power relationships concerning ageing, gender and sexualities within and across different contexts. Chapter Seven, 'All change please: education, mobility and habitus dislocation' by Jill Wilkens forefronts the central importance of social class and mobility, looking particularly at changes in the education system in the 1940s and the impact of these changes on the classed lives of lesbians and bisexual women born between 1940 and 1958. Drawing on Bourdieu's concept of *habitus dislocation*, Wilkens exposes the difficulties and 'cost' of social mobility including feelings of dislocation and 'unbelonging'. The following chapter, by Elham Amini, 'Insider or outsider? Issues of power and habitus during life history interviews with menopausal Iranian women', also draws on the work of Pierre Bourdieu. Amini explores how power shifts between interviewer and interviewee at different points in the interview (while conducting interviews with older women in Iran) and in relation to different *capitals* and *habitus*. In 'Sexual expression and sexual practices in long-term residential facilities for older people' (Chapter Ten), Feliciano Villar addresses intersections between sexual expression and sexual practices alongside ageing, gender and sexual diversity. Villar identifies how the sexual citizenship of older citizens living in residential care might be limited at these intersections. Finally, in Part Three, Finn Reygan and Jamil Khan's chapter 'Sexual and gender diversity, ageing and elder care in South Africa: voices and realities' addresses the junctures of race and class across urban and rural settings and against the backdrop of the apartheid legacy. They consider implications from a social justice perspective as these factors intersect with the lives of LGBTI elders in South Africa.

Part 4, 'Health and well-being', is the final section of the book and comprises three chapters which explore how different aspects of health and well-being intersect with ageing, gender and sexualities. Chapter

Twelve by Mark Hughes is titled 'Health and well-being of lesbians, gay men and bisexual people in later life: examining the commonalities and differences from quantitative research'. In this chapter, Hughes provides an important overview of current international studies of health and well-being research concerning older lesbians, gay men and bisexual people, but in doing so also highlights important inter-group differences. Hughes shows the importance of exploring intersections of ageing, gender and sexualities using quantitative data. In the following chapter, 'Questioning the sexy oldie: masculinity, age and sexuality in the Viagra era', Raffaella Ferrero Camoletto explores the ways in which Italian medics police the prescription of drugs for male sexual dysfunction by drawing on cultural resources around age and relationship-status appropriate behaviours, including newer notions of 'positive ageing' and ageless sexuality. Chapter Fourteen, 'Intersecting identities of age, gender and sexual orientation in gay and bisexual men's narratives of prostate cancer' by Julie Fish is the final chapter in the book. Fish adopts an intra-categorical intersectional approach, undertaking a fine grained analysis of older gay and bisexual men's experiences of prostate cancer. Fish shows how although they are not privileged by heterosexual gender relations, their narratives do draw on discourses of hegemonic masculinity in contingent and temporal ways.

Significance

We hope that the points we have made so far in this chapter illustrate the significance of a collection of this form. Certainly, many of the chapters in the collection point to the theoretical, methodological and policy ramifications of what they discuss. As editors, it is our assertion that this collection has significance across many disciplines and between them because it demonstrates the multiple and complex ways that ageing, gender and sexualities intersect, at both structural, interactional and subjective levels. A real strength is therefore the possibility of sparking debate in the future and we certainly hope that this is only the first of many publications to explore the aforementioned intersections, alongside others.

References

Almack, K., Seymour, J. and Bellamy, G. (2010) 'Exploring the impact of sexual orientation on experiences and concerns about end of life care and on bereavement for lesbian, gay and bisexual older people', *Sociology*, 44(5): 908–24.

Arber, S. and Ginn, J. (1991) *Gender and Later Life: A Sociological Analysis of Resources and Constraints*, London: Sage Publications.

Calasanti, T. (2009) 'Theorizing feminist gerontology and sexuality: an intersectional approach', in V.L. Bengtson, M. Silverstein, N.M. Putney, et al. (eds) *Handbook of Theories of Ageing*, New York: Springer: 471–86.

Calasanti, T.M. and Slevin, K.F. (2001) *Gender, Social Inequalities and Aging*, Walnut Creek, CA: Alta Mira Press.

Connell, R. (2007) *Southern Theory*, Cambridge: Polity.

Cook-Daniels, L. (2006) 'Trans aging', in D.C. Kimmel, T. Rose and S. David (eds) *Lesbian, Gay, Bisexual and Transgender Aging: Research and Clinical Perspectives*, New York: Columbia University Press: 20–35.

Crenshaw, K. (1993) 'Mapping the margins: intersectionality, identity politics and violence against women of color', *Stanford Law Review*, 43(6): 1241–99.

Cronin, A. and King, A. (2010) 'Power, inequality and identification: exploring diversity and intersectionality amongst older LGB adults', *Sociology*, 44(5): 876–92.

Hill-Collins, P. (2000) *Black Feminist Thought: Knowledge, Consciousness and the Politics of Empowerment*, New York: Routledge.

Jackson, S. (2006) 'Interchanges: gender, sexuality and heterosexuality: the complexity (and limits) of heteronormativity', *Feminist Theory*, 7(1): 105–21.

Jones, R.L. (2011) 'Imagining bisexual futures: positive, non-normative later life', *Journal of Bisexuality*, 11(2–3): 245–70.

King, A. (2016) *Older Lesbian, Gay and Bisexual Adults: Identities, Intersections and Institutions*, London: Routledge.

Launius, C. and Hassel, H. (2015) *Threshold Concepts in Women's and Gender Studies*, London: Routledge.

May, V.M. (2015) *Pursuing Intersectionality: Unsettling Dominant Imaginaries*, London: Routledge.

Taylor, Y., Hines, S. and Casey, M.E. (2010) *Theorizing Intersectionality and Sexuality*, London: Palgrave Macmillan.

Part 1
Theoretical interpolations

Part 1: introduction

As we noted in the introduction to this book, the critical relationship between ageing and gender, ageing and sexuality and gender and sexuality have been investigated in a number of different disciplines for at least the past 20 years. However, we also argued that the intersection of ageing, gender and sexualities, alongside other forms of social division, privilege/oppression and power, have been considered less often and therefore been subject to less debate. The chapters that make up this section of the book all interpolate, or introduce, new insights into the relationship between ageing, gender and sexualities. They do this by drawing on several important theoretical traditions, including but not limited to intersectionality, queer theory and life course theory.

In Chapter Two, Toni Calasanti draws attention to the need for an intersectional approach in gerontology and the sociology of later life. Calasanti urges gerontologists to look beyond singular categories, and indeed beyond approaches which simply add up categories as if that could produce a summation of in/equality. Calasanti argues that an intersectional approach to ageing, gender and sexualities is able to demonstrate the complex, situated dynamics of power as they are refracted through these different, yet related, forms of social division and identity. This is achieved in the chapter by two case studies of spousal caregiving: gender and heterosexual spousal caregiving and same-sex partner caregiving. Calasanti concludes that an intersectional approach to ageing is vital if we are really to understand how contexts shape later life and generate new forms of social justice.

In Chapter Three, Yvette Taylor questions normative notions of time and the notion that life events are on-time or out-of-time, and indeed, the very notion of a life course and how it relates to subjectivity. Taylor's chapter interpolates a number of theories in order to do this. She juxtaposes queer notions of time in the work of Halberstam, with more class-inflected critiques of time emanating from the work of Bourdieu, Skeggs and Adkins. In so doing, Taylor demonstrates how queer times and neoliberal times converge, diverge and intersect. Taylor then demonstrates the usefulness of this theoretical position by reflecting on three cases: queer families, caring and the queering of care, and the queer spaces of academia.

In Chapter Four, 'Transgender ageing: community resistance and well-being in the life course,'Vanessa Fabbre and Anna Siverskog add to knowledge about trans ageing, a much under-researched area and also address this theoretically. They begin by outlining what largely North American studies tell us about trans ageing, before making a theoretical interpolation of their own in order to advance current understandings. Specifically, like Taylor, Fabbre and Siverskog draw on queer theory, but they also include life-course theory as a way to further question the normative conceptions of time that often get reproduced when ageing, gender and sexualities are discussed. Hence, like Taylor, Fabbre and Siverskog demonstrate that theoretical juxtapositions are fruitful to develop our understanding of intersections of ageing, gender and sexualities. Similarly, they then demonstrate the productivity of such theoretical moves, by applying it to their own data regarding older trans people in the US and Sweden. Moreover, Fabbre and Siverskog show how community is important to shaping the life-course experiences of trans people, avoiding reductive and individualistic accounts.

TWO

On the intersections of age, gender and sexualities in research on ageing

Toni Calasanti

Despite its widespread usage in the social sciences, intersectionality remains an uncommon and unclear approach in ageing. This chapter lays out general contours of what an intersectional framework does (and does not) entail, and then briefly applies this approach to explore how age, gender and sexual inequalities might shape spousal/partner caregiving.

Intersectionality

Although intersectionality may be a 'buzzword', it is a somewhat ambiguous and open-ended concept (Davis, 2008). Debates concerning how it should be conceptualised are ongoing (Carbado, 2013), and journals have devoted special issues (for example, *Gender & Society*, 2012; *Signs: Journal of Women in Culture and Society*, 2013; *DuBois Review*, 2013) to them. Still, common themes underlie intersectional frameworks, and these are outlined later.

Scholars and activists had discussed the ways that black women's experiences were rendered invisible or marginalised since the 1960s (Davis, 2008; Collins and Bilge, 2016), but legal scholar Kimberlé Crenshaw was the first to apply the label ‹intersectionality› to characterise these. She used this term to suggest how 'the intersection of racism and sexism factors into Black women›s lives in ways that cannot be captured wholly by looking at the race or gender dimensions of those experiences separately' (Crenshaw, 1991: 1224). Of importance to the discussion here, Crenshaw was drawing attention to the ways in which two *systems of inequality*, race and gender, combine to produce unique social locations and experiences.

Intersectionality is simultaneously a theoretical and methodological approach to understanding inequalities (Choo and Ferree, 2010; Clarke and McCall, 2013); an analytic tool for 'understanding and analysing the complexity in the world' (Collins and Bilge, 2016: 25). It does not only look at different outcomes and what might cause these, nor does it just refer to interactions among variables. What makes an approach intersectional is, first, its explicit focus on social inequalities, such as race and gender; and second, the lens through which these inequalities are explored, one which recognises that, 'people's lives and the organization of power in a given society are better understood as being shaped not by a single axis of social division, be it race or gender or class, but by many axes that *work together and influence each other*' (Collins and Bilge 2016: 2; emphasis added). This dual focus on inequalities and how they are interrelated is what distinguishes an intersectional framework from other approaches to differences.

First, *social inequalities* comprise power relations in which members of naturalised social categories, such as those defined by race, gender, age, sexuality, and class, lose authority, status, and wealth, and are stigmatised by others/those who garner such status. Further, those disparities in life chances are justified as natural, divinely ordained, or rational and thus beyond dispute (Calasanti and King, 2015). These social hierarchies are relational in that the privileges of any one group are tied to the disadvantages of at least one other. Thus, those with privilege are as important to study as are those who are disadvantaged (McCall, 2005; Choo and Ferree, 2010). Caught in relations of power, each is tied to the other.

The naturalisation of social inequalities (for example, women are 'naturally' nurturing, men are 'naturally' aggressive) stems in great measure from their embeddedness in *social institutions*: patterned behaviours, expectations and values that are geared at achieving widely shared social goals, such as reproducing citizens or producing and distributing goods and services. For instance, such social institutions as family or education involve behaviours and values repeated so frequently that they are taken for granted as 'normal'. At the same time, power relations, such as those based on gender, shape such patterns and values in ways that reinforce men's privileges and women's disadvantages.

The second aspect of an intersectional framework relates to *how* it examines these inequalities. The premise is that social hierarchies are interwoven such that, for instance, gender is raced, and race is gendered. Thus, it focuses on the interactions among various categories (Browne and Misra, 2003; Collins and Bilge, 2016), but no one intersection or social location is more important than another (Carbado, 2013). For example, all those bound together within systems defined by gender, sexuality and age need to be included as the explanations that apply to those disadvantaged by these systems also point to ways that others are advantaged.

The relational nature of intersectionality distinguishes it from an additive perspective that implicitly puts together inequalities based on gender and on race and derives a particular 'score' or picture of inequality that translates across groups (Crenshaw, 1991; Carbado, 2013). As an example, and focusing on just these two systems of inequality: a black man and a white woman are each privileged and disadvantaged on one status characteristic, either race or gender. Yet it would make no sense to *equate* their experiences. Indeed, the intersections of generally disadvantageous locations (for example, woman, black or old) can produce relative strengths that would otherwise remain invisible to theory, as in the case of black women's advantages in education relative to black men in the US (US Department of Education, 2017), or women's longevity in old age relative to that of men (Calasanti and Slevin, 2001). Thus, the notion of intersectionality indicates the *simultaneity* of categorical statuses. While any one status might be most salient in a particular context, we experience our gender, race, class, sexuality and age simultaneously.

Finally, intersectional frameworks take social context into account (Choo and Ferree, 2010; Carbado, 2013; Collins and Bilge, 2016). Social inequalities are dynamic, and the meanings of social categories and outcomes will vary by place (local, national, global), time and the like (Browne and Misra, 2003). In the US, for instance, who counts as 'white' has changed over time, often decided by Supreme Court rulings. The ways in which inequalities are related to one another are also contextual and dynamic such that they can be configured differently in varying contexts. Indeed, 'some forms of inequality seem to arise from the same conditions that might reduce other forms' such that strategies that might reduce inequality *between* men and women might increase it *among* women (McCall, 2005: 1791).

Interactions between variables or demographic traits are thus not the same as intersectionality, which is concerned specifically with systems of social inequalities. Viewing gender, for instance, as a demographic or personal attribute is qualitatively different from seeing it as a power relation. This does not mean that other characteristics or variables are not important to the question at hand; they may influence outcomes of interest, but they are not intersections. For example, marital status can influence such things as financial stability or various indicators of well-being in later life. Further, this influence can vary for heterosexual women and men. But marital status *itself* is not a system of inequality. Its impact may derive from the ways that family, as a social institution, is shaped by gender and sexual inequalities. For instance, heterosexual married men have advantages in families, such as not being responsible for domestic labour, that are not shared by unmarried men or married women. However, marriage, while influenced by social inequalities, is not a naturalised power relation in itself and thus not an intersecting inequality, though it can still matter and play another role in a theory.

An intersectional lens to ageing

Why use an intersectional lens? One impetus for an intersectional approach to understanding such inequities comes from the insight that, when we focus on one inequality alone, for example, merely reporting aggregate life chances of such large groups as women and men, we miss opportunities to understand the complex ways in which distributions of income and other resources differ systematically within such groups (McCall, 2005). Similarly, we also miss seeing and theorising inequalities among the lesbian, gay and bisexual population when we focus only sexuality as basis of group membership (Cronin and King, 2010).

If we take age relations seriously, and explore how these intersect with such statuses as gender or sexuality, it means that disadvantage does not double with age but alters in complex ways, which include not only structural constraints but also potential sources of strength or opportunities. For instance, old age is a time of many hardships for women; but being old does not mean that all aspects of womanhood alter in the same ways across different groups of women who are further stratified by such statuses as class, sexuality and race. Older women may find themselves cast aside from sexual markets, less often subject to the compulsory heterosexuality that saddles and exploits younger women. At the same time, they may also find that they are relatively invisible, and have fewer material resources. And this situation varies in complex ways when we further intersect gender with class relations; older women of higher classes may still command significant resources and even be able to stave off the invisibility of later life.

Thus, an intersectional approach moves us beyond observation of difference to specify relations of inequality between groups. Though it implies diverse experiences of ageing, intersectionality does not designate independent groups to be studied separately, but instead *relates* groups theoretically, in terms of institutionalised activities that maintain inequality.

Clarke and McCall (2013: 350) argue that intersectional explanations can be 'constructed at the interface of research that is explicitly intersectional, and that which is not.' That is, one can make use of research that does not explicitly use an intersectional approach by engaging in different interpretations of their findings. This is accomplished 'by putting multiple social dynamics in conversation with one another' (2013: 350) The remainder of this chapter pursues the kind of project they describe, using findings from spousal caregiving research that is both intersectional and that which is not in order to suggest ways an intersectional approach might be fashioned. First, however, is a brief description of the social inequalities highlighted in this chapter.

Age relations

Although gerontologists often assume the presence of ageism, they rarely theorise or incorporate this into analyses of later life experiences. But age categorical status affects life chances. Societies organise on the basis of age such that those who are seen as 'not old' gain privileges at the expense of those deemed 'old'.[1] As is the case with other systems of oppression, old people lose authority, autonomy and status that they had enjoyed in younger decades; are excluded from the networks/institutions in which those with privilege manage money and other resources; are stigmatised and devalued; and those with privilege regard these inequalities as determined by a natural order and thus beyond dispute. For instance, equations of old age with decline and frailty justify limiting the autonomy and authority of old people, who find themselves marginalised in the labour market and then find it more difficult to be heard and to influence decisions made about their bodies (Calasanti, 2003; Calasanti et al., 2006). We see this in relation to formal institutions and medical care, and also with informal care; for instance, when family care providers – spouses/partners, children – intervene in what an elder may or may not do. Their adulthood and rights to decide are denied. And the stigma and exclusion attendant on old age is such that people seek to avoid it at all costs, even distancing themselves from associating with those who are seen to be old (Hurd Clarke, 1999).

Gender relations

Societies organise on the basis of gender such that popular ideals of manhood and womanhood, as naturalised in routine interactions, both stem from and affirm gendered divisions of labour, authority

---

[1] Children are also oppressed by age, but they differ from those who are old in that their position is temporary. By contrast, old people are marginalised forever.

17

and status. Rather than being determined by biology, gender is socially constructed according to what people collectively agree that natural sex attributes mean. 'Doing gender' by appearing competently to conform to the dictates of biological givens influences everyday categorisations, assignments of responsibilities and resources, and thus life chances in the sense of access to further resources (West and Fenstermaker, 1995). Such daily affirmation of difference flows from, and reaffirms, structural inequality.

Gender relations are embedded in social institutions such that they are generally invisible, taken for granted and unquestioned. They become naturalised as they reflect the way that people normally 'do' paid work or family (Calasanti, 2009). For instance, men and women are influenced across their life courses by the ways that families divide and value labour, first through workplace experiences of respect and earnings levels, and later in retirement. Pensions in the global North tend to be based on (white, middle-class, heterosexual) men's occupations and patterns of work, assuming careers in the public realm and unpaid reproductive labour support at home (usually from women). Because men's positions within families are naturalised, most people see men's resultant higher retirement incomes as only fair. At the same time, the different meanings that women and men give to 'freedom' in retirement reflect this unequal division of labour, such that men feel free to pursue a range of activities, in part because of women's domestic labour that they also retain in retirement (Calasanti and Slevin, 2001; Repetti and Calasanti, 2017). Such privilege also tends to remain unquestioned.

Relations of sexual inequality

Often, when scholars talk about relations of sexual inequality, they focus on identity, the discrimination that occurs when one identifies as non-heterosexual. Identity gains its salience and import to the extent that it is tied to systemic inequalities embedded in social organisation.

The labels 'heterosexual' and 'homosexual' only came into common usage and with them, sexual identity and social relations of sexual inequalities, at the end of the 19th century, in relation to changing forms of labour within industrial capitalism (Calasanti, 2009). Moral reformers concerned with disciplining labour and consumption created labels for what they deemed reckless, instinctual and unproductive activity, such as masturbation, prostitution and homosexuality, and they posed these as threats to social order (Greenberg, 1988; Laqueur, 1990; Bristow, 1997). As a basis for social organisation, sexuality was thus distinct from the gender relations of that era that constrained women from professional status and full citizenship (Rubin, 1984).

At the same time, within the present political economy, relations of gender and sexuality reinforce each other in some respects. Within capitalism, reproductive labour is central to production in the public realm; and the gender division of labour assures that women will be responsible for this unpaid, reproductive work that benefits production – men's paid work. The exploitation of women's labour rests on *compulsory heterosexuality* – the set of institutionalised pressures on women to form sexual relationships with men, ranging from social exclusion to eugenics to rape (Rich, 1986). Thus, heteronormativity (norms, beliefs and practices that naturalise heterosexuality), aided by compulsory heterosexuality, helps to shape a social order in which women are to provide unpaid, reproductive labour that benefits men and bolsters their status in the public realm.

In modern societies, people who are categorised as affiliating erotically outside the heterosexual system are often viewed as unnatural sexual deviants, and they are stigmatised and subjected to methods of control including violence. In the US, relations of sexuality govern labour practices and family organisation and thus influence status, income and wealth. For instance, gay men earn less than their heterosexual peers (Baumle et al., 2009), a situation that, until quite recently, was exacerbated by the fact that same-sex marriage was not recognised federally. Although same-sex marriage no longer disqualifies one from such federal benefits and rights as Social Security and Medicare, many states still legally allow other forms of discrimination. Contemporary arguments against eliminating such discrimination often draw from ideologies that maintain that which is not heterosexual is unnatural (in terms of nature or god) or goes against the social good (maintenance of family).

The remainder of this chapter uses this understanding of age, gender, and sexuality to think about a model for exploring how these intersecting inequalities might influence spousal care work in later life. This framework is meant to help us to understand experiences of both marginalised and privileged groups. It begins with a discussion of gender and heterosexual spousal caregiving, and then presents an overview of same-sex partner care to suggest how considering this intersection can alter what we understand to be gendered approaches to care.

Gender and heterosexual spousal caregiving

Spousal care work provides an interesting venue for exploring these intersections as, first, spouses are the preferred caregivers for those who need it (Muraco and Fredriksen-Goldsen, 2014). Second, unlike other caregiving relationships, husbands and wives are quite similar in the amount and type of assistance that they deliver to their spouses (Arber and Ginn, 1995). They also express similar motivations for the care they give, such as love, marital duty and reciprocity.

Still, gender differences also emerge among caregiving spouses, and research, including my own study of 22 spouses who cared for their partners with Alzheimer's disease and related disorders (see Calasanti, 2006; Calasanti and King, 2007), has indicated that husbands and wives differ in their caregiving approaches: how they perceive the tasks, which ones they find troublesome, how they respond to these, and how they deal with stress (Russell, 2004; Calasanti, 2006). I attributed these differences to *gender repertoires*: sets of skills and resources learned over the life course that affirm gender identities formed in relation to the gender division of labour (Calasanti, 2010). For instance, contemporary older men bring a paid work orientation to caregiving, and thus tend toward more managerial styles, performing care work in a more task-oriented, problem-solving fashion (Rose and Bruce, 1995; Russell, 2004; Calasanti, 2006; Calasanti and King, 2007). Here is how one of the men I interviewed spoke of his care for his wife:

> Gil[2] (age 75): 'At first ... you know, you don't know exactly how to do it, take care of a woman. I don't believe anybody would. You just have to pick it up like you do a trade. Like laying brick or finishing concrete. You don't go in there and do it as smooth as you do after you do it for a while. You learn a whole lot of shortcuts that helps you out [on] how to do things. You wouldn't have to go back over it if you do it right the first time.'

Such caregiving husbands report relatively little distress because they focus on tasks and find satisfaction in the accomplishing these, feel a greater sense of control and are better able to compartmentalise the loss of marital reciprocity (Rose and Bruce, 1995; Calasanti and King, 2007; Hayes et al., 2009). When challenges arises, husbands who

---

[2] All interviewee names are pseudonyms.

use problem-focused coping strategies thus report positive caregiving experiences (Baker and Roberston, 2008).

Wives also uphold gender divisions of labour across the life course, which designate them as primarily responsible for such domestic labour as care work. Their previous experiences as caregivers and the emphasis on women's nurturing lead older wives to approach care work with empathy and concern for the care receiver as a whole and with the emotional dynamics of the relationship (Rose and Bruce, 1995; Hayes et al., 2009). Performing physical tasks are important, but they also expect that they will care for spouses emotionally, and effortlessly (Rose and Bruce, 1995; Calasanti, 2006). In explaining their expectations of themselves, most of the interviewed women noted simply that they were used to giving care, and presented their identities as bounded by carework. Janet (age 65) said, "I am basically a caretaker at heart, and so it's kind of my nature ...". Joyce (age 77) simply stated, "I was a mom."

The belief that women are natural caregivers appears to create higher standards against which many women hold their care work, resulting in greater stress when problems arise, including grief for lost emotional relations (Rose and Bruce, 1995; Calasanti, 2006; Hayes et al., 2009). By contrast, men convey that they work hard at giving care but it is not integral to their self-concepts as men; experienced difficulties did not detract from their senses of themselves as competent (Calasanti and King, 2007). Other research also suggests that caregiving husbands will discuss instrumental and less likely affective matters (Russell, 2004), a tendency that also fits with the task- or managerial-orientation.

However, all these findings take for granted that heterosexual gender norms regulate these gender repertoires and the caregiving context. For purposes of this chapter, I focus only on older gay men and lesbians caring for partners. Lesbians and gay men (LGs) are socialised in the same culture and gender roles as their heterosexual counterparts, but same-sex couples may not rely on heteronormative notions of 'husbands' or 'wives' as they engage in their intimate relationships (Heaphy, 2007). They must negotiate their division of labour, including who will perform paid and domestic labour, and how they will share these forms of labour. Given LGs' potentially different relationships to the division of labour, the extent to which the gender repertoires found among heterosexual spouses develop in the same ways and result in particular approaches to care work in non-heterosexual contexts is unknown.

Same-sex partner caregiving

We have little knowledge of the extent to which the finding of gendered caregiving approaches is similar among LG partners, who until very recently have been denied the opportunity to marry. Research on LG populations finds that, just like their heterosexual counterparts, most say that they would turn to their partners, if available, when need for care arises (Heaphy, 2007; Muraco and Fredriksen-Goldsen, 2014). However, our understanding of older partner caregiving remains limited, as most research has been conducted on younger LG populations; even when the focus is on older groups, samples tend to be ages 50 and over (for example, Cantor et al., 2004; Hash, 2006). Given age relations and ageism, and cohort differences among the LGs (Cronin and King, 2010), those aged 65 and over can be expected to represent a qualitatively different group.

Further, research on older caregiving partners has not considered gender relations, and so has not shown how the division of labour might affect gender repertoires and caregiving approaches. Research has found that gay and lesbian couples tend to be relatively egalitarian in relation to domestic labour (Solomon et al., 2005; Peplau and Fingerhut, 2007), though some traditional gender assumptions may be retained (Heaphy, 2007). Thus, gender matters, but differently in contexts of LG-committed relationships. For instance, gay men may develop both the workplace skills and identities noted above, while they also learn aspects of domestic labour that heterosexual husbands are relatively likely to forego, because they cannot assign responsibility for it to wives. But this is also only one possible scenario, depending on how the division of labour is allocated, and personal biography. How such repertoires influence care work may thus show similarities as well as differences among same-sex partners.

Sexual orientation does not influence care receivers' impairments per se (though there may be impacts for gay men living with HIV/AIDS), and studies suggest that caregivers for LG elders have similar needs and challenges as their heterosexual counterparts (Hash, 2006). Still, sexual minority status may create specific challenges for caregiving partners and may shape the resources at their disposal, their responses, and ultimately experiences of stresses. For example, the lack of uniform legal recognition faced by many couples can influence caregiver access to healthcare decision making and visitation. Moreover, discrimination can make partner caregivers reluctant to request services, especially medical or in-home services, even if they can afford these, for fear of neglect, rejection or other humiliations (Cantor, et al., 2004; Brotman et al., 2007; IoM, 2011). Variation in publically acknowledged partner status, as well as partial, contextual or repeated disclosure, can impose additional sources of stress and can limit caregiver advocacy for the care receiver (Brotman et al., 2007; Price, 2010). Finally, gender intersections can mean that older lesbians in particular can lack money to buy services, given labour market discrimination based on both gender and sexuality (Barker et al., 2006; Heaphy, 2007). Thus, caregivers for lesbians may have fewer resources on which to draw for help with their care work.

But scholars have also identified aspects of LGs' lives that might provide resources to caregivers, including the presence of 'families of choice' (non-kin, long-term friends), which play important roles for many LGs (Barker et al., 2006; de Vries and Megathlin, 2009; Muraco and Fredriksen-Goldsen, 2014); resilience born of coping with discrimination; and previous experience with care work as a result of HIV/AIDS (Barker et al., 2006; de Vries and Megathlin, 2009; Muraco and Fredriksen-Goldsen, 2011; de Vries, 2015). This chapter follows Cronin and King's (2010) call to explore the interplay of these challenges and strengths, and how gender and age might further shape these.

Age and partner caregiving

The ageism that results when one is designated 'old' by others can influence caregivers' experiences. For instance, the social devaluation of care work is amplified when it is performed for someone considered 'old' (Calasanti, 2006). Care work for children is simultaneously honoured as important *and* devalued as women's work. It is cheapened that much more when the care is given to an older person – someone deemed to be relatively worthless, lacking the 'future contribution' seen to accrue to children – and when it is also performed by an older person. Ageism also may affect older LG caregivers in unique ways, such as through the potential loss of community support. When research looks beyond families of choice, a significant minority of LGs report feeling isolated from community supports; older gay men in particular feel as if they lack emotional support, and some cite ageism within the gay community as the cause (Shippy et al., 2004; Brotman et al., 2007; Heaphy 2007). Thus, although LG communities provide some support and resources for older members, how these informal supports play out in caregiving contexts in later life remains relatively unknown.

Ageism can also have negative impacts on those who care for partners with Alzheimer's disease and related cognitive disorders (AD), as this disease is often further stigmatised as an old person's condition (MacRae, 2008). In combination with the reasons noted above, caring for a partner with AD results in unique sources of stress. Caregivers for those with cognitive issues are likely to have to meet basic physical needs, deal with co-morbidities and negotiate the medical system, sometimes without legal recognition for their decision making. They also face challenges related to the cognitive impairment itself, such as wandering or other difficult behaviours. For partner caregivers of LG elders, AD may raise additional issues of sexual identity and discrimination as the care receiver may no longer be aware of the relationship with the caregiver. This can be especially important if there are no legal ties between the couple, such as marriage.

A heuristic model

This brief literature review suggests a conceptual framework through which we might see ageing, gender and sexuality as intersecting, relational statuses that apply to everyone, and which necessarily shape spousal/partner caregiving. In this model, sexual orientation and gender intersect to influence the division of labour earlier in life: (1) between paid and domestic labour (other forms of unpaid work are important but not a focus here); (2) within paid jobs, in relation to broad occupational types; and (3) within domestic labour, in terms of amounts and types of tasks performed. Typically, today's older heterosexual men were the primary breadwinners, and older heterosexual women were primarily responsible for domestic labour, a pattern that, despite women's contributions to dual earner families, has not changed radically within the US. Within the paid work sphere, women were segregated into feminised jobs with less autonomy, task diversity and income. In the domestic sphere, men specialised in tasks that were occasional rather than daily, and out of doors rather than in the house. These divisions influenced their repertoires: the identities, resources and skills that accumulate over time.

In positing the importance of the intersections of sexual orientation to this division of labour, and examining same-sex couples who are less likely to divide labour in traditional ways, we expand the list of repertoires in a variety of ways. For instance, same-sex partners might divide their labour such that one person takes the primary breadwinning role and the other domestic labour, or they might divide domestic labour in varying ways, including both doing it or neither doing it, instead hiring others to do it for them. Each of these divisions of labour has implications for the skills and resources that form repertoires. And having the income to pay others to perform domestic labour would depend upon the nature of one's paid labour; and here we see a possible intersection with gender in relation to paid labour. Gay men and lesbians may or may not be employed in male- or female-dominated occupations, with ramifications both for income but also for the kinds of skills and resources one acquires from paid work. In turn, these repertoires influence approaches to caregiving, which situations are challenging or stressful, and which strategies might be employed. People are most likely to find most stressful tasks that do not respond well to their particular skills and resources.

Social support, both formal and informal, is an important resource for care work, and the intersections of gender and sexual orientation may influence sources and extent of such support. Heterosexual couples are more likely than gay couples are to have children who may help give care. However, research suggests that children and other family members often assume that the spouse provides any care required and needs no help. And both children and friends can be reluctant to be involved, even at a distance, when care receivers have AD (Calasanti, 2006).

Other research suggests that husbands gain access to friends and kin relations through their wives, and thus they may lack their own sources of emotional support (Russell, 2004), regardless of the care receiver's condition. Gay men, by contrast, though less likely to have children, may enjoy much stronger sources of support when giving care, based on their strong ties to families of choice. However, as previously noted, ageism may be implicated in varying levels of such support, and such ageism may be felt more quickly by gay men than by either heterosexual men or lesbians. As well, ageism can influence the informal support caregivers receive due to stigma attached to the older recipients of care. In all of these ways, intersections of inequalities affect the ways in which organisations and institutions, from family to social services and medical industries, treat caregivers and receivers in old age. Only by looking through this intersectional lens can we appreciate variation in the ways institutions handle needs of old people.

Conclusion

This chapter has sought to illustrate what an intersectional analysis comprises, how it differs from looking at interactions between phenomena other than inequalities, and what it offers researchers on ageing. In offering a preliminary model for care work, it suggests how an intersectional approach can help us address the complexity of social life; such understanding moves us forward in a quest for social justice. In my example, I have tried to show that, by exploring the intersections of sexual orientation with gender in the context of later life, we can both gain a greater understanding of issues faced by same-sex spousal/partner caregivers, and also expand our understanding of how the heterosexual context influences gendered caregiving experiences. We can better theorise how contexts shape caregiving, how they lead to similar and different sources of reward and stress, and how these relate to similar and disparate caregiver needs. This model reveals that truisms about gender are contextual: women are not naturally nurturing, for instance, and men are capable of providing care that includes emotional labour. Exploring the intersections of gender, sexual orientation and age can demonstrate how contexts shape caregiving experiences, allowing for the development of policies and programmes that understand these, so that, for instance, available social supports for caregivers both speak to their needs and are utilised.

References

Arber, S. and Ginn, J. (1995) 'Gender differences in informal caring', *Health and Social Care in the Community*, 3(1): 19–31.

Baker, K.L. and Robertson, N. (2008) 'Coping with caring for someone with dementia: reviewing the literature about men', *Ageing and Mental Health*, 12(4): 413–22.

Barker, J.C., Herdt, G. and de Vries, B. (2006) 'Social support in the lives of lesbians and gay men at midlife and later', *Sexuality Research & Social Policy*, 3(2): 1–23.

Baumle, A.K., Compton, D.R. and Poston, D.L. (2009) *Same-sex partners: the social demography of sexual orientation*, Albany: SUNY Press.

Bristow, J. (1997) *Sexuality*, London: Routledge.

Brotman, S., Ryan, B., Collins, S., Chamberland, L., Cormier, R., Julien, D. and Richard, B. (2007) 'Coming out to care: caregivers of gay and lesbian seniors in Canada', *The Gerontologist*, 47(4): 490–503.

Browne, I. and Misra, J. (2003) 'The intersection of gender and race in the labor market', *Annual Review of Sociology*, 29: 487–513.

Calasanti, T. (2003) 'Theorizing age relations' in S. Biggs, A. Lowenstein and J. Hendricks (eds) *The Need for Theory: Critical Approaches to Social Gerontology for the 21st Century*, Amityville, NY: Baywood Press: 199–218.

Calasanti, T. (2006) 'Gender and old age: lessons from spousal caregivers', in T. Calasanti and K. Slevin (eds) *Age Matters: Re-Aligning Feminist Thinking*, New York: Routledge Press: 269–94.

Calasanti, T. (2009) 'Theorizing feminist gerontology and sexuality: an intersectional approach', in V.L. Bengtson, M. Silverstein, N.M. Putney and D. Gans, (eds) *Handbook of Theories of Ageing*, New York: Springer: 471–86.

Calasanti, T. (2010) 'Gender and applied research on ageing', *The Gerontologist*, 50(6): 1–15.

Calasanti, T. and King, N. (2007) 'Taking 'women's work' 'like a man': husbands' experiences of care work', *The Gerontologist*, 47(4): 516–27.

Calasanti, T. and King, N. (2015) 'Intersectionality and age', in J. Twigg and W. Martin (eds) *Handbook of Cultural Gerontology*, London: Routledge: 193–200.

Calasanti, T. and Slevin, K. (2001) *Gender, Social Inequalities, and Ageing*, CA: Alta Mira Press.

Calasanti, T., Slevin, K. and King, N. (2006) 'Ageism and feminism: from "et cetera" to center', *NWSA Journal*, 18(1): 13–30.

Cantor, M.H., Brennan, M.G., Shippy, R.A. and Network, P.S. (2004) 'Caregiving among older lesbian, gay, bisexual and transgender New Yorkers', National Gay and Lesbian Task Force Policy Institute.

Carbado, D.W (2013) 'Colorblind intersectionality', *Signs: Journal of Women in Culture and Society*, 38(4): 811–45.

Choo, H.Y. and Ferree, M.M. (2010) 'Practicing intersectionality in sociological research: a critical analysis of inclusions, interactions, and institutions in the study of inequalities', *Sociological Theory*, 28(2): 129–49.

Clarke, A.Y. and McCall, L. (2013) 'Intersectionality and social explanation in social science research', *Du Bois Review*, 10(2): 349–63.

Collins, P.H. and Bilge, S. (2016) *Intersectionality*, Cambridge, UK: Polity

Crenshaw, K. (1991) 'Mapping the margins: intersectionality, identity politics, and violence against Women of Color', *Stanford Law Review*, 43: 1241–99.

Cronin, A and King, A (2010) Power, inequality and identification: exploring diversity and intersectionality amongst older LGB adults', *Sociology*, 44(5): 876–92.

Davis, K. (2008) 'Intersectionality as buzzword', *Feminist Theory*, 9(1): 67–85.

de Vries, B. (2015) 'Stigma and LGBT ageing: negative and positive marginality', in N.A. Orel and C.A. Fruhauf (eds) *The Lives of LGBT Older Adults: Understanding Challenges and Resilience*, Washington DC: American Psychological Association: 55–71 de Vries, B. and Megathlin, D. (2009) 'The meaning of friendship for gay men and lesbians in the second half of life', *Journal of GLBT Family Studies*, 5(1–2): 82–98.

Greenberg, D.F. (1988) *The Construction of Homosexuality*, Chicago: University of Chicago Press.

Hash, K. (2006) 'Caregiving and post-caregiving experiences of midlife and older gay men and lesbians', *Journal of Gerontological Social Work*, 47(3–4): 121–38.

Hayes, J., Boylstein, C. and Zimmerman, M.K. (2009) 'Living and loving with dementia: negotiating spousal and caregiver identity through narrative', *Journal of Ageing Studies*, 23(1):48–59.

Heaphy, B. (2007) 'Sexualities, gender and ageing', *Current Sociology*, 55(2): 193–210.

Hurd Clarke, L. (1999) '"We're not old!": older women's negotiation of aging and oldness', *Journal of Aging Studies*, 13(4): 419–39.

IoM (Institute of Medicine) (US) Committee on Lesbian, Gay, Bisexual, and Transgender Health Issues and Research Gaps and Opportunities (2011) *The Health of Lesbian, Gay, Bisexual, and Transgender People: Building a Foundation for Better Understanding*, Washington DC: The National Academies Press, www.ncbi.nlm. nih.gov/books/NBK64806/

Laqueur, T.W. (1990) *Making Sex: Body and Gender from the Greeks to Freud*, Cambridge, MA: Harvard University Press

MacRae, H. (2008) '"Making the best you can of it": living with early-stage Alzheimer's disease', *Sociology of Health & Illness*, 30(3): 396–412.

McCall, L. (2005) 'The complexity of intersectionality', *Signs: Journal of Women in Culture and Society*, 30(3): 1771–800.

Muraco, A. and Fredriksen-Goldsen, K. (2011) '"That's what friends do": informal caregiving for chronically ill midlife and older lesbian, gay, and bisexual adults', *Journal of Social and Personal Relationships*, 28(8): 1073–92.

Muraco, A. and Fredriksen-Goldsen, K.I. (2014) 'The highs and lows of caregiving for chronically ill lesbian, gay, and bisexual elders', *Journal of Gerontological Social Work*, 57(2–4): 251–72.

Peplau, L.A. and Fingerhut, A.W. (2007) 'The close relationships of lesbians and gay men', *Annual Review of Psychology*, 58: 405–24.

Price, E. (2010) 'Coming out to care: gay and lesbian carers' experiences of dementia services', *Health & Social Care in the Community*, 18(2): 160–8.

Repetti, M. and Calasanti, T. (2017) '"Since I retired, I can take things as they come. For example, the laundry": gender, class and freedom in retirement in Switzerland', *Ageing and Society*, onlinefirst [no pagination].

Rich, A.C. (1986) 'Compulsory heterosexuality and lesbian existence', in *Blood, Bread, and Poetry: Selected Prose, 1979–1985* (1st edn), New York: Norton: 23–75.

Rose, H. and Bruce, E. (1995) 'Mutual care but differential esteem: caring between older couples', in S. Arber and J. Ginn (eds) *Connecting Gender and Ageing: A Sociological Approach*, Maidenhead: Open University Press: 114–28.

Rubin, G.S. (1984) 'Thinking sex: notes for a radical theory of the politics of sexuality', in C. Vance (ed), *Pleasure and Danger: Exploring Female Sexuality*, Boston: Routledge: 267–319.

Russell, R. (2004) 'Social networks among elderly men caregivers', *The Journal of Men's Studies*, 13(1): 121–42.

Shippy, R.A., Cantor, M.H. and Brennan, M. (2004) 'Social networks of ageing gay men', *The Journal of Men's Studies*, 13(1): 107–20.

Solomon, S.E., Rothblum, E.D. and Balsam, K.F. (2005) 'Money, housework, sex, and conflict: same-sex couples in civil unions, those not in civil unions, and heterosexual married siblings', *Sex Roles*, 52(9–10): 561–75.

US Department of Education, National Center for Education Statistics (2017) https://nces.ed.gov/programs/raceindicators/indicator_rec. asp

West, C. and Fenstermaker, S. (1995) 'Doing difference', *Gender and Society*, 9(1): 8–37.

THREE

The queer subject of 'getting on'

Yvette Taylor

Introduction

This chapter aims to address the theme of intersections of ageing, gender and sexualities as matched to – or far from – the particular research projects which I have undertaken, often involving intersections of class, gender and sexuality. In considering what to present at the related conference and write-up in this chapter, I wanted to question (myself), and had to resist (my own), urges to pull data from particular aged research participants, as older or, indeed, younger; certainly I could have done this as my research has usually involved participants across diverse age ranges. In my current project, Making Space for Queer Identifying Religious Youth, I am seeing how *young* people inhabit particular times, places, bodies as aged subjects with certain rememberings of the past and projections for the future (Taylor and Snowdon, 2014a, b; Taylor, 2015). To think of these intersections involves a consideration of the 'queer subject' of 'getting on' in the context of international equalities legislating supposedly making new 'sexual citizens'.

In this chapter I want to explore three cases: 'queer families', 'queer cares' and the queer spaces of academia, to inflect ideas of 'moving on' and becoming as interrupted and interrupting of linear trajectories of, for example, becoming sexual citizenship, becoming adult and becoming academic. I interweave these examples to explore interruptions to normative career-caring trajectories by highlighting work–life balances and the effort of 'getting on' as applied in research–researched–researcher exchanges, experiences and biographies.

To think of 'age' is perhaps often to think of the embodied subject who has aged. On a more collective level, sexualities research is replete with metaphors of 'coming of age', of maturing into disciplines, of appearing in social policies and claiming full-citizenship rights and entitlements, arguably grappling with a new 'world we've won' as sexual citizens (Weeks, 2007). This becoming 'someone' as a self-actualised and entitled subject is apparent within celebrations of the 'world we've won' as lesbian, gay, bisexual, transgender (LGBT) groups and individuals realise sexual citizenship in the realms of family and working lives (Weeks, 2007; McDermott, 2011). In 'arriving' in places of sexual citizenship, young people are often seen as the beneficiaries of previous generations' struggles but they are often simultaneously 'invisiblised' because they are 'not yet' fully in the worlds of family and employment (Taylor et al., 2010; Taylor, 2017).

On an everyday level, particular gendered and sexual subjects are constructed as *on time*, say for reproduction and maternity, planned alongside work–life balance and situated against anticipated life-course trajectories, as endorsed in social policies, institutional practice and normative imaginings. The recent and highly publicised warning by a senior NHS doctor[1] not to wait until the age of 30 to have a baby (or face a 'fertility time bomb') would be an obvious example of the saliency of normative gendered trajectories.

I want to pause on the idea of a 'time bomb' as that which disrupts normative time, which explodes ideas of what is done 'at the right time', and question who, if anyone, can dwell in, or with, what seems like an obviously dangerous construction. In considering intersections of age, sexuality and gender, as bringing forward certain subjects, while rendering others as out of time, backwards, behind and redundant, I want to draw on different projects, in order to empirically situate the 'queer subject of "getting on"'.

First, I introduce some concepts from Bourdieu, and ideas of 'queer temporalities', to explore how normative and non-normative personhood is produced (and ruptured). Next, I consider these research themes, while locating myself in and through research, as inevitably

---

[1] A leading National Health Service doctor in the UK has said that women hoping to conceive should try for a baby before reaching 30 to stop a 'fertility time bomb'. Professor Geeta Nargund warned that fertility issues were placing a "costly and largely unnecessary burden on the NHS" as increasing numbers of women in their thirties and forties sought IVF treatment. She wrote: "I have witnessed all too often the shock and agony on the faces of women who realise they have left it too late to start a family ... For so many, this news comes as a genuine surprise and the sense of devastation and regret can be overwhelming ... Information is power and the best way to empower people to take control of their fertility is through education. Ideally, if a woman is ready for a child, she should start trying by the time she is 30. She should consider having a child early because as a woman gets older, her fertility declines sharply." (www.telegraph.co.uk/news/health/news/11641694/Senior-NHS-doctor-tells-women-have-baby-before-30.html).

intersecting my own cares, biography, and personal and professional identities (as also a queer subject getting on).

Throughout this chapter, I present some examples of what happens when normative time is disrupted: when 'family time' encroaches on 'work time' and makes non-sense of 'work–life' balance; when this is reversed so that the person being cared for is not a child but a grandmother, when the queer feminist academic arrives 'too soon' in academia; when the 'child-as-future-citizen' is placed as needing 'active planning' (and pre-birth) – and when they collide with institutional timelines for maternity recognition and care entitlements.

Theoretical overview

In order to situate the intersecting subjects of 'queer families', 'queer cares' and the 'queer spaces of academia', it is important to think about the place of contemporary neoliberal capitalism in shaping subjectivity, where what is 'normal' is arguably driven by a very particular and narrow mode of being, relating and valuing, driven by competition, inequality and rational self-interest. We will recognise this in – as well as from – academia.

Such a mode of being is also governed by a temporality that values reproductive maturity and wealth accumulation. Adkins (2009; 2012) has argued that capitalism is governed by 'clock time' where certain time scales, cycles and life stages are naturalised and internalised. Conditions of contemporary neoliberalism demand, and thus shape, a future-oriented, enterprising, capital-accruing subject (Skeggs, 2004), operating in an exchange value economy where capital is accrued in the person and generative of future value. Bourdieu (1984) argues that as people move through social space they encounter possibilities for increasing their overall value through the acquisition and formation of capitals, where relationships can be quantified, measured and are exchangeable.

In this model, individual worth is tied to economic and reproductive worth, and relationships are based on exchange value. From a classed perspective, questions can be asked about social inequality, while from a queer perspective we might be concerned with alternative values with queer theorisations of 'strange' temporalities and futurities: ways of relating to people that are not oriented around exchange and accumulation or around reproduction or productivity (Halberstam, 2005). We might be concerned with both of these reproductions, and ruptures, as I am. In the 'clock time' of capitalism (Adkins 2009) certain time cycles (leisure, recreation, work, family, domesticity), and life stages (birth, growing up, partnering, parenting, careers, retirement, death) are naturalised and internalised (Halberstam, 2005), reproducing not only heteronormative ideals but a 'chrononormativity'.

Empirically, research on the middle classes tends to substantiate Bourdieu's capital-accruing model. The middle classes are seen converting their time and energy into activities to generate cultural and social capital, protecting and projecting certain futures. However, Skeggs (2011) argues that Bourdieu's theories do not explain working-class personhood, or any other personhood without (legitimised) social value. Like others, Skeggs asks if people live in different material conditions, why would they not have different forms of association and value practices, different ideas about the future? Qualitative studies of working-class groups demonstrate that this is the case. Working-class personhood is found to be defensive, not acquisitive, protectionist rather than proprietorial (Skeggs and Loveday, 2012), involving living with precarity and 'getting by', rather than oriented towards futurity and 'getting on' (Skeggs, 2011; Taylor, 2012; McKenzie, 2015).

Caring is often seen an essential way to live with others, as making the best of limited circumstances. These conditions have been identified as 'supportive connectivities' not sources for 'self-accumulation' (Skeggs, 2011), involving non-utilitarian affects of care, loyalty and affection, rather than competition, strategy or accumulation. Valorising relationships made from local and familial sociality, can involve, for example, valuing the gift of attention over time, and we may think of this as 'alternative circuits of value' (Skeggs 2011; Skeggs and Loveday, 2012).

Alongside research on class, queer theory provides useful tools to consider alternative ways of relating, challenging the equation of a 'successful' or 'happy' life in heteronormative capitalist society, so often reducible to forms of reproductive maturity, combined with wealth accumulation (Halberstam, 2005). Queer theory – which troubles the reification of innate gender categories, and the imperative of reproduction – aims to 'articulate an alternative vision of life, love and labour' (Halberstam 2005: 6). 'Queer' is about ways of being that stand outside conventional understandings of success and the ways these successes – or 'failures' – are politicised, inhabited, felt and embodied, such as 'embodied moment[s] of becoming Otherwise' (Renold, 2008: 130).

Queer uses of time and space thus question linear and homogeneous time, highlighting instead the transient, fleeting and the contingent. In alternative temporalities, chance, or the untimeliness of the event are often seen as key elements in any political effort to 'bring into existence futures that dislocate themselves from the dominant tendencies and forces of the present' (Grosz, 2004: 14). This represents a useful shattering of chrononormative and 'clock time' logic (Adkins, 2009), but it is also necessary to take account of the material contexts of such stretches and subversions.

Edelman (2004) and Halberstam (2011) argue that queer subjects should embrace non-productivity, and resist narratives of futurity bound into capitalist accumulation. However, this sidelines the practical and pragmatic (im)possibilities for certain subjects, with Renold (2008) noting that 'queer subversions' are also sustained from places of power. For the purposes of this chapter, how might 'getting on' queerly intersect with varied social divisions, involving more than an age-count of who we 'get' as researchers, acting instead to pull us away from the temptation to count older and younger research subjects, and situate ourselves more fully in research–researched–researcher exchanges.

Queer families

I want to turn to some examples from *Lesbian and Gay Parenting: Securing Social and Educational Capital* (Taylor, 2009), which explored changing welfare regimes and recognitions in the UK context, as to how it affected 'queer families', and interviewed 60 self-identified lesbian and gay parents from self-defined middle class and working-class backgrounds. Weeks (2007) explores the 'coming forward' of certain subjects in moments of sexual citizenship, a 'winning of worlds' in which LGBT citizens are now capacitated and filled with life (as parents, citizens, recognised subjects) as opposed to death (as criminals, deviants, sick subjects). To some extent these new rights represent a success and a securing of (feminist) futures in so far as claims can be made on the state and new existences can be secured and materialised: further, individual and family futures are also protected and legitimised in these socio-cultural transformations. But even seemingly subversive 'winning' practices often project specific futures aligned to – rather than the challenging of – societal and educational inequalities.

In the broader project, I argued that middle-class parental practices seek to bring forth a future, capacitated citizen, as a measure of queer parents' *sameness to* and even *success against* their heterosexual counterparts: (re)producing a certain future involves a turn from social difference, disgust and abjection to one of sameness, inclusion and a desirable diversity (Taylor, 2007, 2009). Within this process of resourcing the good, succeeding child, others are positioned as failing, excessive and culpable. This has an embodied and spatial dimension where (social, parental) 'disgust' is re-located onto working-class bodies and practices. The shaping of children's bodies/spaces as a (middle-class) caring act involves 'choice', 'balance' and 'discernment' as indicators of diversity and difference, and as claims on a new improved version of good parenting. By positioning working-class families as failing children, the implication is that they are also failing to bring forth a certain future, capacitated citizen; working-class families' choices and realities remain fixed through notions of risk and blame. While queer parents were once positioned rather homogeneously as gambling with social futures, I found that, within my sample, this judgement firmly attached itself to working-class parents, re-embedding current injustices.

Middle-class interviewees spoke of the importance of 'active planning', to reinforce the fact that parental and care decisions had not been taken lightly, and that their sexuality actually *compelled*, rather than negated, the following of proper, well-thought-through routes. This parallels the arguments regarding the relationship between the 'social' and the 'biological' in terms of how family is made and who counts as a parent – at once gays and lesbians are seen as too sexual (embodying the 'wrong kind' of sexuality) or too restricted by the biological to 'do parenting'. This leaves many contradictions, whereby parenting may be perceived as an entirely social, asexual project, which the interviewees themselves negotiate, resist and repeat. Many middle-class interviewees spoke of being active choosers in planning their routes to parenthood, foregrounding their own sense of responsibility, as against that which 'just happened' all too easily. Having become pregnant through assisted insemination, Gemma[2] claims an 'active choice' where family does not easily 'just come packaged', positioning herself against that which 'just happens' to 'het [heterosexual] people':

> 'You make an active choice … and the vast majority of het people, it just sort of happens to them. You know, very rarely do they actively make the choice. It's interesting talking to women who go for fertility treatment because they are having to make the active choice.' (Gemma, age 50, middle class)

Jacqui also foregrounds her own responsibility, contrasted with drunkenness and a profound lack of planning, recognisable in more

---

[2] All interviewee names are pseudonyms.

conservative discourses. In both Jacqui's and Gemma's accounts it is difficult to reconcile notions of 'good planning' alongside other interviewees' experiences, where they would not be recognised via this 'redemption':

'I think that if you're going to that much trouble to have a child, it must be really wanted. I think that if it's a question of you going down the pub, you're getting pissed and you get laid and you come home pregnant, that child hasn't really been thought about or chosen, or decided on, or anything. I think that when gay people decide they want to have children they put a lot of thought and a lot of effort into it, so it's not just happening to them, they are making choices and I think that's a good thing.' (Jacqui, age 43, middle class)

Immediate, excessive, gratification is set alongside long-term planning and efforts. Similarly, Kevin (age 36, middle class) spoke of "project planning" his parenting of Ruby, in conjunction with her mother, aiming to create the "right environment" which had been well "thought through" and, crucially, resourced. Again, Carol (age 53, middle class) affirms her "active choice" of parenting almost against that which just happened, in youthful times, by 'traditional means' and in doing so repositions in terms of rightful, respectable routes. The trope of 'the family' is one of the longest standing within sociological discussion, and it is ever (re)circulated, in terms of rights and wrongs. Conceptualisations of family 'choices', particularly prevalent in the literature on lesbian and gay parented families, have frequently foregrounded a reflexive, agentic subject politically mobilised against expected attacks on their incapacity to parent – and we might want to extend this into 'caring' in general (as with the ideas of 'families of choice). Nonetheless, the articulation of (queer) 'choice' may serve to recirculate very similar notions of who is and who is not capable of caring; even queer subjects might reproduce static and normative, rather than subversive, futures.

'I think the danger of it is that I think it's fantastic for people that want to do it, I've been to lots [civil partnerships]. But I think the danger of it is that it's creating a sort of two-tiered world where you are kind of jolly and out and no problems and equal to straight people and then the kind of slightly grotty ones who decide not to. You know, like an

underclass, and I'm in that! [laughter] I'm in that underclass
… again! Back in the margins. And I think, I mean, that's
one way of looking at it, and also, because I've done that,
I've been married and I spent most of my adult life married
… you're not really going to start wandering back into
that world and, you know, I don't care about the legal and
the financial links really.' (Katerina, age 52, working-class)

Queer cares

I now want to turn to quite another case of 'queer cares': having
deconstructed the cares of others, I should dwell on my own, and here
I return to the idea of the embodied subject who has aged, in this case
myself and my grandmother. In doing so, I want to again think about
the politics of storytelling – for in researching, writing and presenting
we are telling stories – alongside the complexities of care, as so often
required at certain points of the life course. The above examples situate
the complexities of parental care, but caring for a parent or grandparent
can interrupt and reverse these normative stories.

Despite being convinced about the necessity of reflecting on the
personal as political, I do have a certain authorial ambivalence about
the reach and significance of doing so, about whether this does
justice to a particular methodological approach and to a specific
set of sociological – and personal – concerns. The positions of
researcher and granddaughter are navigated in relating an account
of my grandmother's (mis)positioning as an Alzheimer's 'patient', as
'senile' and 'unknowing', and her subsequent status as recipient of a
National Health Service (NHS) 'care' package. My grandmother is
unable to tell her story, on the academic page and in medicalised (read
'authoritative', 'reasoned', 'capable') knowledge constructions.

> The relation between memory and caring … is, I maintain,
> an internal relation – a relation that could not fail to
> obtain between those two concepts since memory is partly
> constitutive of the notion of care. If I care for someone or
> for something, and then I forget that person or that thing,
> this means that I have stopped caring for him or it. (Margalit,
> cited in Taylor, J., 2008: 318)

In contrast to the above linkage between remembering, recognising
and caring, between seeing and being seen, Janelle Taylor (2008) relates
how these connections result in a misrecognition of the 'cares' of those

who no longer remember – where memory, history and knowledge is reduced to simplified recall, a question of 'Does she recognise you?' Does the patient recognise the daughter, the granddaughter, the significant others? In seeking to understand the repeated question of whether her mother, who is living with progressive dementia, still recognises her, Taylor interrogates how claims to social and political recognition are founded on the demonstrable capacity to 'recognise' people and things, where those who 'don't remember' can be discarded as lost, as inhabiting permanent patienthood, rather than as mothers, sisters, grandmothers, and ones with 'cares', histories and futures.

My grandmother, as a person living with Alzheimer's, was 'lost' to her family as she was 'cared' for: made a resident of a hospital and returned, not to her family home, but to a residential care home, against her family's wishes – and against her own expressed wishes, communicated when she could, officially, consent. Consequently, the removal of memory, history, knowledge and cares occurred through years of institutional care, marked by conflict, error and misunderstanding, by the misrecognition of her as only a patient and not a person, not a grandmother. If social and political recognition are founded on the provable capacity to 'recognise' people and things, might the narration of the complexities of care enforce a new kind of recognition for those deemed lost and gone, who can no longer 'get on'? There are structuring contexts beyond individual tales; research cares also force a consideration of the complexities of care as differently told, practised and authorised.

My gran became a patient, or a 'client', depending on what carers – social workers or nurses and doctors – were 'intervening' to provide the most efficient, least costly 'care package': she was a number added to NHS lists, she was 'pending' care. I was often annoyed by the infantilisation of her, as a manifestation of such care. Many, mostly female, carers were affectionate and tactile. This was, probably, good for her, in an otherwise clinical and sterile environment. I have myself worked as a carer in a nursing home and have cared efficiently, professionally and often with affection. But she was not theirs – just as this story is mine and not completely my granny's. If she was telling this story I'm sure it would be different, she'd tell the present differently and remember the past differently; I try to be mindful of this, and of silences, slippages (Gill and Flood, 2009), as I attempt to recall her wishes and desires, as well as my own.

The failure of a 'care plan', as a legalised, consensual document signed by my grandmother pre-Alzheimer's, denied rather than guaranteed her choice. This care package enveloped and even eclipsed her own concerns, her own choices and cares; as an expert of 'good enough' care, a fine balancer of stretched resources and seemingly infinite demands, my granny was relegated to the bottom rung of 'care', wheeled into a demarcated ward, labelled 'gerontology'. Her body and mind were diagnosed as 'elderly', an open-and-shut case, nothing more to say, no more decisions. Is care release or relief, if so, for whom? If reflexivity is generationally bound, to be awarded and deployed by the younger, female academic, should one fear its removal post-retirement, when what one knows and who can no longer be commanded? From esteemed and knowing ('grandmother', 'academic') to out-of-date and strangely 'junior'. The relevance of social positioning and inequality are relevant in the rendering, and securing of, self and subjecthood, and we reach vulnerable positions with the weight of past dispositions; if an aging self embodies a potential vulnerability, it does so via other materialities and subjectivities. My gran's story speaks to the intersection of class, gender and generation in the complexity of caring across and at the end of the life course.

As I saved multiple letters in negotiating the care system via the NHS complaints procedure, applying relatively care-free processes to a personal, rather than academic concern, I often paused to think what I should save correspondences as, where should I place these, what folder does it belong in? This disjuncture speaks of the connections and disconnections in embodying academic and personal concerns, identities and speaking positions: I consciously aimed to mobilise and 'perform' an authoritative, knowing self, to be drafted, considered and redrafted in written communications to medical institutions. I demanded recognition for family connections and knowingness, for memories materialised across generations, and known without being diagnosed; I liaised with medical professionals, care organisations, social workers, nurses, community providers, residential nursing homes, and I asked them to hear my story too. I also speak their language; I understand budgetary constraints, the complexity of care provisioning, competing 'best interests', and I asked "Where does my gran fit in these tales?"

That I am called on to intervene, to question and cajole in this respect may well say something about broader familial patterns of, for example class and gender; where my ultimate failure, or lack of success, can be seen to confirm rather than escape social 'fixity' and structured hierarchies, as opposed to demonstrating mobility and agency. Over the years I added a whole new 'Granny' folder in my files. It is still filled with facts, complaint and pleads, with indignation, anger and despair. These letters were sent to care authorities, organisations, providers and campaigning groups for older people. I sent them to newsletters, support groups, friends and family, and they leave a trace in connecting the cares. My everyday academic spaces and tools (A4 lever arch file, now filled; photocopies of replies and forwarding correspondences; search engines now exhausted of the words 'health', 'old age' 'NHS complaints') used to provide assurance that something would be done. Yet actively mobilising academic credentials, technologies and knowledges uneasily aligned me with other professionals, everyone in pursuit of and conflict over the 'right thing to do'. But this 'right thing to do' doesn't work as a rule book or policy document (prefaced with a 'that's what happens' section) in a safely guarded, hierarchical bureaucracy, where consultants fear losing their professional status and prestige (but perhaps not their gran). My claims to knowledge hope to pay heed to the complexity of positioning, but this is not always a safe – or useful – stance: (medical) doctors often do not care in this respect (in utilising 'Dr' as a signature I have been called to account as having no real, that is medical, knowledge).

I have presented a brief consideration of the complexities of my grandmother's story, of the movement and misplacement from 'grandmother' to 'patient'; a movement in time punctured and effaced by medical diagnosis and 'expert' erasure (Taylor, J., 2008). These punctures also exist in the spaces of academia, affecting who can 'get on'.

Queer spaces of academia

In a recent academic forum, I was happily engaged in collegial conversations. In these settings, exchange can become 'conversions', allowing us to display, convey and circulate career capitals – or not. Such conversions, moving from conversations to careers, are perhaps more subtle than bringing out the curriculum vitae. But recent experiences have left me wondering if reaching for the paper version of the academic self would cut out, condense or confirm ratings of worth, measures of success, feelings of (im)perfection and (in)secure academic arrivals. Everyday judgements and distinctions are always manifest in social interactions, and academic settings are no exception. Many have written passionately and provocatively about the awkward encounters in academia, where some seem to be versed and conversant, while others occupy marginal positions – and others are not even in the room (Taylor, 2013). We know this is a matter of structural inequality rather than simply not being able to appear and perform. If feminism is itself caring, as a generative commitment to families, interviewees, audiences and publics, embodied in labours and cares, what happens when that is interrupted and challenged? I was made to think about this possible – and rather deathly – *descent* recently when a colleague asked me if I thought I had 'peaked too soon?' Consider the following fictionalised auto-ethnographic account.

> Institutional benefits accrue to the young academic in the form of promotion, career and geographical mobility: she moves from there to here and seems to fit in and take up her space. Even this requires an explanation. Surely this is too soon? Surely she must be too ambitious, too individualist, too removed from The Family or any emotional cares, that she is instead able to just invest in herself? Does she have children? A partner? Does she have work–life balance or just works too hard? Even (feminist) successes may be recast as failures in normative measures of fitting in, moving, achieving and (not) caring, and as she considers this the question of what it means to live out, activate and be present in and through academia become pressing issues ...

At a time of continued and profound social division in academia, effecting who climbs and gets ahead, I find snapshots of individual career acceleration (and deceleration – as the summit slips) rather disturbing – and as another kind of time bomb. As with gendered material inequality, many feminists have highlighted gendered cultural climates within academia where:

> there is a cultural climate that favours men ... Women are not recognised for their talents or abilities and are often forced to do low-level, high-volume administrative work, while many more men assume external-facing roles that have immediate ... career gains ... (Morley, 2013: [not paginated])

In the same article, Morley asks 'why are so many women missing from leading institutions, particularly at senior management levels?' When this absence becomes a potential presence it is still rendered culturally peculiar and questionable, both reduced and inflated, as a 'peak' too soon.

We see supposed measures of productive labour all around us, ever-rehearsing what comes to count (as academic, activist, feminist). The neoliberal university is increasingly a site that demands a mobility of practice and an entrepreneurial orientation to local–global markets; the academic is encouraged to extend her reach, to outreach to 'diverse communities', and to do so as the responsive-responsible 'engaged' one – to stay on top, ahead, ascending, active. These processes efface the material and affective labour and vulnerability in 'coming up against' blockages (or 'coming out') which means the queer researcher-teacher gets 'stuck' (Taylor, 2013).

We might ask what happens to the feminist herself (post 'peak')? In academic presentations across the career-stage, we are endlessly displaying and building our own value, with presentations apparently announcing an arrival (even as we ask ourselves 'what next?', moving from 'early' to 'mid' to 'established' career). As we appear on the page (in the magazine, journal, book) and in the lecture theatre we create certain presences and we have to be careful to ask 'what and who else is carried with us?' In times when some are rendered excessive (in need of 'cutting back'), including individual academics, whole disciplines and entire institutions, our presence must be resituated as mutual and collective, rather than singular and embodied in moments of individual success (or failure). Once more to the following fictionalised auto-ethnographic account:

> Our same young academic – with emphasis on 'young' – receives an email from her PhD student. It's several pages long and a potential chapter in itself. She realises this could be serious and jumps down the paragraphs, trying to find the urgency in her inbox (and there are many urgencies in her inbox). The message is this: the student is going to have a baby; she knows this is a shock, she hopes it won't affect opinions of her or her commitment to work, she questions if this will be recognised, if her funding will continue, her deadline extended, her employability ended ... She wonders if her potential is already being recast as that of a failure, and the sense of being in the wrong time (too young to mother, too young to be a successful academic) is transmitted ...
>
> Work is done by the young academic in reading between the lines of emails, policies and funding guidance, which speak of equal opportunities, a commitment to diversity, an 'investors in people' status. Forms are completed, procedures are followed and pregnancy is declared at the appropriate time – being 'pregnant enough' (for recognition, extension, advice) is stated as 22 weeks, the official time when institutional recognition can begin. 'You're not the first person to have a baby' is the relayed response to the student's concerns and questions.

The phone rings – funding has been received and a research associate vacancy advertised. The potential candidate is ringing to ask if she is still eligible to apply. She's just found out that she is pregnant. The lecturer is thinking equal opps, she's thinking HR.[3] And she's thinking funding deadlines. What would you be thinking? Her research associate gives birth, takes time out. She's not entitled to institutional benefits having not served enough time. But she's extending her maternity leave nonetheless ...

Conclusion

Certain time scales, cycles and life stages are naturalised and internalised, as 'clock time' governs our movements in 'getting on' or 'getting by' (as, for example career mobility, citizenship recognitions, institutional rights). In this chapter, I've presented some examples of what happens when normative time is disrupted: when 'family time' encroaches on 'work time' and makes non-sense of 'work–life' balance; when this is reversed so that the person being cared for is not a child but a grandmother; when the queer feminist academic arrives 'too soon' in academia; when the 'child-as-future-citizen' is placed as needing 'active planning' (and pre-birth), but when this collides with the timeline of '22 weeks' for maternity announcements and entitlement. When these things, feelings, bodies, dislocations circulate in and as queerer spaces of academia, they can appear as 'time bombs', exploding commentaries on what should-be-done-when, often as an instantaneous solution demanding that we act on time ('have a baby before you're 30 years old').

What could happen if, instead, we took our time? Readers may well suspect me of a degree of fraudulence, or hypocrisy at this point, but I seriously do still intend to take – and repeatedly fail in doing so – my own advice, while acknowledging complexity and complicity in the processes that govern us as researchers, carers, citizens (and sometimes the material impossibility of slowing down). Bringing these three positions together, while locating myself in and through research, as inevitably intersecting my own cares, biography, personal and professional identities (as also a queer subject getting on), involves for me at least ongoing 'intersections' of age, sexuality and gender, as themselves moving rather than as static material and subjective positions.

---

[3] Human resources.

References

Adkins, L. (2009) 'Sociological futures: from clock time to event time', *Sociological Research Online*, 14: 1–5.

Adkins, L. (2012) 'Out of work or out of time? Rethinking labor after the financial crisis', *South Atlantic Quarterly*, 111(4): 621–41.

Bourdieu P. (1984) *Distinction: A Social Critique of the Judgement of Taste*, London: Routledge.

Edelman, L. (2004) *No Future: Queer Theory and the Death Drive*, New York: Duke University Press.

Gill, R. and Flood, R. (2009) *Secrecy and Silence in the Research Process. Feminist Reflections*. London: Routledge.

Grosz, E. (2004) *The Nick of Time*. New York: Duke University Press.

Halberstam, J. (2005) *In a Queer Time and Place*, New York: NYU Press.

Halberstam, J. (2011) *The Queer Art of Failure*. Durham: Duke University Press.

McDermott, E. (2011) 'The world some have won: sexuality, class and inequality, *Sexualities*, 14(1): 63–78.

McKenzie, L. (2015) *Getting By: Estates, Class and Culture in Austerity Britain*, Bristol: Policy Press.

Morley, L. (2013) 'Global Gender Index', Times Higher www.timeshighereducation.com/features/global-gender-index-2013/2003517.article

Renold, E. (2008) 'Queering masculinity: re-theorising contemporary tomboyism in the schizoid space of innocent/heterosexualized young femininities', *Girlhood Studies*, 1(2):129–51.

Skeggs, B. (2004) *Class, Self and Culture*. London: Routledge.

Skeggs, B. (2011) 'Imagining Personhood Differently: Person Value and Autonomist Working-Class Value Practices', *The Sociological Review*, 59(3): 496–513.

Skeggs, B. and Loveday, V. (2012) 'Struggles for value: value practices, injustice, judgment, affect and the idea of class', *British Journal of Sociology*, 63(3): 472–90.

Taylor, J. (2008) 'On recognition, caring and dementia', *Medical Anthropology Quarterly*, 22: 313–35.

Taylor, Y. (2007) *Working-Class Lesbian Life: Classed Outsiders*, Basingstoke: Palgrave

Taylor, Y. (2009) *Lesbian and Gay Parenting: Securing Social and Educational Capital*, Basingstoke: Palgrave

Taylor, Y. (2012) *Fitting Into Place? Class and Gender Geographies and Temporalities*, London: Routledge.

Taylor, Y. (2013) 'Queer encounters of sexuality and class: navigating emotional landscapes of academia', *Emotion, Space and Society*, 8: 51–8.

Taylor, Y. (2015) *Making Space for Queer Identifying Youth*, Basingstoke: Palgrave.

Taylor, Y. (2017) 'Mediating 'aspirant' religious-sexual futures: in God's hands?', *Sociological Research Online*, 22(1): 13 [not paginated].

Taylor, Y. and Snowdon, R. (eds) (2014a) *Queering Religion, Religious Queers*, London: Routledge.

Taylor, Y. and Snowdon, R. (2014b). 'Making space for young lesbians in church?', *Journal of Lesbian Studies*, 18(4): 393–414.

Taylor, Y., Hines, S. and Casey, M. (eds) (2010) *Theorizing Intersectionality and Sexuality*. Basingstoke: Palgrave.

Weeks, J. (2007) *The World We Have Won: The Remaking of Erotic and Intimate Life*, London: Routledge.

FOUR

Transgender ageing: community resistance and well-being in the life course

Vanessa Fabbre and Anna Siverskog

Introduction

A small but growing field of social research is emerging on the topic of trans[1] ageing. This scholarship is situated within the larger field of LGBTQ (lesbian, gay, bisexual, transgender and queer) ageing and highlights the challenges to health and well-being that many transgender adults experience as they age. In this chapter we will briefly summarise the empirical landscape concerning the well-being of transgender older adults, present the theoretical perspectives we are using, and then present insights from two social science projects carried out in Sweden and the US. We derive these insights by using queer and life-course perspectives on the intersections of age, gender and sexuality and conclude with a discussion of the meaning of well-being for transgender adults whose lives exist at these intersections.

Trans ageing: empirical landscape

The Trans MetLife Survey on Later-Life Preparedness and Perceptions in Transgender-Identified Individuals (TMLS) is the largest internationally distributed online survey to date of trans-identified

---

[1] For reference, the term trans (or transgender) is an umbrella term used to describe people whose gender identity and/or gender expression differs from expectations based on the sex they were assigned at birth. For a comprehensive review of LGBTQ terminology, we recommend the resources provided by the Safe Zone Project (https://thesafezoneproject.com/), the National Center for Transgender Equality (NCTE) (https://transequality.org/issues/resources/understanding-transgender-people-the-basics), Gender Identity and Research & Education Society, www.gires.org.uk/resources/terminology/, and The Swedish Federation for Lesbian, Gay, Bisexual, Transgender and Queer Rights, www.rfsl.se/en/lgbtq-facts/lgbtq/glossary/

people (N=1,963) that addresses how ageing affects perceived possibilities to live accordingly to one's gender identity (Witten, 2013). Respondents, who were majority white (92%), reported significant fears of becoming ill and being involuntarily outed and not receiving the care they will need at the end of their lives. Many respondents (who were not lesbian, gay and bisexual identified) also expressed worry that they would be 'lumped together' with lesbian, gay and bisexual (LGB) ageing services where they did not feel comfortable (Witten, 2009, 2013; Witten and Eyler, 2012). These experiences vary by age, sexual orientation, and gender identities (Witten, 2016), religious affiliation and spiritual practices (Porter et al., 2013), and experiences of family and community (Witten, 2009).

The Caring and Ageing with Pride project, a survey study in the US of 2,560 LGBT adult respondents aged 50 and older (159 of whom identified as transgender), also offers insights into the health and well-being of transgender older adults (Fredriksen-Goldsen et al., 2011). This study found that transgender older adults are at significantly higher risk of poor physical health, disability, depressive symptomatology and perceived stress in comparison to non-transgender LGB older adults (Fredriksen-Goldsen et al., 2013). Fear among participants to access health-care services, coupled with internalised stigma and victimisation, were significant mediators in the relationship between gender identity and health outcomes (Fredriksen-Goldsen et al., 2011; 2013). Similarly, the Still Out Still Aging (Met Life) study, also conducted in the US, which comprised 1,201 LGBT respondents aged 45-64 years old (60 of whom identified as transgender), found that only 39% of transgender respondents reported being 'completely' or 'mostly' out, only 42% of these respondents' families are 'completely' or 'very' accepting, and 28% of trans respondents are 'guarded' about their gender identities (MetLife Market Institute, 2010).

The findings highlighted in these larger studies are supported by additional investigations into transgender ageing that draw attention to the challenges of living and ageing in contexts where cisnormativity and transphobia are dominant social forces and where many trans people have been criminalised and pathologised (Witten, 2004, 2013). These contexts have shaped people's experiences throughout life, have consequences for physical and mental well-being, and shape an elder care workforce that is unprepared to provide competent care for transgender older adults in later life (Siverskog, 2014). Yet, while these studies highlight important knowledge about the social welfare needs of trans older adults and demonstrate the detrimental effects of ageing in a transphobic society, the literature lacks a focus on resistance, empowerment, and community-level actions to support well-being on the part of transgender people. These forces may help to more fully illuminate how the intersections of age, gender and sexualities affect the life course for transgender older adults.

Trans ageing: theoretical perspectives

In light of the severe consequences of ageing in a transphobic society, we offer insights developed from two studies we conducted that explored the life narratives and community well-being of transgender older adults in Sweden and the US. For both studies, we combined a life-course perspective with queer perspectives in order to advance our conceptualisations of ageing and well-being in these two contexts. The life-course perspective helped us to emphasise the timing of key events and experiences, the interdependence of human lives, and the nature of human agency within socio-historical contexts (Elder, 1994). We also built on Dannefer and Settersten's argument that this perspective offers 'a departure from the conventional practice of thinking about age in normative terms – reflected in ideas of "normal ageing" or natural "stages" of life' (Dannefer and Settersten, 2010: 3). In order to explore how these expectations of what a normative life course should look like, not only in relation to age, but also in relation to expectations of cisgender status and heterosexuality, we also turned to queer and trans scholars such as Sara Ahmed (2006, 2010) and Jack Halberstam (2005, 2011). Ahmed's work on 'orientation' invites the body into analysis and explores how bodies are situated in time and space, where being 'orientated' means being comfortable and able to feel at home. Ahmed talks about normative life courses in terms of following the 'straight line', or following the expected path where happiness is promised to follow if you 'live the right way' (Ahmed, 2006; 2010). Halberstam similarly illuminates how the construction of the life course rests on normative expectations for reproduction and life stages, which are 'ruled by a biological clock for women and by strict bourgeois rules of respectability and scheduling for married couples' (Halberstam 2005: 5). By queering notions of time and 'success' in the life course, Halberstam offers interpretations of the life course that do not rely on normative cultural meanings. Thus, the life-course perspective combined with queer perspectives facilitated a critical exploration in our studies of how expectations and notions around normative life are created and reproduced. These theoretical perspectives also sensitised us to the ways in which community-level resistance shapes ageing experiences and affects well-being for trans older adults.

The Swedish study

The varied social, economic and political forces in Sweden and the US shape the contexts in which trans people live and age. In Sweden, trans people have had the right since 1972 to pursue hormone treatment or sex reassignment surgery, and to change their legal gender if they participated in a two-year psychiatric investigation and were diagnosed with transsexualism (Svensk författningssamling, 1972). While this civil right was seen as radical when it was adopted, activists criticised it for reliance on binary and normative notions of gender. Until the law changed in 2013, it also required that one be a Swedish citizen, unmarried and sterilised. As a result of many years of activism, the requirement of forced sterilisation was finally removed and therapies have been made available to people who do not meet the criteria for 'transsexualism' as well as to people who identify outside the gender binary. Even though there is an increasing privatisation of health and care services in Sweden, care is still publicly funded and heavily subsidised which makes trans care more accessible here than in many other countries. In recent years trans figures have also been more present in films, television series, and the news media. However, greater visibility and representation have not necessarily translated to well-being for members of the trans community. A study from the Public Health Agency in Sweden found that transgender people's health has not improved over the last 10 years, and in some areas it has even declined. Every third person in this study was found to have seriously contemplated suicide in the past year, and half of the respondents reported experiencing harassment in the previous three months and avoided everyday activities due to fear of discrimination (Folkhälsomyndigheten, 2015). Against this backdrop, the Swedish interviews referenced in this chapter were conducted with six transgender people born between 1933 and 1950 (62–88 years old at the time for the interviews)[2] who participated in life story interviews

---

[2] The participants live in both urban and rural areas in Sweden. They are all white, but differ in relation to class, (former) occupation, health status, integration within social networks, engagement in transgender groups, sexuality, partnership status and gender identities. Three of them identify as transsexual, two of which came out and started their transitions in later life, and one who transitioned in his twenties. One person identifies with his legal male gender while dressing and appearing as a woman full time. One person previously identified as a woman during long periods of his life and was out as trans earlier in life, but now lives as a man and rarely cross-dresses. The last person identifies as genderqueer, and thus does not want to be identified according to binary gender categories.

that lasted for three to six hours and were then analysed using a thematic approach (for a more detailed description of the methodology and description of the Swedish context, see Siverskog, 2014, 2015).

Trans resistance in Sweden

Siverskog's study participants described their youth as a time when transgender identities were invisible and when there were no concepts or words to describe their feelings and experiences. Any deviations from dressing, acting or behaving in ways not consistent with their legal gender were strongly regulated and disciplined within their surroundings, leading them to understand that their identities were not tolerated in society (Siverskog, 2014, 2015). Most of the participants that Siverskog interviewed concealed their trans identities for the majority of their lives, which raises questions about how they made sense of their gender identities and how they managed to find other trans people, community, and the courage to come out in their lifetimes.

Early trans groups

Trans older adults recall early trans organisations in Sweden as places where anonymity was very important and where people were not supposed to be open with their trans identities. Lena,[3] a transsexual woman aged 65, describes these protocols from memory:

'When they started this organization, no one was allowed to talk about them being trans. They were not supposed to show themselves, never go out ... It was closed. Nobody could come in, the doors were locked and they sat in there and talked and drank coffee and beer and so on. Today it is different, luckily.'

The meeting that Lena described was modelled on an early US-based organisation, FPE (Foundation for Personality Expression), where gatherings were secret and held in people's homes or in hotel rooms (Stryker, 2008). Lily, also aged 65, applied for entrance to a group and started receiving information by mail:

---

[3] All names in this chapter are pseudonyms to protect the confidentiality of study participants.

'It was so exciting. And the information in question was based on men who wanted to dress in women's clothes but did not want to be women, but wanted to be able to go back to their male role. That was perhaps not something that was, it was okay how they reasoned, but it didn't really feel like mine … But it was the contact I had back then and it gave me an outlet for my feelings and thoughts.'

Lily's quote exemplifies the importance of what Ahmed calls other *lines*, other ways of living that move beyond the well-trodden heteronormative line (Ahmed, 2006: 18 ff.), in which cisgender identity and expression are required. Even if this 'line' was not really 'at home' for Lily, it was better than the alternatives at hand, where no expressions outside the gender binary were possible in mainstream society. These resources became very important for Lily and facilitated visualisations and representations of what she was feeling – but which were impossible to enact in her life. As Kath Weston (1991) has pointed out, to find community is, above anything, about knowing you are not alone in the world. Later in life, Lily went on a longer trip to participate in a trans week in the US, where she could be "Lily the entire time." Lily described this experience as a "liberation, it was simply a relief".

In a cisnormative society it is hard for people with bodies that do not easily fit binary gender norms to take up space and feel comfortable, without risks of harassment and violence. In this reality, alternative spaces and contexts become critical to developing resistance to these norms. These trans contexts work as spaces where other norms of gender are produced, where a cisgender binary model is disrupted and creates circumstances where one can be affirmed in alignment with one's identity. However, these possibilities are not guarantees of having congruent experiences.

When home doesn't really feel like home

Lily reminds us that while the trans organisation she joined fitted her needs better than a cis-normative society, they still did not align with how she perceived herself. Susan Stryker addresses the limits to these early groups in the US, arguing that they were often created by white and middle-to-upper class people who avoided relating to the gay rights movement, minority ethnic communities, public places and the police (Stryker, 2008). Thus, it is important to note that being able to experience these trans meetings as liberating and empowering was not only about gender, but also about class and race among other power relations.

Sture, a 76-year-old interviewee, had identified as a trans woman during previous parts of his life, but now, due to his ageing body and living situation, says he "lays low" in his trans identity. He recalls trans groups in the early 1980s where it was very important that the group not be connected to the gay community, and when he came out as bisexual it "was not appreciated at all within this trans group." There were still strict norms within these trans groups that members identify as straight men who were cross-dressing. We see in Sture's experience that while trans groups developed resistance to transphobia in society, they also simultaneously perpetuated social forces like homophobia. Similarly, even though the largest gay rights organisation in Sweden, RFSL – the Swedish Federation for LGBT Rights – officially included trans people as a target group in 2001, some of the respondents in this study experienced a lack of knowledge of trans issues within the organisation (Siverskog, 2014). Sture conveys how he, when he been visiting the social space of RFSL, felt "looked at" by other people there and that "there were just as many prejudices" in that space. Thus, what was constructed as 'home' for some (that is, lesbians and gays) became something else when one's body couldn't take up space and truly feel at home. As Ahmed (2006: 11-12) argues, 'some spaces extend certain bodies and simply do not leave room for others', thus leaving those others to feel out of place. Given these tensions, trans groups and organisations in Sweden have historically had different purposes from those of lesbian and gay groups. Some straight-identified cross-dressers, who often were married and had families, aimed to create 'breathing room' for people to dress as they liked and to socialise. This contrasted with lesbian and gay communities that, to a large degree, developed spaces and contexts where one could 'come home' and find 'chosen families' (Weston, 1991).

Community in later life

The nature of early trans organisations had consequences for ageing as a trans person in Sweden. Older lesbians and gays who participated in lesbian and gay movements during the 1970s and since often have strong networks of families and friends from this time, while their trans counterparts struggled more often to find this social connection. Many older adults that Siverskog interviewed believed that while trans groups were a place to find refuge from an inhospitable society, 'family' was still something you were expected to have outside the group. This experience echoes Fredriksen-Goldsen et al.'s (2011) findings where many trans people reported that they did not always feel they belonged to the LGBT community. Among the people Siverskog interviewed, only one lives with a partner while the rest live alone, and none of them lives in a bigger city with access to trans groups or networks, which makes the absence of supportive networks even more acute.

Lena is responsible for a support phone line for trans people, and often receives calls by older people who are not open about their trans identities. Some of these people are afraid to even buy the clothes they want in case someone might find them after they die. Lena describes this reality as a "prison that is out of this world" and says she is encouraging people to "not give a crap about that". Instead she tells them "buy yourself a dress and feel good while you are alive". Klas, 62 years old, who transitioned when he was aged 20 to escape this sense of "prison" was encouraged by his doctor to move away and not talk about his trans identity. Thus, he has never been involved in any sort of LGBT community, but revealed he is dreaming about Stockholm, about the groups and the community. He says he has been trying to convince a friend to go to Pride with him some year: "Still, I feel, no I don't think I belong there. But who the fuck does? But it would be fun just to be there, see it and experience that." Lena and Klas's narratives illustrate a refusal to accept the idea that being in old age means they should not hold dreams about livable lives and meanings beyond both age norms and heteronormativity.

The US study

The US context for trans issues is similar to Sweden's in that it has evolved rapidly in recent years, and yet serious welfare concerns for transgender people remain. Despite recent attention to trans issues in the US, a survey by the National Center for Transgender Equality suggests that trans people are four times more likely to have a household income of less than $10,000/year compared with the general population and 41% of respondents reported attempting suicide, compared with 1.6% of the general population (NCTE, 2016a). In addition, racism in the US affects the way trans issues are framed and exerts additional barriers and inequalities for trans people of colour. At the national level, there are no employment non-discrimination protections that include gender identity; at local levels some states have passed such legislation while others use religious freedom legislation to uphold discrimination against trans people (NCTE, 2016b). Yet progress has been made through major governmental programmes, such as Medicare that now covers some transition-related care, and Social Security, which allows gender markers to be changed on identification documents. Recently, the US Department of Veterans Affairs disseminated trans-positive guidelines for care through its health system (NCTE, 2016c). This mix of affirming policies for care on the part of institutions, coupled with persistent and devastating social marginalisation and stigmatisation of trans Americans makes for a complex and multi-faceted context in which transgender adults are ageing. For the US study, Fabbre used the extended case method (Burawoy et al., 1991; Burawoy, 1998) to examine the case of gender transitions in later life. Fabbre conducted in-depth biographical interviews with 22 male-to-female identified adults[4] who had contemplated or pursued a gender transition over the age of 50 and conducted 170 hours of participant observation at three national transgender conferences in the US (fieldwork took place in 2012. For a more detailed description of the methodology used in this study, see Fabbre, 2014, 2015, 2017).

Trans resistance in the US

The experiences of participants in Fabbre's study echo those illuminated in Siverskog's study in that many experienced gender conflicts over many years, often in extreme isolation before connecting with others. In the US, trans groups have served to facilitate connections and challenge the heteronormative social forces and pressures experienced in mainstream society. Many of Fabbre's study participants felt that their decisions about a gender transition were directly affected by

---

[4] Eighteen participants were European American, three were African American and one was Asian American. Five expressed ongoing socioeconomic challenges, six expressed a sense of socioeconomic stability, and eleven shared that their socioeconomic position afforded stability and some luxury. Twelve participants were between 50–60 years old, seven were between 61–70 years old, two were between 71–80 years old, and one participant was 82 years old. Seven participants were currently married, eleven were previously married and divorced, two were partnered, and two were never married or partnered. Language of the participants themselves was used to discuss identity and transitions. The term 'transition' referenced the process through which a person decided to change from living 'part time' (expressing their preferred gender identity as female in private or only in some aspects of their lives) to 'full time' (expressing their preferred female gender 100% of the time). At the time of the interviews, fifteen of the participants were living full time, three were living part time and were not sure about transitioning, three were living part time and had decided not to transition, and one person was living part time and considered herself in preparation for transition.

decades of transgender community organising that over time made transitioning in later life a realistic possibility for many older adults.

Contemporary trans groups

In the US, many national transgender conferences are week-long events that take place at large host hotels, offering daily seminars and social events for those who identify on the transgender spectrum. Fabbre observed several conferences that were first organised in the 1980s and 1990s by a variety of cross-dressing organisations and transsexual support groups and were initially geared toward male-to-female identified participants. Many participants have attended or followed the conferences over time as they have aged. During the first week of one such conference, Fabbre observed and participated in a popular roller derby night. The social significance of this event was embodied by Amber, a 72-year-old fellow attendee living "part time" (expressing her female identity in only some parts of her life), who was observed getting ready to participate in a light-hearted match between conference attendees and the local roller derby team. Amber received encouragement from the team members on the side of the rink, "You got this girl. You look great in those tights!" Amber then reminded her younger counterparts that she used to skate weekly in the 1950s, but admitted "It does feel great to wear a skirt and tights this time." Social events like roller derby night exist because of the focus within transgender communities on creating alternative spaces that embrace a range of individual gender identities and desired expressions. Many conference attendees do not experience this kind of liberation and acceptance in their everyday lives, and experiences such as Amber's capture the essence of many of these conferences where people are given time and space to build a stronger sense of agency and self-acceptance.

At the start of The Art of Getting Out, a conference workshop aimed at helping people to feel more prepared and confident leaving the house in female-mode, the speaker presented a cartoon image of Popeye the Sailor and asked what he might have to teach cross-dressers and transgender women about embracing their identities. The audience laughed at the notion that this hyper-masculine character had anything to teach about embracing one's femininity in the social world. The speaker added one of Popeye's famous quotes to the image: "I am what I am, and that's all that I am." A collective nodding and murmur signalled the connection the audience made with this quote, a poignant sentiment from an unlikely source. For many attendees, conferences provide a space in which to practice a newfound self-acceptance and explore both sides of the conflict many feel about their urge to present or live in the world as women. Seminars such as this one provide immediate social forces that run counter to the one's many experiences in work and family life, and thus facilitate time and place for participants to reflect, consider opportunities, try new gender expressions, and think about how to translate lessons learned to their home and work lives. This construction of both time and place to explore one's gender supports Halberstam's argument that queer lives thrive on *queer time and place* not regulated by normative scripts and life stages.

Many conferences that Fabbre observed were billed in their early years as retreats, or vacations, from a larger social world that was not accepting of gender variance or encouraging of exploring transgender identities. This retreat-like nature is still important today. Fabbre noted that one organiser stated, "A lot of the ladies who come here live in pressure cookers; they need a place to breathe." In addition to offering a form of release for attendees, conferences have also expanded and increasingly serve as places to learn about transgender civil rights and logistical possibilities for transitioning or expressing one's preferred gender presentation in the world. Most conferences now host informational sessions with physicians who perform gender-affirming surgeries, authors who write publicly about their own gender and family relationships, and consultants who offer advice for those who may be contemplating a gender transition at work. This extends the purpose of the conferences to more than just a vacation from a constraining social world. For many attendees who experience 'pressure cookers' in their everyday lives, the social forces generated at conferences directly affects their sense of agency as they age.

Over time, these conferences have encouraged attendees to exert their rights as transgender persons. The ways participants narrate this history highlights the significant role of conferences in changing social forces in ways that shape new opportunities for those who participate. An excerpt from Fabbre's field notes demonstrates a common narration of conference history by participants:

> Met Victoria ... who has been coming to [this conference] for 14 years, she [noted that] it has changed, 'the core used to be cross-dressers, and now that core are more transsexuals. It's becoming more transsexuals.' We discussed how the conference has changed over the years and she said 'it's individuals who set the change in motion, then that change

ends up affecting them' – referring to how the early cross-dressers creating [this conference] have made it possible for more people to transition. (Field notes, 2012)

For some, attending conferences such as these allowed for direct participation in these environments; for others, they experience these places indirectly through community blogs, newsletters and social networks. Many who attended conferences recalled experiencing bursts of emotional awareness, like Carly, who recounts her first experience at one such conference:

> '… and oh my god, that first time I walked into the ballroom at [the conference] my jaw dropped. Everyone was so free, so beautiful, it made me feel like a Hollywood starlet! The women just looked so amazing. And I mean, I felt like one of them, almost, though I knew I had some work to do to feel so free.'

Beyond trans groups

For some participants in this study, and many of their peers, attending a conference is not possible due to financial or geographic limitations or family responsibilities. The rapid proliferation of internet-based resources, blogs, newsletters and chat rooms since the 1990s has helped to disseminate much of what happens at conferences to the larger community. For example, one interviewee for this study shared a popular blog she had written and disseminated through online communities. Several excerpts from this blog demonstrate the type of stories that gain traction in the community:

> As the day approached to go to my first [conference] I became more and more apprehensive…it was the stuff of my fantasies back in the 70s and 80s when I was a young closeted cross dresser trying to imagine what it would be like to live as a woman…
>
> The volunteers were patient and helpful, and they represented a cross section of the TG [transgender] life, from passable transsexuals to awkward CDs [cross dressers]. I'm okay here, I think. I can fit in…Early in the first hours, a fire alarm at the hotel goes off…while we loitering outside, several non-conference people arrive. One male studies me intently from a distance…for some reason, in this situation,

surrounded by many other t-girls, I am not intimidated. Think what you will, I say to myself, this is part of who I am, lo and behold, at this moment I am really enjoying it...I am a different person as I drive away. I knew more about myself and a little more about my community.[5]

The broad dissemination of blogs like this on popular sites for transgender older adults, especially those on the male-to-female spectrum, point towards the direct effects of attending a conference and also demonstrate how community-level actions affect the broader collective consciousness in transgender communities. This shifting consciousness facilitated by trans conferences echoes Halberstam's notion of 'queer failure', wherein gender and sexual minorities embrace their so-called 'failure' to be normal and renegotiate what it means to be queer in a heteronormative society.

Trans resistance and well-being in the life course

Our findings illuminate the varied nature of trans resistance through community organising and have implications for understanding the well-being of trans older adults. Specifically, an understanding of the role of community organising in shaping the life course experiences of trans older adults helps to make sense of welfare concerns and guide potential interventions. For example, current research has demonstrated that lower levels of social support and community belonging among transgender older adults account for poor mental health outcomes and that social support can be a protective factor against the deleterious effects of victimisation (Fredriksen-Goldsen, 2013). Our findings point towards the importance of understanding the *nature* of this social support and highlight the need for social support that explicitly counteracts heteronormative social forces in order to be effective. Further, this social support is complicated by tensions at the intersection of several social identity domains as evidenced in part by the homophobia recalled in early trans groups and the separate development of gay and lesbian organisations. Scholars have noted that access and participation in gay and lesbian organisations reflect power dynamics and negotiations of social capital (Cronin and King, 2010), and trans groups are no different. Therefore, the experiences of older transgender adults who have participated in these organisations and gatherings over time will vary along multiple identity fronts.

---

[5] The blog is not identified in order to protect the participant's confidentiality.

In addition to the role that these trans groups, conferences and organisations have had in individuals' lives as they age, they also affect the larger societal level context for trans ageing. In this regard, scholars have noted the mutually constituting link between trans identities and social opportunities for such identities. For example, Valentine (2007) argues that as the category of 'transgender' has been rapidly adopted and accepted, this influences the social opportunities for those who take on this collective identity. Similarly, Gagné et al. (1997) note that the process of coming out as transgender is inextricably linked to community relationships and socially constructed options for transgender identity. Thus, the trans organisations and groups that played a role in promoting well-being for the trans older adults we interviewed also play a role in shaping the broader social context for intersections around gender, sexualities and ageing. The role of the internet in disseminating information and generating connection among trans people will certainly continue to shape and be shaped by the progression of these communities. Although, based on the intensity and impact that in-person meetings have had in our study participants' lives, we must continue to examine and understand how in-person relationships and gatherings affect the well-being of trans people as they age.

References

Ahmed, S. (2006) *Queer Phenomenology: Orientations, Objects, Others*, Durham, NC: Duke University Press.

Ahmed, S. (2010) *The Promise of Happiness*, Durham, NC: Duke University Press.

Burawoy, M. (1998) 'The extended case method', *Sociological Theory*, 16(1): 4–33.

Burawoy, M., Burton, A., Ferguson, A.A., Fox, K.J., Gamson, J., Gartrell, N., Hurst, L., Kurzman, C., Salzinger, L., Schiffman, J. and Ui, S. (1991) *Ethnography Unbound: Power and Resistance in the Modern Metropolis*, Berkeley, CA: University of California Press.

Cronin, A. and King, A. (2010) 'Power, inequality and identification: exploring diversity and intersectionality amongst older LGB adults', *Sociology*, 44(5): 876–92.

Dannefer, D. and Settersten, R.A. (2010) 'The study of the life course: implications for social gerontology', in R.D. Dannefer and C. Phillipson (eds) *The SAGE Handbook of Social Gerontology*, London: SAGE Publications.

Elder, G. (1994) 'Time, human agency and social change: perspectives on the life course', *Social Psychology Quarterly*, 57(1): 4–15.

Fabbre, V.D. (2014) 'Gender transitions in later life: the significance of time in queer aging', *Journal of Gerontological Social Work*, 57(2–4): 161–75.

Fabbre, V.D. (2015) 'Gender transitions in later life: a queer perspective on successful aging', *The Gerontologist*, 55(1): 144–53.

Fabbre, V.D. (2017) 'Agency and social forces in the life course: the case of gender transitions in later life', *Journal of Gerontology: Social Sciences*, 72(3): 479–87.

Folkhälsomyndigheten, 2015, *Hälsan och hälsans bestämningsfaktorer för transpersoner – en rapport om hälsoläget bland transpersoner i Sverige*, Folkhälsomyndigheten. Retrieved from www.folkhalsomyndigheten. se/publicerat-material/publikationer/Halsan-och-halsans-bestamningsfaktorer-for-transpersoner---en-rapport-om-halsolaget-bland-transpersoner-i-Sverige.

Fredriksen-Goldsen, K.I., Hyun-Jun, K., Emleet C.A., Muraco, A., Erosheva, E.A., Hoy-Ellis, C.P. and Petry, H. (2011) *The Aging and Health Report: Disparities and Resilience among Lesbian, Gay, Bisexual, and Transgender Older Adults*, Seattle: Institute for Multigenerational Health.

Fredriksen-Goldsen, K.I., Cook-Daniels, L., Kim, H-J., Erosheva, E.A., Emlet, C.A., Hoy-Ellis, C.P. and Muraco, A. (2013) 'Physical and mental health of transgender older adults: an at-risk and underserved population', *The Gerontologist*, 54(3): 488–500.

Gagné, P., Tewksbury, R. and McGaughey, D. (1997) 'Coming out and crossing over: identity formation and proclamation in a transgender community', *Gender & Society*, 11(4): 478–508.

Halberstam, J. (2005) *In a Queer Time and Place : Transgender Bodies, Subcultural Lives*, New York: New York University Press.

Halberstam, J. (2011) *The Queer Art of Failure*, Durham, NC: Duke University Press.

MetLife Market Institute (2010) *Still Out, Still Aging. The MetLife Study of Lesbian, Gay, Bisexual and Transgender Baby Boomers*, Westport: Mature Market Institute.

Porter, K.E., Ronnegberg, C.R. and Witten, T.M. (2013) 'Religious affiliation and successful aging among transgender older adults: findings from the Trans MetLife Survey', *Journal of Religion, Spirituality & Aging*, 25(2): 112–38.

Siverskog, A. (2014) '"They just don't have a clue": transgender aging and implications for social work', *Journal of Gerontological Social Work*, 57(2–4): 386–406.

Siverskog, A. (2015) 'Ageing bodies that matter: age, gender and embodiment in older transgender people's life stories', *NORA – Nordic Journal of Feminist and Gender Research*, 23(1): 4–19.

Stryker, S. (2008) *Transgender History*, Berkeley, CA: Seal Press.

Svensk författningssamling, 1972, Svensk författningssamling 1972:119 Lag (1972:119) om fastställande av könstillhörighet i vissa fall – riksdagen.se. Retrieved from www.riksdagen.se/sv/DokumentLagar/Lagar/Svenskforfattningssamling/sfs_sfs-1972-119/.

Valentine, D. (2007) *Imagining Transgender: An Ethnography of a Category*, Durham, NC: Duke University Press.

Weston, K. (1991) *Families We Choose: Lesbian, Gays, Kinship*, New York: Columbia University Press.

Witten, T.M. (2004) 'Life course analysis – the courage to search for something more: middle adulthood issues in the transgender and intersex community', *Journal of Human Behaviour in the Social Environment*, 8(2–3): 189–224.

Witten, T.M. (2009) 'Grateful Exits: Intersection of Aging, Transgender Identities, and the Family/Community', *Journal of GLBT Family Studies*, 5(1–2): 35–61.

Witten, T.M. (2013) 'It's not all darkness: robustness, resilience, and successful transgender aging', *LGBT Health*, 1(1): 24–33.

Witten, T.M. (2016) 'Aging and transgender bisexuals: exploring the intersection of age, bisexual sexual identity, and transgender identity', *Journal of Bisexuality*, 16(1): 58–80.

Witten, T.M. and Eyler, E.A. (2012) 'Transgender and aging: beings and becomings', in R.M. Tarynn and E.A. Eyler (eds) *Gay Lesbian, Bisexual and Transgender Aging: Challenges in Research, Practice and Policy*, Baltimore: The John Hopkins University Press, 187–269.

Part 2
Representations

Part 2: introduction

The chapters in this second section focus on representations of ageing, gender and sexuality. Representations matter because they shape discursive possibilities: what can be imagined and what actions seem possible and viable. All the chapters in this section draw on textual sources. In their chapters, Elizabeth Barry and Maricel Oró Piqueras draw on texts from English literature by authors such as Virginia Woolf, Penelope Lively, Angela Carter and Doris Lessing, while Kinneret Lahad and Karen Hvidtfeldt draw on material from online web columns and magazine articles.

In Chapter Five, Elizabeth Barry employs a reading of Virginia Woolf's *Mrs Dalloway* as a lens to think about cultural and scientific representations of the menopause. She responds particularly to Germaine Greer's criticisms of Simone de Beauvoir's representations of the menopause. Greer argues that de Beauvoir's characterisation of the menopause as a time of loss of agency and weakness demonstrated a sexual double standard. However, Barry argues that in making this critique, Greer herself draws on pathologising understandings of the menopause and of the sexuality of older women. Barry suggest that, while not always sympathetic towards the experiences of other women experiencing the menopause, Woolf's *Mrs Dalloway* ultimately offers scope for a more nuanced and complicated understanding of this underrepresented aspect of older women's lives. Barry thus demonstrates that literature offers resources for new ways to imagine menopause and later life sexuality.

Maricel Oró Piqueras too uses literature to explore the intersection of ageing, sexuality and gender. In Chapter Six she takes an interdisciplinary approach, starting with social scientific studies of the common discursive resources for talking about older women's sexuality (a dichotomy between 'asexual' and 'sexy oldie'). Oró Piqueras then examines three contemporary British stories that focus on the sexual experiences of women in their seventies and eighties, asking whether they offer new ways of thinking about later-life sex. She demonstrates that these stories do indeed offer resources for new ways of imagining older women's sexuality which are less binary and less heteronormative than common representations.

Kinneret Lahad and Karen Hvidtfeldt also draw on textual sources to explore issues around representations in Chapter Seven, but in everyday texts rather than literary ones. They examine Danish and

Israeli magazine articles and online web columns that focus on midlife motherhood, exploring how older 'midlife' mothers negotiate around normative expectations about the 'proper' time to become a mother. Lahad and Hvidtfeldt draw on the notion of 'ageing capital' to discuss how women are able to employ notions of the gains of ageing (such as greater experience and patience, and increased economic and emotional stability) to counterbalance their 'off-time' transition to motherhood. The comparison of Denmark and Israel demonstrates that, despite very different political and cultural contexts, remarkably similar discourses around age, gender and sexuality and their relationship to good mothering are found in both settings.

Taken together, the chapters in this section demonstrate that both literature and everyday texts can offer resources for thinking about ageing, gender and sexuality in more nuanced ways.

FIVE

Endogenous misery: menopause in medicine, literature and culture

Elizabeth Barry

In her oft-cited essay 'The double standard of aging' (1972), a key text for questions of intersections between gender and ageing, Susan Sontag contrasts the 'genuine' *condition of old age*, which 'men and women undergo in a similar way', with *growing old*, the latter 'an ordeal of the imagination – a moral disease, a social pathology' which 'afflicts women much more than men' (Sontag 1972: 285). It is a truism that old age in men is seen to confer distinction and esteem, whereas in women it bespeaks confusion, frailty and physical decline. This inequality is compounded by the cultural constructions of age according to which youth is synonymous with beauty and personal value, and even virtue is tacitly (and perhaps increasingly explicitly) with associated physical health and attractiveness – again, associations that 'afflict' women in a manner disproportionate to men.

While Sontag's argument seems unfailingly true to contemporary women's experiences of ageing, her use of the metaphor of disease points up the dilemma explored in this chapter. One aspect of ageing in particular, the menopause, reverses the metaphor, being constructed socially as a literal instance of illness, such a definition itself reflecting attitudes that pathologise so many aspects of ageing for women. Menopause is in one regard 'simply' biology, the cessation of reproductive capacity at an age (for the majority) when one has long since renounced reproduction in any case. Yet this biological event has a cultural corollary: women who have fought to attain what Betty Friedan has called a 'fully human personhood' (Friedan, 1993: 496) beyond the biological role of bearing children (or feeding sexual desire) seem at this milestone to be newly and unquestioningly defined in relation to biology once more. A natural and inevitable process is conceived of as a disease, and a disease that reflects on the soul as well the body of the sufferer. The rise of psychoanalysis has only compounded this association of sexual identity crisis and psychic failure. Psychoanalyst Helène Deutsch famously observed that 'Woman's last traumatic experience as a sexual being is an incurable narcissistic wound' (Deutsch 1945: 457). Menopause is unique in the ageing process for Simone de Beauvoir, much influenced by Deutsch, in being a discrete event, an interruption of fertility, where the rest of ageing is a 'continuous development' (de Beauvoir 1997: 33); and it is also unique to women in this. As Hilary M. Lips has commented, making this what Margaret Morganroth Gullette has called the 'magic marker' of ageing can have the effect of 'making it appear that women, as the menopausal sex, are the only ones who age!' (Lips 2016: 431). As such, this process constitutes an asymmetry in the perception of the experience of ageing for men and women on which the double standard of ageing itself can seem to rest.

As has been suggested, the medical discourse about menopause has categorised the condition as an illness that begins with physical 'deficiency' but extends to mental weakness and often, in a further (unwarranted) step, to moral failing. The discourse of medicalisation and its ideological underpinning has been highlighted by prominent scholars of gender (Martin, 1987), and ageing (Gullette, 1997), and in accounts of menopause by Louise Foxcroft (2009) and Roe Sybylla (1997). Ironically, however, while the objectivity of scientific accounts of menopause is compromised by ideological metaphor, cultural treatments of menopause, while purporting to offer a more critical perspective, can conversely borrow from scientific discourse in ways that unsettle and complicate their position of historical and social critique. This latter tendency will be the focus of the current enquiry.

Betty Friedan wrote in relation to the menopause in *The Fountain of Age* that 'eternal vigilance is needed to ward off both a reversion to the feminine mystique, and a passive acquiescence to the medical model which reinforces the mystique of age even as it seems to defend against it' (Friedan, 1993: 496). Even while the biological account of women's ageing is demonstrably rife with value judgements and affective metaphor, cultural commentators find it hard to resist the patina of medical science in their critique of such an account. This is arguably in part because of an uncertainty in the value given to female sexuality in the story of women's ageing. If women lose both sexual desire and the bodily markers of femininity – to the extent that they do, which is itself questionable – is this a cause for celebration or mourning? Literature, this chapter argues, might be able to offer a more nuanced picture of the experience of menopause than either (pseudo)scientific generalisation or polemical cultural critique, holding the felt contradictions of the condition in play.

To this end, the chapter begins with a discussion of the literary representation of menopause in Virginia Woolf's early 20th century novel *Mrs Dalloway*. Menopause is portrayed there as a medical condition, an 'internal ailment', but is also conceived of by implication as what Sontag calls a 'moral disease': a shameful experience about which men cannot speak directly, and from which even women distance themselves. In a wider sense, however, its ambivalent affect provides the very emotional tenor of the novel as a whole. This has several dimensions: the ambivalent feelings of the menopausal woman towards both being invisible and being seen; the renunciation of sexual life received with both mourning and celebration; the mask of illness as both a stigma to shun and an identity to embrace. The contradictions of this particular 'time of life' for the individual and the social discourse are probed and laid bare. At the end of the novel, however, we witness a surprising twist. Rather than being the occasion of seclusion and retirement that it has seemed for both minor and central characters earlier in the narrative, Clarissa Dalloway's change of life marks the embrace of a new life and an ongoing commitment to social identity. The party with which the novel culminates is in effect a commemoration of this turning point and a renewed turn outwards, as Elizabeth Hirsh has argued (2005). Menopause is seen here, for all its complexities and aversive aspects, as a facet of Friedan's 'fully human personhood' for women, rather than its limitation.

The chapter will go on to discuss the treatment of menopause in the social critique of Simone de Beauvoir, a treatment read by Germaine Greer as displaying a sexual double standard which equates life for post-menopausal women with weakness, passivity and loss of agency; in short a kind of death-in-life. This characterisation of female ageing is, as the chapter outlines, one authorised by scientific and medical discourse: women's ageing is a story of deficiency and decay. The discussion then looks at the way that this scientific discourse pervades and destabilises even the kind of cultural critique practised by Greer, whose reading of de Beauvoir's account of female old age diagnoses its pessimism as the universal 'endogenous disappointment' of the menopause itself, unintentionally aping de Beauvoir's pathologising characterisation. Both these thinkers, despite their feminist intentions, seem bound to reinscribe certain patriarchal notions of women's sexuality and its perceived loss in old age. Finally, the chapter looks at what is nonetheless done in such discussions, and in fictional representations such as Woolf's *Mrs Dalloway*, to 'lift the veil' on women's experience of menopause, and combat the taboo created by the interaction of ageism and sexism in both medical and social discourse at large.

'It is probably *that*': Virginia Woolf and menopause as disease

To begin, however, I want to think about the early drafts and opening pages of Woolf's novel, where menopause is treated at once as physical disease and social pathology, a condition to be censored in conversation and hidden away in nursing homes. Louise Foxcroft has observed that in the late 19th and early 20th centuries 'to the medical profession woman was her biological self and no more, and from this cruelly simplistic "fact" flowed assumptions of femininity, virtue, morality and wider social ideas about who and what she was or might be' (Foxcroft, 2009: 134). Virginia Woolf, writing in the 1920s, explores such ideas and their implications for the ageing woman, destined to be invisible once her sexual appeal had diminished, and discovers the collusion of both men and women in their circulation. In a short story that formed the basis of Woolf's 1925 novel *Mrs Dalloway*, 'Mrs Dalloway on Bond Street', the heroine, Clarissa Dalloway, bumps into a friend, the diplomat Hugh Whitbread, in the street. Enquiring after Hugh's wife Milly, Clarissa learns that she is in London to see a doctor for an unnamed ailment about which Hugh is somewhat cagey:

> 'Of course, [Clarissa] thought, walking on, Milly is about my age – fifty, fifty two. So it is probably *that*.' (Woolf, 2010: 88)

Woolf's unidentified relative pronoun prefigures Germaine Greer's (1992: 5) 'undescribed experience', the unspoken and invisible process that Greer's book so trenchantly brought to light.

Woolf – who had somewhat unhappily followed doctors' advice not to have children – was both troubled and fascinated by the menopause, what she calls the 'turn of life'. On Tuesday 24 November 1936, when she was 54 years old, she recorded in her diary that she was glad to be dining with her friend Helen Anrep so that:

> 'I shan't be alone, alone I fall into those trances, comas, which are I suppose t. of l. [*turn of life*]: but so frustrating, when I want to be clear & to read. A curious throbbing this disease produces. But I've been on the whole vigorous and cheerful.' (Woolf, 2008: 399; cited in Foxcroft 2009: 238-9)

The condition is described as a 'disease', but here too there is uncertainty: we hesitate to take the idea of 'trances', let alone 'comas', literally and these symptoms, if such they are, reside somewhere between the physical and the mental – as Woolf's experience of mental illness also perennially did. In a characteristic verb, characteristically used to hover between the somatic and the psychological, Woolf describes the symptoms as a kind of 'throbbing'. This is associated here with a kind of absence, experienced through 'trances' and antithetical to vigorousness, but elsewhere the surrender to the body that is 'throbbing' is a kind of energy tantamount to life itself. As Woolf writes in *Mrs Dalloway*, 'Whatever is alive is throbbing; the pulse is the one "vital" sign of life' (Woolf, 2000 [1925]: 35). To be subject to the body and its animal life is, in a final twist, also to be something akin to a machine, however; another entity that 'throbs' in Woolf's writing in the form of the oil tanker, described later in the novel with its "oily throbbing sides" (2000 [1925]: 105), that carries Peter Walsh to and from India. In the passage about 't. of l.' she is at the mercy of her physiology, but unsure nonetheless whether the effects of the condition are felt in the mind or the body.

In the final draft of *Mrs Dalloway*, there is more – and at the same time less – about the subject of menopause. Early in the novel, Woolf writes:

> They [Hugh Whitbread and his wife] had just come up [to London] – unfortunately – to see doctors. [...] his wife had some internal ailment, nothing serious, which, as an old friend, Clarissa Dalloway would understand without requiring him to specify. Ah yes, she did of course; what a nuisance; and felt very sisterly and oddly conscious at the same time of her hat. (Woolf, 2000 [1925]: 6)

Clarissa feels 'sisterly' about this, presumed to be some gynaecological issue connected to the menopause, which made Hugh's wife (now named Evelyn rather than Milly) 'a good deal out of sorts' and had previously led to a spell 'in a nursing home'. Later in this section of the novel she comes across as rather less sisterly, however, referring to Evelyn as 'that indescribably dried-up little woman' with whom she 'settled down for the usual interminable talk about women's ailments' (Woolf, 2000 [1925]: 10). Even at this earlier moment Clarissa's thoughts pass swiftly from Evelyn to the appearance of her hat, and in the later reference is concerned (in an implicit contrast to Evelyn) that 'people should look pleased as she [Clarissa] came in'.

Clarissa, so conscious of Hugh's gaze, and her own social identity in general, replicates the stereotypical discourse about menopausal women of the time (and often persisting today): that they are 'dried-up', out of sorts and preoccupied by their ailments, and that they somehow shrink in stature, if not disappear from society altogether, once their role as mother is lost to them. Acutely conscious of her own potential invisibility at this stage of life, she famously spends the novel organising a party – an event at which, ironically, the hostess herself can become all but invisible, the party running best when the labour implicit in its smooth operation is unremarked and out of sight. Even the famous opening of Woolf's novel, often read as a positive assertion – and continued flowering – of Clarissa's selfhood and freedom, can be read as an empty gesture. 'Mrs Dalloway said she would buy the flowers herself' (Woolf, 2000 [1925]: 3): no one will, in the event, know (or care) whether it was Clarissa or one of her servants who had purchased the flowers for the party. There are more positive readings of this and other aspects of Clarissa's day (the subject and span of the whole novel): small but significant self-determinations in the face of society's perceived indifference. Her condition is at this time of life finely balanced, however, between momentary pleasure and threat of despair, a condition characterised even for affluent women by a freedom that has society's indifference as its price and a very narrow theatre of operation as its sphere.

A complex and ambivalent affect is produced both by the images that pertain to Clarissa's situation and the use of free indirect discourse, whereby such images hover between her conscious self-ascription and a separate narrative voice. We learn that Clarissa herself sleeps in an attic room, signalling the end of sexual relations with her husband Richard, after an illness that appears to be something to do with the heart, but may also be linked to, and is certainly coincident with, the menopause. When the socially and economically superior Lady Bruton asks Richard Dalloway but not Clarissa to a lunch party, Clarissa has a kind of crisis of confidence connected to her age and this withdrawal from life (linked as it is to her physical transformation):

> she feared time itself [...] feeling herself suddenly shrivelled, aged, breastless [...] Like a nun withdrawing, or a child exploring a tower, she went upstairs [...] There was an emptiness about the heart of life; an attic room. [...] Narrower and narrower would her bed be. (Woolf 2000 [1925]: 33)

Despite the apparent bleakness of this depiction, there is a saving ambiguity here: she is like a nun, but she is also like a child on the brink of a new (and even magical) existence. Even the idea of a nun is not necessarily a negative one here: the nun is an agent, her withdrawing a choice. The different voices of the narrative assume different attitudes to the rituals of her life, the ceremonies of party and social call, allowing the novel to keep both irony and reverence in play. Peter Walsh belittles their value in comparison with the love which grips him ('Oh these parties, he thought; Clarissa's parties. Why does she give these parties, he thought' (Woolf, 2000 [1925]: 52-3)), and Clarissa later feels 'desperately unhappy' at the dismissiveness that he and Richard display towards them (133). She also feels a thrill, however, at the idea of keeping alive what she discerns as a 'beating, a stirring' of London life, at the prospect of preparing to 'kindle and illuminate; to give her party' (Woolf, 2000 [1925]: 52-3).

Elaine Showalter emphasises Clarissa's condition as a 'menopausal woman' (Showalter, 2000: xxxv) in linking her with the traumatised Septimus Smith, suggesting the idea that this phase of life might make one unhappy and unstable (if not suicidal). Yet the novel offers a series of epiphanies that take place not in spite of but in part because of Clarissa's age, and Elizabeth Hirsh has read Clarissa's party, with which the novel ends, as a ritual celebration of Clarissa's change of a life, a transition from one stage to the next rather than an ending (Hirsh 2005: 76, 80). Seeing herself in the strange symbol of a 'post', a 'stake driven in at the top of the stairs', which she feels she has become in making the party happen, Clarissa admires this prosaic object, and feels that it 'marked a stage' (Woolf, 2000 [1925]: 187). This moment of her life is a marker in the flow of time, a marker that betokens a future as well as a past.

The figure of menopause as such is referenced obliquely in Woolf's novel, but is central to the emotional narrative. In one sense Woolf seems to have little sympathy for those who might experience it as an 'ailment', like the 'dried-up' and invisible character of Evelyn Walpole. Instead she favours a character like Clarissa who has weathered the 'change' better and still seeks the authorised mode of male approval, continuing to present a pleasing physical spectacle to men – at least at the parties to which she is invited (namely her own). Clarissa's unsisterly recoil from Evelyn and her predicament is part of the complex affective texture of Woolf's novel, however. She also experiences the invisibility of old age, the waning of social capital that it entails, in her case too, given the correlative of an ambiguous 'illness' that starts in this era to become the catch-all answer for the 'problem' of what to do with women of a certain age. In the end, however, she escapes a passive acquiescence to the medicalised model of menopause and old age to make a commitment to the future and to a 'change of life', whatever it may bring, in the most expansive sense.

Germaine Greer reading Simone de Beauvoir: ageing is not dying

Virginia Woolf features rather curiously in the philosopher Simone de Beauvoir's ground-breaking and still famous 1949 study, *The Second Sex* – a relatively early work to explore women as positioned as socially and materially *other*, object to the male subject, and discriminated against as such. De Beauvoir uses Woolf's writing in this work to exemplify many facets of female experience which might seem frivolous to later feminists, but which could confer genuine pleasure: the excitement of a young girl at a party; the 'sexual initiation' of a country girl; the giving of a dinner party (de Beauvoir, 2010 [1949]: 390–1, 596–7). The flip side of such social pleasures is, however, the process whereby they wane for or are explicitly denied to women 'of a certain age', as Clarissa is denied recognition by being excluded from Lady Bruton's luncheon. An already limited sphere of experience is further compromised by the intersection of age and gender. Ironically, Lady Bruton is of course older than Clarissa, demonstrating an exception whereby the wealthier you are, the more immune you are to the losses of ageing – an inverse intersectionality of which de Beauvoir is very well aware, writing as she does in her later monumental volume on the ageing process itself, *Old Age*, about the economic factors significant to well-being in old age (de Beauvoir, 1997 [1972]: 36–7). In the main, however, de Beauvoir's female subjects in *The Second Sex*, like Clarissa, feel unfeminine and invisible as they get older: the feminine pleasures she attributes to Woolf's younger heroines are, for de Beauvoir, a case of making a virtue out of necessity, and it is a virtue that has a short shelf-life.

Germaine Greer makes a caustic reading in her book on the menopause, *The Change: Women, Ageing and the Menopause* (1992) of de Beauvoir's depiction of ageing in *The Second Sex*, her autobiography *The Force of Circumstance* and the later *Old Age*. The radical feminist import of *The Second Sex* indeed seems all but undone by the unhappy intersection of gender and ageing. The political and social prejudices that confine and oppress women come to seem for de Beauvoir like hopeless inevitabilities when these women age. She asks of 'woman', offered without an article as the universal exemplar of her sex, 'What is to become of her when she no longer has any hold' on her sexual partner (de Beauvoir, 2010 [1949]: 588). About her own ageing in particular, Greer suggests, de Beauvoir is negative, bleak and even phobic. There is a naturalisation of the disgust that one might feel about ageing, which is presented as an illness that medicine cannot palliate – 'when I look, I see my face as it was, attacked by the pox of time for which there is no cure' (de Beauvoir, 1997 [1972]: 656). It is presented as a moral disease in the (literal) sense that one has somehow brought it on oneself, as one does a sexual 'pox'. This echoes the moment in *The Second Sex* where de Beauvoir criticises 'woman' for 'gambl[ing] much more heavily than the man on the sexual values she possesses' (de Beauvoir, 2010 [1949]: 587–8), or the enjoinment in *Old Age* to stop 'cheating' (de Beauvoir, 1997 [1972]: 5) in denying that we will age. A few pages further on in *Force of Circumstance,* thinking of her younger self, she blames that self for the delusion that it could have a continuously fulfilling life: 'turning an incredulous gaze towards that young and credulous girl, I realise with stupor how much I was gypped' (de Beauvoir, 1975 [1963]: 658). Women are, she implies, guilty for hoping for more than their lot as sexual object. As Helen Small has observed, de Beauvoir is condemned to portray the experience of old age as the converse of her theme in earlier works, the freedom of the subject, her book on ageing reading instead as a 'record of constraint' (Small, 2010: 15).

We also find in all of de Beauvoir's writing about ageing the recurrent idea that death has already begun with menopause (or even earlier); alluding to Sainte-Beuve she observers caustically that 'We harden in some places and rot in others. We never ripen' (de Beauvoir, 1997 [1972]: 380). After menopause, the woman becomes one 'whose life is already finished even though death is not imminent'; old age can be 'summed up by the words decrepitude, ugliness and ill-health' (de Beauvoir, 1997 [1972]: 60). Greer comments in *The Change* that 'Characterizing ageing as dying is the kind of category mistake that a woman as well instructed as de Beauvoir should blush to make' (Greer, 1992: 281).

Yet biological and – in its wake – medical science has conspired to label ageing as dying for at least a century by the time de Beauvoir is writing. The ageing body is, as Stephen Katz has observed in his Foucauldian study of ageing, *Disciplining Old Age*, always already a dying body from the mid-19th century onwards, scientists drawing out the implications of the discovery of universal apoptosis or 'an inexorable devolution of cells' (Katz, 1996: 43). The account of women's ageing and in particular its pervasive discourse of (hormone) deficiency compound this newly direful turn in the science of life course (now a science of death). Gynaecologist Robert Wilson, for instance, influential for decades in the study and medical treatment of menopause, echoes this conflation of ageing and dying in his warning that 'no women can be sure of escaping the horror of this living decay' (Wilson, 1966: 43). The language of death and decay, applied to post-menopausal women, is, as Wilson's comment suggests, a radically misogynistic one, drawing on centuries of patriarchal association between women, sexuality and death, but recasting these ancient cultural associations as modern medical science. In Wilson's writings, and many others of the mid-20th century, women encountered a moral tone and an encouragement to self-revulsion (as well as some very bad science). There is a persistent and pervasive gender bias in the most apparently scientific discussions of menopause fed by and in its turn feeding the prevailing sexual ideology.

De Beauvoir, in *The Second* Sex, describes the dilemmas of ageing in the terms of existentialist philosophy: the female cannot escape the objectification and immanence that bars her from access to true freedom and transcendence; in short, she cannot escape association with and confinement by the body. The female invests in the work of 'species' (reproduction), in domestic work and in sexual pleasure (as a route to power or security – de Beauvoir has little to say about pleasure for its own sake). De Beauvoir critiques these investments and their dangers are explored, but there is no hint of an alternative. The fleeting references to work, for instance, hold little weight against the experiences of the flesh, or in de Beauvoir's words the 'fleshly object that she [all women] identifies with herself' (de Beauvoir, 2010 [1949]: 588).

The idea of an inner life in which a woman might be seen to develop emotionally, spiritually and creatively, towards which Woolf gestures in her novel, is also seen as somewhat flimsy, and certainly fleeting. De Beauvoir notes those moments of happiness that Woolf affords her female protagonists:

> These are the moments of luminous happiness that Virginia Woolf – in *Mrs Dalloway*, in *To the Lighthouse* – that Katherine Mansfield all through her work, grant to their heroines as a supreme recompense. The joy that is a surge of freedom is reserved for the man; what the woman knows is an impression of smiling plenitude. (de Beauvoir, 2010 [1949]: 631)

These are, however, no more than the 'impression of smiling plenitude' – 'smiling' here a matter of appearance and thus a strangely negative quality – rather than true freedom. They are ultimately the *absence* of something: *ataraxia*, will-lessness, 'the pleasure that comes when the mind is at rest' (de Beauvoir, 2010 [1949]: 632). This ataraxia can be a release from the tension of 'denial, recriminations and demands', but it is 'a delusion to try to find here the true definition of the hidden soul of the world'. Women's access to the freedom of purposeful action does indeed wither in old age, for de Beauvoir, in a way that is not seen to be true for men.

The Wilsons and menopause as endogenous misery

Furthermore, what de Beauvoir casts as rest from anxieties and responsibilities can all too easily be equated with both passivity and unproductiveness. Robert Wilson and his wife Thelma (a nurse in his practice) wrote an article in the *Journal of American Geriatrics Society* in 1963 in which they argue that even without the discomfort or depression regularly felt to attend menopause:

> a large percentage of women who escape severe depression or melancholia acquire a vapid cow-like feeling called a 'negative state'. It is a strange endogenous misery [...]. The world appears as through a gray veil, and they live as docile harmless creatures missing most of life's values. (Wilson and Wilson, 1963: 353)

This quality of ataraxia also pervades the tropes used about the menopausal phase and its aftermath – tropes of emptiness and invisibility that unconsciously reproduce the more extravagantly sexist language of the medical discourse about the menopause or 'climacteric', language that came to its heyday not in the 19th or early 20th century, but in the 1960s (and which is still detectable today). This language is underpinned by the deficiency hypothesis – that the menopause represents a somehow unnatural, even pathological deficiency of oestrogen – and the ideology that attends it. The title of the Wilsons' article, claiming to chart women's decreasing powers from 'puberty to grave' also demonstrates that death is ever-present in such accounts.

Ironically, as Margaret Lock has noted, Robert Greenblatt, writing the foreword to Robert Wilson's 1966 book *Feminine Forever*, the infamous work advocating HRT as the necessary alternative to 'senile decay', cites the feminist de Beauvoir herself in support of Wilson's argument. Greenblatt observes that the ideas of Wilson were in tune with those of the author of *The Second Sex*, who had written about the 'pathetic urgency of those who have staked everything on their femininity to turn back the flight of time' (Wilson, 1966: 13, cited in Lock, 1993: 349). De Beauvoir's first book, published in English just a year before Wilson's, is indeed hardly a call to arms, her berating of her fellow women reproducing the charge of apathy which male gynaecologists have been all too ready to use:

> ... my species is two-thirds composed of worms, too weak
> ever to rebel, who drag their way from birth to death through
> a perpetual dusk of despair. (de Beauvoir, 2010 [1949]: 654)

As Germaine Greer comments in *The Change*, de Beauvoir's disappointment with life seems 'endogenous' (Greer, 1992: 283); it appears to arise in her rather being imposed from outside.

Yet – as the term 'endogenous', echoing (of all people) Robert Wilson, indicates – Greer herself falls into the same trap. Her observation of de Beauvoir's 'endogenous disappointment' is perilously close to Wilson's own diagnosis of 'endogenous misery' in menopausal women. Greer medicalises this defeatist condition, partly condemning de Beauvoir, partly empathising with her in their fellow suffering, in the common plight of their common species ('woman'). She writes of de Beauvoir that these 'self-defeating mental processes, her vivid awareness of death, her nightmares and obsessions, *are* the misery of the climacteric' (Greer, 1992: 283; my emphasis). On the one hand, this 'unnatural' behaviour is 'pathologically' disordered according to Greer: it is a 'toxic' disillusionment, it is 'anophobia' (that is, in Greer's own coinage, an irrational fear of the old woman), there is 'something radically wrong' with 54-year-old Simone de Beauvoir. On the other, these pathologies belong to all women, at least for the term of this transitional phase of life.

Even Greer, then, cannot resist a medicalised account that suggests the inevitability of both physical discomfort and depression at the same time as she blames others for failing to consider that everyone's menopause is different and so, implicitly, that such suffering is by no means inevitable (or even – as many studies show – the norm). It is ironic that while the so-called medical accounts are often value-laden, metaphorical and beholden to dominant narratives of female decline and decay, the cultural examinations by literary figures such as Greer and de Beauvoir, while not short on their own ideological metaphors, pursue the spurious authority of medical language even as they critique the medicalisation of menopause.

Kathleen Woodward has commented (in the Introduction to her collection on female ageing, *Figuring Age*) on the 'oddly archaic biological essentialism' of Greer's work (Woodward, 1999: xiv). She identifies this quality in Greer's argument not in terms of the quasi-medical vocabulary discussed here, but in terms of the way in which Greer wants to mark the menopause as a transition between the 'before' of reproduction (as if this is the basis of every woman's identity) and the 'after', a life of quiet, asexual 'reflection'. Greer echoes the Victorian image of menopause as a 'sure haven' in which women might be 'safely anchored', as gynaecologist Edward Tilt wrote in 1870, sexual activity a danger from which such women are now happily inured (Tilt, 1870: 68, cited in Sybylla, 1997: 204).

Greer is caught here, of course, between the two polarised positions imposed on women in relation to sexuality since the beginning of the 19th century. The first position, epitomised by Tilt as well as other doctors such as Samuel Mason and the now indirectly famous J. Braxton Hicks, was that women of reproductive age were in danger of instability, insanity and even death if subject to a disordered uterus, a condition associated with 'animal spirits' that might 'fuddle' the brain (Tilt, 1870: 203). In the period after menopause, when sexual activity should be 'extinct', as French gynaecologist Marc Columbat put it in 1850, the woman was therefore both safer and also, in becoming more 'masculine', concomitantly seen to be (and – crucially – permitted to be) more mentally vigorous (Tilt, 1870: 27) and capable (Hicks, 1877: 475-6).

The second position, wherein women were not only permitted but exhorted to continue to be sexually active, while continuing to equate femininity exclusively with sexual characteristics and behaviour, at least appears to value their femininity. This same – flawed – conception of what is 'feminine' flips to the other extreme, however, in making sexual activity, often connected to both youthful appearance and pliability (that is, not being 'moody', a euphemism for sexual refusal), an inescapable duty. Women may be valued in being different from men, then, but only if they continued to define themselves, as men did, purely in terms of bodily appearance and sexual availability. Both Greer and de Beauvoir seem to capitulate to some extent to the terms of this forced choice, Greer opting for Tilt's asexual and invisible safe haven, and de Beauvoir, as Roe Sybylla has observed, also leaning towards the first option in appearing to endorse and favour the 'masculinising' of the menopausal woman: 'And while they are not males, they are no longer females. Often, indeed, this release from female physiology is expressed in a balance that they lacked before' (de Beauvoir, 2010 [1949]: 43, cited in Sybylla, 1997: 318, n. 17).

What, therefore, is the alternative to this biological essentialism, which seems even in the most feminist of accounts to impose the unenviable choice of invisibility, a poor approximation of masculinity or continued sexual objectification? Even invisibility can be an asset, according to Greer (like, as she says, 'calm or indifference') but she also admits that she is making a virtue out of what she sees as a necessity, this invisibility something the post-menopausal woman is, according to Greer, 'forced to accept' (Greer, 1992: 430). Kathleen Woodward, on the other hand, calls for something other than invisibility – what she calls 'taking the veil' – for the years of menopause. This is not, after all, a veil that is easily lifted, once it falls. And here in fact is where de Beauvoir's work can serve in a more positive fashion. Her monumental study *Old Age* has many problems for the feminist and age scholar alike. It does not escape the revulsion and fear that she betrays for ageing in general. It is also especially ironic that it is male ageing that takes centre stage there, the loss of identity as she sees it so much harder for men, the implication being that they have much more identity to lose. However problematic this study is, however, it does say 'look'. Its abiding message is that society must not, as de Beauvoir puts it, 'turn away' (de Beauvoir, 1997 [1972]: 603). It removes the veil. And Woolf, too, makes the reaffirmation of visibility the crowning moment of her famous novel, which ends with Clarissa, in all her contradictions, simply *there*:

> It is Clarissa, he said.
> For there she was. (Woolf, 2000 [1925]: 213)

Conclusion

Both Simone de Beauvoir and Germaine Greer are asking us to look at female old age as constructed by society in relation to a sexist ideology both fearful of female sexuality and dismissive of womanhood beyond sexual behaviour. This ideology and the practices of control that have followed from it have been authorised and administered by a scientific and medical establishment drawing in the case of menopause on the spurious science of deficiency. It is well understood, thanks to the work of scholars such as Gullette (1997), that this pseudoscience, pressed into service by global capitalism to sell pharmaceutics and costly medical procedures, has demonstrated a value-laden tone and a floridly morbid rhetoric of distraction, decay and incapacity in its imagery and narratives until late in the 20th century. Such has been the authority of medical science, however, since the mid–19th century, that even the critiques of this pathologising discourse, such as those of leading feminists like de Beauvoir and Greer, can find themselves using the spurious concepts of science as their own, and naturalising the idea of mental and even spiritual deficiency as an inevitable attendant to this physical change. Woolf's novel is by no means free of these ideas and associations, of course, and her protagonist is far from 'sisterly' towards those who suffer physically and socially in relation to the condition. The literary treatment of Clarissa Dalloway's mid-life transition is, however, able to capture some of the nuances and the contradictions, as well as the subjective experience of this phase of life, and all three of these feminist icons in their different ways are concerned at the very least to describe Greer's 'undescribed experience', to talk about *that*.

References

de Beauvoir, S. (1975 [1963]) *Force of Circumstance*, trans. R. Howard, Harmondsworth: Penguin.

de Beauvoir, S. (1997 [1972]) *Old Age*, trans. P. O'Brian, Harmondsworth: Penguin.

de Beauvoir, S. (2010 [1949]) *The Second Sex*, trans. C. Borde and S. Malovany-Chevalier, London: Vintage.

Columbat, M. (1850) *A Treatise on the Diseases and Special Hygiene of Females*. Philadelphia: Lea and Blanchard.

Deutsch, H. (1945) *The Psychology of Women*, New York: Grune & Stratton.

Foxcroft, L. (2009) *Hot Flushes, Cold Science: The History of the Modern Menopause*, London: Granta.

Friedan, B. (1993) *The Fountain of Age*. London: Jonathan Cape.

Greer, G. (1992) *The Change: Women, Ageing and the Menopause*, Harmondsworth: Penguin.

Gullette, M. (1997) 'Menopause as magic marker: discursive consolidation in the United States and strategies for cultural combat', in P. Komesaroff, P. Rothfield and J. Daly (eds) *Reinterpreting Menopause: Cultural and Philosophical Issues*, London: Routledge: 176–99.

Hicks, J.B. (1877) 'The Croonian Lectures on the difference between the sexes in regard to the aspect and treatment of disease', *British Medical Journal*, 21 April 1(851): 475–6.

Hirsh, E. (2005) 'Mrs Dalloway's menopause: encrypting the female life course', in K.V. Kukil (ed) *Woolf in the Real World: Selected Papers from the Thirteenth International Conference on Virginia Woolf*, Clemson, SC: Clemson University Press: 86–91.

Katz, S. (1996) *Disciplining Old Age: The Formation of Gerontological Knowledge*, London: University Press of Virginia.

Lips, H. (2016) *A New Psychology of Women: Gender, Culture and Ethnicity*, Long Grove, Illinois: Waveland Press.

Lock, M. (1993) *Encounters with Aging: Mythologies of Menopause in Japan and North America*, Berkeley: University of California Press.

Martin, E. (1987) *The Woman in the Body: A Cultural Analysis of Reproduction*. Boston: Beacon.

Showalter, E. (2000) 'Introduction', *Mrs Dalloway* (Virginia Woolf), London: Penguin.

Small, H. (2010) *The Long Life*, Oxford: Oxford University Press.

Sontag, S. (1972) 'The double standard of aging', *Saturday Review*, 23 September: 29–38.

Sybylla, R. (1997) 'Situating menopause within the strategies of power', in P. Komesaroff, P. Rothfield and J. Daly (eds) *Reinterpreting Menopause: Cultural and Philosophical Issues*, London: Routledge: 200–24.

Tilt, E. (1870) *The Change of Life in Health and Disease*, London: John Churchill.

Wilson, R. (1966) *Feminine Forever*, London: W.H. Allen.

Wilson, R. and Wilson, T. (1963) 'The fate of the non-treated postmenopausal woman: a plea for the maintenance of adequate estrogen from puberty to grave', *Journal of American Geriatrics Society*, 11(4): 347–62.

Woodward, K. (1999) *Figuring Age: Women, Bodies, Generations*, Bloomington, IN: Indiana University Press.

Woolf, V. (2000 [1925]) *Mrs Dalloway*, London: Penguin.

Woolf, V. (2008 [1953]) *Selected Diaries*, London: Vintage.

Woolf, V. (2010 [1923]) *Mrs Dalloway's Party: A Short Story Sequence*, London: Vintage.

SIX

Representations of female ageing and sexuality in Penelope Lively's *Moon Tiger*, Angela Carter's *Wise Children* and Doris Lessing's 'The grandmothers'

Maricel Oró Piqueras

Introduction

In her *Out of Time: The Pleasures and Perils of Ageing*, Lynne Segal (2014: 7) explains that Simone de Beauvoir despaired when she turned to her fifties since she thought she would never be able to 'experience new desires or to display her yearnings publicly'. As de Beauvoir herself explains, 'it is not I who am saying goodbye to all those things I once enjoyed, it is they who are leaving me' (Segal, 2014: 7). Despite the exponential ageing of Western populations, there are a number of deep-rooted cultural ideas that contribute to present late-middle age and old age as a time of unstoppable decline in which certain emotions and human drives, together with the biological ageing of the body, seem to magically disappear all of a sudden. This is the case with regard to desire and sexuality. However, in recent years, this limited understanding of old age and sexuality has been counterbalanced by an image of ageing and sexuality which can be found at the other extreme of the spectrum, namely, that of the 'sexy oldie' (Gott, 2005: 23). Research conducted by Gott and Hinchliff (2003) and Katz and Marshall (2003) shows how, in recent years, the message has proliferated that looking and staying sexy and having an active sexual life is the best way of fighting against the losses of ageing.

This chapter aims to present these two extremes of the continuum in relation to how sexuality and ageing have been culturally presented, especially with regard to female ageing, within the fictional texts of three contemporary British authors, namely Penelope Lively's *Moon Tiger* (1988), Angela Carter's *Wise Children* (1996) and Doris Lessing's short story 'The grandmothers' (2004). The protagonists portrayed in these three texts, all of them women in their seventies and eighties, neither conform to these models of female ageing and sexuality nor to a normative understanding of relationships. The fictionalised form of the two novels and the short story allow the readers to get into the inner thoughts of the protagonists in order to witness how they think and feel, as well as to understand the ways in which they establish an interrelationship with their social background and communities. In this sense, cultural and sociological studies on the experiences of sexuality in later life will establish a dialogue with the fictional texts analysed here in order to discern to what extent and in what ways these two discourses are challenged in the texts analysed.

From the asexual old woman to the 'sexy oldie'

For Kathleen Woodward, the restricted meanings attached to old age and to the ageing body come from two different sources: an over-valorisation of youth and an almost automatic association of the ageing body to decline and death. As Woodward (1991: 19) contends, 'we cannot detach the body in decline from the meanings we attach to old age'. In this respect, desire and sexuality are related to the young body and are perceived as disgusting and inadequate when felt and experienced by someone past their youth. In their article 'Sex and ageing: a gendered issue', Merryn Gott and Sharron Hinchliff (2003: 64) explain that despite the fact that sex has been integrated as a part of normal behaviour within societal norms, 'old age remains outside this "sexualized world"'. Through their research, they argue that 'sex remains important to quality of life until the point where people do not think they will have another sexual partner during their lifetime' (Gott and Hinchliff, 2003: 65). Thus, despite the fact that the informants within their study show that 'sex was perceived as something "natural" and "normal" for "adults", including for older people', the reasons why a few of them had become 'sexually retired' was because they had lost their partners and thought they would not find a new one; otherwise, sex and desire was seen as a '"normal" and "pleasurable" aspect of life, as one of the informants put it' (married woman, aged 63) (Gott and Hinchliff, 2003: 68).

In other studies, mainly based on heterosexual relationships, Woodward (1999) and Gott (2005) research further the relationship between ageing, old age and sexuality, with a special emphasis on female ageing in the case of Woodward. Starting from the premise that sexuality, which is frequently described as 'the most natural thing about us' (Gott, 2005: 79), is actually socially and culturally constructed in complex ways, Gott argues, in that 'sexual attitudes and behaviours of older women and men' have to be explored and studied 'within a wider socio-cultural and historical context' (2005: 79). In this sense, Woodward develops her argument following the seminal texts of Simone de Beauvoir (1997 [1949]) and Susan Sontag (1972), according to which women are considered to age sooner than men due to the cultural and social meanings attached to the female ageing body. As Woodward contends (1999: xiii), 'in the West, female attractiveness has long been associated with youth, and the older woman has been thought of in disparaging terms as menopausal and post-menopausal'.

Thus, both authors highlight the still close relationship between attractiveness and sexuality at the turn of the 21st century. As the biological body ages, interest in sex is thought to decline too. However, different studies have proved that this is one of the prevailing narratives associated with a restricted view of the ageing process. Contrarily to this view, Gott refers to Barbara Sherman's study, *Sex, Intimacy and Aged Care*, published in 1998, in which she concludes that 'sexuality and making love are part of the fabric of our lives; part of the very essence of being human – even for older people' (Shermann, 1998, cited Gott, 2005: 16). Similarly, Rebecca L. Jones challenges other limiting cultural ideas related of older women and sex in her study '"That's very rude, I shouldn't be telling you that": older women talking about sex' in which she departs from the 'dominant cultural storyline' (Jones, 2002: 125), according to which academics and practitioners believe that older people are expected to have lost interest in sex and, moreover, they are believed not to talk about sex. Through her research, Jones proved that there actually existed a counter-narrative, with its complexities, which determined that interest in sex was lifelong and that older women talked about sex in quite a natural and straightforward way. In a more recent article, Maggie Syme (2014: 5) states that 'older adult sexuality is often ignored' among healthcare professionals, who prove to still rely on stereotypical beliefs which make old age, sexual attractiveness and, thus, interest in sex, utterly incompatible. Syme includes 'intimate partnerships' within what she calls 'quality social connections' (2014: 36), which contribute to ensure a good quality of life throughout the life course. Thus she supports the idea that professionals need to incorporate a holistic view of sexuality that extends across the lifespan, in which emotional, social and intellectual experiences go hand in hand with sexual experiences within the relationship context, with both pleasure and sexual dysfunction as part of the picture.

In her study, Syme (2014: 38) also refers to 'body image and sexual self-esteem' as factors that affect sexual interest in a negative way, especially in women. However, as other researchers have argued, these factors are mainly triggered by ageist views in relation to youth and beauty. As pointed out in the introduction, this stereotype has been counterbalanced by the notion that nowadays citizens, especially women, entering or in old age have the obligation to keep youthfully 'sexy' with the aim of having an active sexual life which is read as a sign of health in old age. Gott refers to the myth of the 'sexy oldie' as a stereotype whose key message is that 'being sexual is fundamental to mental and physical well-being at any age, but particularly as a means to stave off old age' (Gott, 2005: 24). For their part, Katz and Marshall (2003: 4) discern a narrowly defined 'active sexuality', based on 'heterosexual intercourse', as part of an over-optimistic cultural imagery of what has been called 'the new aging'. Gott, Katz and Marshall coincide in recognising media as the main source of the creation and spreading of the stereotype of the 'sexy oldie'. Katz and Marshall, specifically, consider the advertising industry as the main instigator of standardising the ageing experience within a frame of 'timelessness, impermanence, and simultaneity', which can be achieved through consumerism and a healthy life style with fitness and sexual intercourse at its core. As the authors state, 'older individuals must cope with the impossible burden of growing older without aging, with a fundamental part of this burden attributed to the maintenance of sexual functionality and "fitness"' (Katz and Marshall, 2003: 5). In this respect, Dolan and Tincknell (2012: viii) introduce their volume *Aging Femininities* precisely stating that nowadays older women are encouraged to fit in 'a discourse of "successful ageing" which basically encourages women to invest resources, both economic and personal, to achieve a "socially approved identity"'.

Thus the older woman is either invisible or rendered inadequate when trying to express her sexuality if she has accepted the vicissitudes of time on her body; alternatively, she is perceived as a plausible sexual being when she has managed to keep the signs of ageing at bay through the use of consumer products and techniques; in other words, there seems not to be a middle ground for women ageing into old age. In this respect, Lynne Segal (2014: 97) argues that there needs to be a change in the 'youthful iconography of what it is for a woman to be a desirable sex object'. Segal refers to one of Penelope Lively's characters, the protagonist of *Spiderweb*, Sarah Durham, a recently retired archaeologist, who, starting to experience invisibility after moving to the country on her own, considers that 'if you have been a beauty, ageing must be intolerable … the process is bad enough as it is' (Lively, 1998: 187). This quote shows to what extent the cultural references of sexual attractiveness and desire are still narrow and mainly focus on youthful looks.

Fictionalising female sexuality in later life

The potential and value of fictional contemporary texts to look at the complexities of the ageing process and old age from various perspectives has been widely discussed in the last years. Among different scholars, Sara Munson Deats and Lagretta Tallent Lenker and sociologist Mike Hepworth have proved fiction to be a valuable source to establish a constant and dynamic interaction between cultural and social conceptions of old age and the ageing process. As Hepworth (2000: 8) contends, 'stories of ageing should be read as the products of historically established systems of ideas and beliefs'. For their part, Deats and Lenker (1999: 3) consider that 'studying the way in which stereotypes of any kind – gender, race, class, or age – are constructed within a work of art can help us to learn about – and to challenge – the construction of stereotypes within our own society'. In this respect, fictional texts turn to be a valuable source to look at topics which are especially sensitive to being stereotyped and even concealed to some extent, as it is the case of sexuality and desire in old age. As Lynne Segal suggests (2014: 173), 'there are other ways to recognize and value the mixed experiences of old age, in which beauty, pain, resilience and resistance intermingle, while time itself appears more fluid'. In her book, *Out of Time: The Pleasures and Perils of Ageing*, Segal references a wide range of Anglo-American fictional texts from which significant cultural and social conceptions of the ageing experience can be extracted and analysed; at the same time the reader is granted the opportunity to observe the older protagonists and characters from within, through their thoughts and innermost concerns, as well as to witness the social dimension of the characters, through their interaction with other characters. Deats and Lenker, Hepworth and Segal, among other scholars, from their specific disciplines, coincide in pointing to the fact that fictional texts and, actually, popular culture in general, foreground the complexity of the ageing experience within the life course at the same time as they contribute to portraying multiple perspectives and experiences.

At the end of the 1980s, Margaret M. Gullette and Barbara Frey Waxman refer to the emergence of a number of novels in which female characters in their late middle years become not only the main protagonists and, in some cases, narrators of their own stories but they also refuse to succumb to decline narratives once past their fertile years. As Gullette (1988: xiv) states, 'they are not "heroines" or "heroes" in a classical way, but they have resistances, strengths, or sly timely weaknesses, ingenious mental feints'. Waxman (1990) actually identifies a new kind of genre in these emerging novels which she names *Reifungsroman* (novel of ripening), reminiscing the coming of age novel known as Bildungsroman which usually stops when the protagonist reaches young adulthood. As Waxman argues, the biological ageing of the body and the coming to terms with it of the protagonists is not denied; conversely, these novels seek to give voice to female characters that would ordinarily be pushed into the background or silenced, and present their passions and concerns, their longing and resentments through a process which is experienced by all human beings, namely, growing older.

In her most recent study and departing from the premise that 'today's invisible women can only make themselves visible by distinguishing themselves as younger women' (2013: xi), Jeannette King analysed the presence of older female characters in literature in English from the 1850s to the present times. According to King, the stereotypes of either the mother – usually inadequate, with a lack of maternal presence – or the spinster, together with the stereotype of the mad or demented older woman have been prevalent from the end of the 19th century up until the end of the 20th century. Similarly, Traies (2016) acknowledges the silencing and invisibility of same-sex desires between women. King (2013) points out the relationship between madness and female sexuality, particularly in association to the menopause. According to King, up until the 1960s, the menopause was often matched to terms such as hysteria and madness (2013: 58). Actually, both Hepworth and Brennan recognise the 'grandmother' as one of the very few accepted female literary images in old age. After revising and analysing older female literary figures in Anglo-American literary texts, Brennan (2005: 79) argues that

> the virginal stereotype of the grandmother continues to be the most accepted one in popular imagination, either because she is too 'grotesque' for anyone to want as a lover or too wise to be concerned with matters of the flesh.

Thus, both Brennan and Hepworth argue that the main reasons why the figure of the grandmother remains an accepted image of female ageing is the fact that she is devoid of sexual implications; her role being mainly that of carer and emotional support when needed in the family.

Within contemporary British fiction, Doris Lessing's novel *Love, Again* (1996) is among the first to deal with female ageing and sexuality in an explicit way by allowing the readers to go into the inner self of their female protagonists. In the case of *Love, Again* Lessing portrays a 65-year-old woman who falls in love twice, in a short period of time, and with younger men. Sarah Durham is a successful theatre producer who has been a widow for a number of years and, as Brennan (2005: 79) explains, she 'finds herself unexpectedly emerging from a calm she assumed appropriate to the old and falling passionately in love with two younger men'. Indeed, throughout the novel the protagonist goes from considering herself past sexual desire to trying to understand the mismatch between the sexual desire her body feels with her biological age, a mismatch which provokes in Sarah a good deal of anxiety over the fact that the body she scrutinises in front of the mirror is not young and beautiful anymore, according to Western cultural standards. Throughout the novel the reader understands that Sarah's coercion of her desire towards two of her work colleagues is cultural rather than biological. In this respect, literary texts allow a short, but many times intense, glimpse into multiple possibilities and probably new-imagined future, as Marshall (2016: 19) expresses in her recently published *Age Becomes Us*: 'through literature, readers connect with collective histories, and by extension, with shared futures, a potential that can create in the reader a vital and empowering obligation'.

Lively's historian, Carter's sisters and Lessing's grandmothers

Penelope Lively's *Moon Tiger* (1987), Angela Carter's *Wise Children* (1996) and Doris Lessing's 'The grandmothers' (2004) are three fictional texts, two novels and one short story, by contemporary women British writers in which the reader is guided by the voices of three women protagonists in their seventies and eighties. In these texts the reader is invited to go into the inner recesses of five women protagonists – Claudia Hampton in *Moon Tiger*, the twin sisters Nora and Dora Chance in *Wise Children* and the good friends Lil and Roz in 'The grandmothers' – who have not followed the commands and demands of their times, neither during their youth nor in their old age. They are not only strong women with clear voices, but also older women who have enjoyed and enjoy sex according to their own norms. The relationships, love affairs and sexual encounters that are described in the novels, more or less explicitly, present relationships of these women outside a normative understanding of love and sexuality.

The female protagonist in *Moon Tiger*, Claudia Hampton, is presented as an 80-year-old woman who is bed-ridden and who intends to write a history of the world before she dies. Her history of the world will be composed of 'fact and fiction, myth and evidence, images and documents' (Lively, 1988: 1). Claudia is a journalist who claims to have had two big loves in her life: her brother Gordon and her first lover Tom Southern who died in Cairo during the Second World War. The relationship between Claudia and her brother is described as one of having had a mutual crush since they were teenagers. They shared this feeling and knew the other felt the same, but never succumbed to it: 'I saw in Gordon's maleness an erotic flicker of myself; and when he looked at me I saw in his eyes that he too saw some beckoning reflection' (1988: 137). Claudia actually set Gordon as a model to follow against any man she met; as she herself explains: '[u]ntil I was in my late twenties I never knew a man who interested me as much as Gordon did. That was why it was as it was between us. I measured each man I met against him, and they fell short: less intelligent, less witty, less attractive' (1988: 136). The peculiar relationship that Claudia had with her brother up until the moment in which the novel starts, in her death bed, foregrounds Claudia's unique character and her irreverent conceptions of both relationships and family. She believes that both Gordon and her daughter Lisa married the first woman and man who came along, as she states in the novel, and thus conformed to a restricted conception of the family. For her part, Claudia never married although she had a daughter with Jasper, a diplomat she met in her late thirties. She claims not to believe in marriage and describes her relationship with Jasper as quite an informal one, despite having a child in common. After they met and for 'the next ten years we sometimes lived together, sometimes did not, fought, made it up, parted and were reunited' (1988: 9). Apart from Gordon, Tom and Jasper, when she is in her late middle age, Claudia takes Laszlo as her protégée. Even though a sexual or romantic relationship between Claudia and Laszlo is never explicitly mentioned in the novel, they share mutual admiration as well as a common language from which Lisa and Jasper, Claudia's daughter and ex-husband, feel distanced and somehow envious. Throughout the retelling of her personal story and throughout her 80-year-old mind, Claudia's loves and desires are far from what is understood as normative heterosexuality.

In her *Discourses of Ageing*, King (2013: 114) contends that Lively's *Moon Tiger* 'challenges the goal-oriented discourse of the female

Bildungsroman, in which the ultimate goal is marriage, whatever aspirations the protagonist might harbour initially'. In terms of form and narrative, King contends that this is present in the novel in the fact that the love affair which Claudia considers to have marked her life, her relationship with soldier Tom Southern, is set in the core of the novel as well as Claudia's life; however, it does not represent the end of either. On the contrary, after her intense love relationship with Tom, Claudia understands she will never fit into the role of a normative heterosexual relationship. On the other hand, the structure of the novel contributes to portray present and past as simultaneous and coexistent and the idea of 'identity as multiple but continuous' (King, 2013: 120). In this respect, as King argues, 'it suggests that an old woman is not someone who has moved beyond into a distinct stage and category of life, but merely a woman who is old' (2013: 120). Thus in her particular history of the world, which is guided by neither chronology nor order, both the limiting conceptions of youth and old age, as well as a restricted view of relationships and family structure, are undermined.

In Carter's *Wise Children*, the protagonists, Nora and Dora, are presented through a similar lens to Claudia Hampton in Lively's *Moon Tiger*. They are twin sisters and the novel opens with their 75th birthdays. They have lived in London all their lives, on the wrong side of the river, according to Dora's narrative, and had made a living in the music-hall and show business. Despite the fact that they had had love affairs that had marked their lives (as Claudia with Tom Southern), they had always kept a distance from what was understood as normative love and sexuality as well as from the limiting position of women within traditional family structures. As Dora narrates her story in the first person, she confesses that the first man with whom she herself and her sister had fallen in love had been her uncle Perry:

> Ooh, wasn't he a handsome young man, in those days. If I find myself describing him in the language of the pulp romance, then you must forgive me – there was always that quality about Perry ... . It was our Uncle Peregrine from America and we didn't know him from Adam. (Carter, 1996: 30)

The love-hate relationship the Chance twins have with their father, who only recognised them as legitimate children right at the end of his life, on his 100th birthday, as well as the open-minded life philosophy of their adoptive grandmother, who defined herself as a naturist, had inculcated in them the idea of not taking life too seriously. As Dora explains, grandma Chance was 'a convert to naturism' (1996: 27) and used to go around the house naked while she urged the girls to allow their bodies to get some fresh air too. This philosophy allowed them to enjoy their bodies away from cultural constraints and to understand the concept of family in a broad sense. According to Dora, 'Grandma invented this family. She put it together out of whatever came to hand – a stray pair of orphaned babes, a ragamuffin in a flat cap. She created it by sheer force of personality' (1996: 35). The Chance sisters had had multiple love and sexual affairs; they had fallen in love and had suffered for love but had never succumbed to the requirements of a patriarchal understanding of the word family. On their 75th birthdays, they share the Brixton house they had inherited from Grandma Chance and take up family, friends and acquaintances who need shelter and love.

The novel opens with 75-year-old Dora and Nora getting ready to attend their father's 100th birthday party and, as they do so, they retell their story and their family's, from the time they were born to the present time of the novel. The process of getting ready for the party is described by Carter as a process of reconstruction of their younger selves which, in fact, is both comic and rebellious. As Nora explains,

> It took an age but we did it; we painted the faces that we always used to have on to the faces we have now. From a distance of thirty feet with the light behind us, we looked, at first glance, just like the girl who danced with the Prince of Wales when nightingales sang in Berkeley Square on a foggy day in London Town. (Carter, 1996: 192)

The fact that the Chance sisters disguise themselves in the clothes and make-up they used to wear in their twenties blurs the boundaries between young and old. Nora's ironic and humorous narrative simultaneously undermines a narrow image of sexual attractiveness, very much related to youthful beauty, as argued by cultural gerontologists such as Kathleen Woodward and Margaret Gullette. The Chance sisters have physically aged with the century as both actresses and models; however, they have neither lost their sense of humour nor their creativity to keep on reconstructing themselves as women ageing in a time and place in which the physical signs on the body result into limiting one's participation and implication in society. Not only do they still have sexual desire and, comically, try to disguise themselves into 'sexually attractive beings', but also, and following their Grandma's philosophy, they take up any person who needs a family. This is the case of a character they call Wheelchair, the first wife of their father Melchior, who was neglected by her ex-husband and children and who lives with them, as well as a black single mother and her little daughter, Our Cyn and Tiffany.

The ending of the novel precisely reinforces the idea that sexuality is not only the terrain of the young and beautiful, since it finishes with 75-year-old Dora and a 100-year-old Perry making love at Dora's father's birthday party, while the party guests in the dining room below can hear and see the chandelier agitating wildly. The act of making love makes time stop for a while, according to Dora, and for a few minutes Perry

> was himself, when young; and also, while we were making love he turned into, of all people, that blue-eyed boy who'd never known my proper name. ... I saw myself reflected in those bracken-coloured eyes of his. I was a lanky girl with a green bow in her mouse-brown hair. (Carter, 1996: 221)

The sexual act together with the fact that there exists real love and affection between them makes Dora and Perry forget about the biological, but mainly cultural, limitations of their ageing bodies and focus on embracing their desire and enjoying that sexual part that stays with any human being until the end. According to Beth A. Boehm (1994: 88), 'it is not the act itself that makes time stand still, but rather the magic that lies in human desire'. In other words, a desire that can be as vivid in someone's twenties as in someone's seventies. For her part, Zoe Brennan (2005: 77) considers that Dora and Perry 'mock the idea that sexual fantasy and expression in old age is abnormal, taboo or inappropriate, while managing to avoid the pitfall of suggesting the other extreme: that older women should necessarily be sexually active'. Through humour, irony and drag, the Chance sisters undermine both the cultural conception that women past their fifties become 'sexually retired', as expressed by Gott (2005: 68), and the opposite conception, that is, the image of the 'sexy oldie' as the emblem of the sexually active older woman.

In Doris Lessing's 'The grandmothers', the female protagonists are two 60-year-old women, Roz and Lil, and their respective children, Tom and Ian, two men in their thirties. The short story narrates the close relationship that exists between Roz and Lil since they were teenagers and the love affairs and strong bonds between Roz and her friend Lil's son, and between Lil and her friend Roz's son. Despite the fact that the men are married to women their age and had children, they are still in love with the older women. Their desire was contained in what their mother's friends represented, leaving aside limiting conceptions related to old age and the ageing body:

> 'What did you think? We'd all just go on, indefinitely, then you and Tom, two middle-aged man, bachelors, and Roz and me, old and then you two, old, without families, and Roz and I, old, old, old … we're getting on for old now, can't you see?'
>
> 'No, you aren't,' said her son calmly. 'Not at all. You and Roz knock the girls for six any time.' (Lessing, 2004: 50)

In this specific quote and throughout the short story, Lessing focuses on the strong attraction that the boys feel towards their lovers over the years; an attraction that does not diminish with time and the ageing of the women's bodies, but actually grows and becomes stronger. For instance, Tom finds himself fantasising about Lil's body: 'He was thinking of Lil's body that always smelled of salt, of the sea. She was like a sea creature, in and out, the sea water often drying on her and then she was in again' (2004: 41). In this case, it is actually the women who feel inadequate because of their ageing bodies, and they advise the younger men to look for younger women. With this highly suggestive short story Lessing blurs the boundaries of time between the older women and the younger men, and, thus, ageing and the Western limitations attached to the ageing body, in the same way as Carter does in *Wise Children*, through a humorous and ironic tone.

Conclusion

In the three fictional texts, the expression of corresponded desire and sexual interaction between the older female protagonists and other characters supports Gott's, Hinchliff's and Jones's thesis, proved through the respondents in their studies, according to which sex was seen as something natural, normal and pleasurable in healthy ageing. At a narrative level, it must be noted the fact that all the female protagonists speak for themselves, either using a confessional tone, as in the case of Dora, or through an omniscient narrator who tells the story from inside the character's minds and emotions. At a cultural level, the stories are set outside traditional family and patriarchal structures in terms of family structure so that protagonists can express their sexual desires and experiences openly, detached from social and cultural constraints. In this sense, the three stories conform to a concept that

Judith Halberstam (2005: 3) has coined as 'queer time' and 'queer space', in other words, understanding space and time 'in opposition to the institution of the family, heterosexuality and reproduction'. And, indeed, none of the older protagonists in Lively's, Carter's and Lessing's texts conform to a normative understanding of relationships. The fictional form of the texts allows the reader to witness the different ways in which each of the protagonists loves and builds family structures according to their own standards of the affective bonds that define a family. Thus, Claudia Hampton, in Lively's *Moon Tiger*, considers Lazlo a surrogate son when she is in her fifties, while also feeling sexually attracted to the young Polish man; the Chance sisters, in Carter's *Wise Children*, rejected by their legitimate family since their birth, create a family of their own, following their Grandma Chance's example; and Roz and Lil, in Lessing's 'The grandmothers', raise their children and grandchildren without a father figure.

Moreover, Lively's, Carter's and Lessing's stories portray sexuality and desire in a broad sense; in other words, and using Syme's definition of sexuality, the texts 'encompass ... interest, behaviors, functioning, satisfaction, intimate relationships, and sexual self-esteem', and thus move away from a narrow conception of 'hetero-normative behaviour (for example, penile-vaginal intercourse), and heterosexist and ageist assumptions' (Syme, 2014: 36). This goes hand in hand with a representation of old age and the ageing process as part of the life cycle in which different selves, different times and different experiences merge. As Segal (2014: 177) argues, taking her own experience as example, 'it is one thing for me to point out that we can always see continuities across a lifetime, suggesting also that as we age, we retain a certain access, consciously or not, to all the selves we have been'. All in all, the older female protagonists within these texts prove that between the 'asexualised older woman' and the 'sexy oldie' there is a wide spectrum of possibilities that can and need to be explored, leaving aside restrictive and limiting conceptions not only around the ageing body and old age, but also heteronormative organisational regimes.

References

Boehm, B.A. (1994) '*Wise children*: Angela Carter's Swan Song', *The Review of Contemporary Fiction*, 14: 84–90.

Brennan, Z. (2005) *The Older Woman in Recent Fiction*, North Carolina: McFarland & Company Inc.

Carter, A. (1996) *Wise Children*, New York: Quality Paperback Book Club.

Deats, S.M. and Lenker, L.T. (eds) (1990) *Aging and identity: A humanities perspective*, Westport CT: Praeger Publishers.

de Beauvoir, S. (1997 [1949]) *The Second Sex*, trans. H.M. Parshley, London: Vintage.

Dolan, J. and E. Ticknell (eds) (2012) *Aging Femininities: Troubling Representations*, Cambridge: Cambridge Scholars Publishing.

Gott, M. (2005) *Sexuality, Sexual Health and Ageing*, Oxford: Oxford University Press.

Gott, M. and S. Hinchliff. (2003) 'Sex and ageing: a gendered issue', in: S. Arber, K. Davidson and J. Ginn, *Gender and Ageing: Changing Roles and Relationships*, Maidenhead: Open University Press.

Gullette, M.M. (1998) *Safe at Last in the Middle Years. The Invention of the Midlife Progress Novel: Saul Bellow, Margaret Drabble, Anne Tyler, John Updike*, California: University of California.

Halberstam, J. (2005) *In a Queer Time and Place: Transgender Bodies, Subcultural Lives*, New York/London: New York University Press.

Hepworth, M. (2000) *Stories of Ageing*, Maidenhead: Open University Press.

Jones, R.L. (2002) '"That's very rude, I shouldn't be telling you that": older women talking about sex', *Narrative Inquiry*, 12(1): 121–42.

Katz, S. and B. Marshall. (2003) 'New sex for old: lifestyle, consumerism, and the ethics of aging well', *Journal of Aging Studies*, 17(1): 3–16.

King, J. (2013) *Discourses of Ageing in Fiction and Femininity: The Invisible Woman*, London: Palgrave Macmillan.

Lessing, D. (1996) *Love, Again*, London: Flamingo.

Lessing, D. (2004) *The Grandmothers*, London: Harper Perennial.

Lively, P. (1988) *Moon Tiger*, London: Penguin.

Lively, P. (1999) *Spiderweb*, London: Penguin.

Marshall, L. (2016) *Age Becomes Us: Bodies and Gender in Time*, New York: Suny Press.

Segal, L. (2014) *Out of Time: The Pleasures and Perils of Ageing*, London: Verso.

Sontag, S. (1972) 'The double standard of aging', *Saturday Review of The Society*, 23 September: 29–32.

Syme, M. (2014) 'The evolving concept of older adult sexual behavior and its benefits', *Generations: Journal of American Society on Aging*, 38(1): 35–41.

Traies, J. (2016) *The Lives of Older Lesbians*, London: Palgrave Macmillan.

Waxman, B.F. (1990) *From the Hearth to the Open Road: A Feminist Study of Ageing in Contemporary Literature*, New York: Greenwood.

Woodward, K. (1991) *Aging and its Discontents: Freud and Other Fictions*, Bloomington/Indianapolis, IN: Indiana University Press.

Woodward, K. (1999) *Figuring Age. Women, Bodies, Generations*, Bloomington and Indianapolis: Indiana University Press.

SEVEN

'Last-minute mothers': the construction of age and midlife motherhood in Denmark and Israel

Kinneret Lahad and Karen Hvidtfeldt

This chapter examines the question of how age, gender and personal status intersect, as well as the ways in which they are 'done' by analysing the discursive construction of midlife mothers in Denmark and Israel. Drawing on a textual analysis of online web columns and magazine articles interviewing midlife women, we explore women's vulnerability and resilience to ageist stigmas. In this chapter we are particularly interested in how midlife mothers negotiate ageist stigmatisation and normative timelines in general and thus pave the way for alternative knowledge of ageing, age and family life. By incorporating a critical feminist approach, we argue that in both case studies, age relations and age-based hierarchies come about. We have found that both Danish and Israeli mothers increasingly seem to perceive their age as 'ageing capital' (Simpson, 2013) and integrate it with the good mother ideal and the regulatory ideal of intensive mothering (Hays, 1996).

Introduction

During the last decade there has been an increase in the number of women giving birth after the age of 40 in various European and Anglo-American societies. This chapter explores how age is linked to public morality and heteronormativity by analysing textual accounts of 'older mothers' in Denmark and Israel. We perceive the discourse of midlife motherhood as a site through which age, ageing and gender moralities are negotiated and performed, and we argue that they also convey new–old understandings of age, ageing and motherhood.

Comparing Denmark and Israel allows us to make connections with the gendering of age and the national, pro-natal and age-stratified social and moral order in both countries. In both countries, biopolitics seems to follow pro-natal ideologies in which the figure of the good mother plays a central role (for example, Berkovitz, 1997;

Lahad and Hvidtfeldt, 2016). As will be further elaborated, while in Denmark this ideology is strongly connected to the social welfare state, in Israel it is historically connected to Israeli Zionist eugenics and concerns the physical survival of the Jewish people. Within this context, we contend that this comparison highlights the similarities about the global discourse of intensive mothering (Hays, 1996) and the ways in which it interconnects with what Nikolas Rose (1998, 1999a) terms the neoliberal entrepreneurial self, which takes control of its fate and future happiness (Ahmed, 2010). Moreover, in both countries the discourse about 'old mothers' regards heteronormativity and heterosexuality as unmarked features, reflecting their taken-for-granted privilege. This absence is naturalised and unarticulated and thus reflects the ways in which the category of late mothers intersects with age, gender and sexuality.

It is significant to note that the terminology of 'old mothers' is different in Denmark and Israel. In Denmark this age cohort of women is, at times, criticised for what is considered to be 'bad timing' and, more generally, their competence as good and responsible mothers is undermined (Lahad and Hvidtfeldt, 2016), However, in Denmark the term 40+ mothers often seems to be used to avoid the term 'old', and in Israel the terms 'older mothers' or 'late mothers' are regularly evoked. In this chapter, we prefer to use the term 'midlife mothers', which attempts to dismantle the normative and judgemental discourses about women who have decided to give birth and raise children in this phase of their lives.

Our analysis explores two main lines of inquiry: the heteronormative pro-natal discourse in both countries, along with the age- and gender-based moral work performed by midlife mothers. One of the emerging findings in both Danish and Israeli texts is the way in which age emerges as social capital with which to resist stigmatisation (Simpson, 2012, 2013, 2015; Lahad and Hvidtfeldt, 2016). Drawing on our previous research and taking it one step further, we argue here that ageing capital in these accounts is transformed and older age is moralised, contributing to the perception of themselves as moral agents and good mothers.

Our understanding of parental moral agency draws inspiration from McCarthy et al. (2000) and May's studies (2004) about the way that parents present themselves as moral actors. McCarthy et al. (2000: 787) argue for attention to

> the moral content in people's accounts by their use of evaluative language; the use of contrast with the motivations

and behaviour of others and/or self in the past; the use of confessional self-disclosure; and a consideration of the part played by cultural assumptions about what constitutes worthy moral behaviour as a good parent.

On that basis, we argue that the category of midlife mothers does not merely signify or imply chronological age, but also serves as a repository for public concerns and social anxieties about families, ageing and morality, as well as what constitutes a good mother. Put differently, we claim that the discourse around midlife mothers in both countries can be seen as a significant discursive site for representing the ongoing struggle related to meanings of age, gender, 'proper motherhood' and female respectability (Skeggs, 1997).

Theoretical and contextual background

In September 2012, the national Israeli gynaecologist's association launched a campaign to encourage young women to give birth earlier. This campaign included 'bar hopping' by fertility experts who frequented bars in Tel Aviv, during which they gave a short lecture about the recommended age of conception and warned young women about their ticking biological clock (Tures, 2012). Dr Ronit Haimov Kochmann, a senior physician at the fertility unit in Hadassah Hospital who initiated the project, was quoted as claiming that 'the goal is to bring the issue to public attention. We have difficulty in reaching the target audience of women aged 25-35, who are the subject of this project' (Tures, 2012). In Israel this campaign stirred a public debate in the electronic media portals and blogs, and while some voices saluted this initiative, others condemned its patronising and sexist tones.

A similar controversy emerged in Denmark, when in 2014 a Danish travel agency, Spies Rejser, launched the campaign 'Do it for Denmark', which addressed the low birth rate in Denmark as a crisis ('Fewer Danes mean fewer to support the ageing population – and tragically, fewer holidaying with us') and presents 'more sex' as a solution: 'Research shows that Danes have 46% more sex on city holidays and since more sex equals the chance of more kids, we are prescribing a romantic city holiday to save Denmark's future'.[1] In the video, the Eiffel Tower and a sputtering bottle of champagne illustrate the desired potency of the young Danish man on a romantic getaway in Paris with his girlfriend Emma – who was herself 'created' in a

---

[1] www.spies.dk/do-it

hotel room in Paris 30 years earlier. It is said that 10% of all Danes are conceived during holidays abroad and that couples have 46% more sex when on holiday compared with daily life. Spies Rejser even offers 'ovulation discount' and launched a competition whereby couples who succeed in achieving pregnancy can win a supply of nappies and a child-friendly vacation.

In contrast to the above-mentioned Israeli campaign, age is not a direct issue in either the 'Do it for Denmark' video, or the follow-up 'Do it for Mom' video from 2015, but both videos clearly draw on age- and gender-related stereotypes: wrinkled older women mourning their fate as a not-yet grandparent. 'Do it for Mom' advertises sunny holidays, arguing that Danes have 51% more sex on this kind of holiday, and further recommends active holidays as conducive for sexual desire. The website provides opportunity for 'Spies Parents Purchase' ('Forældrekøb': a concept normally known for parents purchasing an apartment for their adult children): 'Send your child and his/her partner on an active holiday and increase your chances of getting a grandchild'.[2]

The explicit heteronormative and ageist tones of the campaigns reflect a pro-natal and youth-oriented culture in both countries. As such, the increasing tendency to postpone childbirth is generally seen as a warning sign, which stands in contrast to conventional heteronormative life schedules. All of the campaigns clearly place parenting within a heteronormative setting, based on age limits and rigid collective timetables. However, within this context it is significant to note that over recent decades both Denmark and Israel have undergone transitions in family life. In common with many European and American societies, both countries have been affected by societal trends, such as the multiplicity of living arrangements, postponement of the age of marriage, rising rates of divorce, LGBT (lesbian, gay, bisexual and transgender) partnerships, single-parent families and single-person households. Yet, despite these far-reaching changes, family values prevail and are ascribed new meaning in both countries (Gundelach, 2002; Fogiel-Bijaoui, 1999; Lahad 2012, 2013, 2014). Sociologists like Giddens (1993) and Beck and Beck-Gernsheim (2002) claim that in the 'post-industrial family' marriage is determined by emotional intimacy. In the post-industrial family, the relative economic equality between the parents and the possibility of divorce are essential. However, feminist scholars have criticised this assumption as overly optimistic (Jamieson, 1998). Both in Denmark and Israel,

---

[2] www.spies.dk/do-it#doitformom

traditional family values are strongly idealised and the strong support for the nuclear family and the strong idealisation of motherhood as an institution seem to be constant (for example, Berkovitch, 1997; Hacker, 2001; Gundelach, 2002; Giese, 2004; Donath, 2011).

As we have shown, the pro-natal regimes in both societies are instilled with strong overtones of panic and blame (Lahad, 2012, 2013, 2014; Lahad and Hvidtfeldt, 2016). For instance, in Israel this tone is vividly illustrated when single women are accused of being 'too selective', marking women as being too slow and wrongly imagining that they have time on their hands (Lahad, 2012, 2013, 2014). In Denmark, the injunction to 'hurry up' is often conveyed and backed up with scientific and popular wisdom, truth claims about ticking biological clocks and expiration dates (Lahad and Hvidtfeldt, 2016). This tone in both countries casts doubt on women who do not follow the heteronormative paths. In particular, their capacity to make rational judgments and reasonable decisions is questioned.

Moreover, couched within these perceptions is a growing tendency to adhere to neoliberal ideology, which promotes responsible decision making. In this light, the choice to become a mother at the 'right age' is connected to new forms of self-governance, in which this choice has become an obligatory way of enacting and performing one's subjectivity (Rose, 1999b; Bauman, 2001). In achieving and maintaining autonomous modes of self-governance, the individual is assumed to be in charge of his/her own well-being and happiness (Rose 1998, 1999a, 1999b; Ahmed, 2010).

Feminist interpretations of this ideological climate point out that nowadays this required form of self-monitoring has become central to women's self-understanding, in which the choice of motherhood is articulated as solely a private and a responsible choice (Crittenden, 2001; Vint, 2007; Hoerl and Casey, 2010). This neoliberal ideology, which accentuates self-responsibilisation, can also be linked to the cultural expectations for mothers to practice intensive mothering (Hays, 1996), in which the mother is responsible for the well-being of her children. For Hays, who coined the term 'intensive mothering', this kind of mothering is wholly child-centred, labour intensive, expensive, emotionally involving and time consuming. Such a view promotes the moral dictum of putting the children first and accordingly creates significant pressure to live up to these binding ideals. In what follows, we further expand these ideas with a close, textual analysis of midlife mothers from Denmark and Israel.

Methodology and analysis

We now turn to a textual analysis of online columns, feature articles and interviews published on Danish and Israeli websites and in printed lifestyle magazines focusing on midlife motherhood. In Israel, the online columns are published on *nrg* and *Mako*, two popular web portals which form part of a flourishing Israeli internet culture, in which questions regarding personal relationships, single life and motherhood come to the fore. In Israel, a wide range of internet portals, blogs and online forums have shown a growing interest in women's personal lives. For example, in previous studies about single women in Israel (Lahad, 2013, 2014, 2017), it has been shown that web portals serve as central cultural platforms, in which women's lives are represented and produced.

In Denmark, Danish articles from the monthly *Magasinet Liv* (*Life Magazine*) of November 2011 and also August 2016 were picked out for close reading. *Magasinet Liv* (LIV) has been published since 2011 as a lifestyle publication, aimed explicitly at 40+ women. It includes articles on beauty, rejuvenation and fashion, and features more mature models than most other magazines. In its print form, LIV is clearly aimed at relatively well-educated, urban, middle-class women and regularly addresses problems related to family and working life of women from similar socioeconomic backgrounds. However, numerous articles are also published online and circulated on Facebook. This means that the articles, like the Israeli online columns, reach a broad audience of readers within society.

The texts were selected following readings of magazines and weeklies, as well as wide online searches and snowballing of blogs and social media debates, in order to identify the main lines of argument. The study of online texts poses new challenges for social research, as it is limited in its ability to assess the socioeconomic characteristics of the writers and bloggers (Press and Livingstone, 2006). Taking this matter into consideration, we do not necessarily regard it as a limitation, but rather a shift in focus. Building on the tradition of critical discourse analysis (Van Dijk, 1993; Huckin, 2002; Fairclough, 2013), this chapter is not meant to capture the social identities of the writers themselves, but extract the cultural meanings that are produced and brought out in these texts. In this light, we perceive these texts as a discursive site of a cultural struggle (Fiske, 1996) that offers a unique prism through which it can be understood how current cultural meanings on midlife mothers are validated and contested. However, we bear in mind that midlife motherhood is a relational category that is dependent, for example, on class, race, sexual orientation and ableness. Here, we explore the gendered, unmarked heteronormative and age-related aspects and we hope our study will guide future studies that will incorporate more intersectional dimensions of midlife motherhood.

A mother or a grandmother? Keeping fit and staying young

In August 2016, the Danish magazine LIV featured an article on the new elasticity of the forties age group. On the cover page of the magazine the article is titled '43 years old and a new mother – or grandmother? We can do it all!' This woman-power, liberatory rhetoric presents two women, both aged 43, with one being the mother of a two-year-old child and the other being the grandmother of an infant whom her 22-year-old daughter gave birth to. The magazine article concludes that age no longer poses limits for midlife women.

Similar themes emerge on online Israeli websites. For example, in an article titled 'Not a grandma, a mother! On motherhood at a late age' (Kadush, 2012). One of the women interviewed for the article is Rivka Shraga, who had her first child when she was 50 years old. In the interview she refers to the social stigma of being perceived as a grandmother and not her child's mother:

> Sometimes I hear phrases like, you have a nice grandchild, or your grandmother was here. In the past I was outraged by these reactions, but today the two of us [Rivka and her child] roar with laughter and exclaim that I am his mother. (Kadush, 2012)

The titles of both the magazine articles emphasise a social reality in which women in their forties can be both grandmothers and mothers. The Danish magazine LIV celebrates this as a new and changing reality: 'New mother or grandmother during the forties? But of course! The forties are the most elastic of our decades and easily includes it all. We can do it all!' (Greve, 2016: 30). In both Danish and Israeli texts, flexible age norms are presented and negotiated. It seems that one of the messages that is proclaimed here is that age is no longer an all-encompassing organising principle in one's reproductive schedules. This flexibility enables one to move in between categories and be a mother and a grandmother at midlife, for example. To some extent, it could be argued that a kind of post-modern utopia of an ageless society (Young and Schuller, 1991) is presented, in which one is liberated from strict age roles, norms and scripts, and granted with temporal agency. However, this discourse also demonstrates how strict age norms rule and regulate women's reproductive timetables. The texts reveal a tension between ageless- versus family-oriented, youth-based norms. This normative view is embedded with the injunction to fit with a certain kind of maternal figure: a young, dedicated and active, kind mother who echoes the culture of intensive mothering (Hays, 1996).

In the *nrg* article, the Israeli journalist comments that 'Meanwhile Rivka tries to keep a young appearance, and last year she lost 40 kilos in weight' (Kadush, 2012). Rivka herself goes on to explain:

'I keep in shape for the sake of my son, and it keeps me young. Now I can go out with him on trips, rave, jump – all steps which I had difficulty because of excess weight. When my girlfriends are enjoying their grandchildren, I spend time with my son in the park and have fun.' (Kadush, 2012)

Rivka's account reflects another source of tension between the ageless 'we can do it all' rhetoric and age-based stereotypes. As evidenced in some of the texts, the women are aware of the stigmatisation they are subjected to as midlife mothers. As Rivka claims, she often hears that she has a nice grandchild. In accordance with intensive mothering norms, she emphasises that she spends her time with her son in the park and is fit for the sake of her son. Similar themes emerge from 43-year-old Helena Mary Lund Aagaard's account from Denmark. She claims not to have met stigmatisation, but is at the same time very conscious of her physical appearance, which enables her to pass as younger than her chronological age: 'It also depends on how you act and how you dress. When people see me with a small child, they automatically assume that I am in my late 30s, and of course that is a nice bonus' (Greve, 2016: 33) .

These accounts reveal that the apparently ageless norms have to follow a strict dress code and 'keep-in-shape' repertoire. Neoliberal ideas concerning active ageing and positive ageing (Katz, 1996; Calasanti and Slevin, 2006; Katz and Calasanti, 2014) fuel the notion of individual responsibility to age 'well' and the significance of passing as younger than one's age. If we follow this line, our contention here is that the logic of active ageing could be extended to *midlife active ageing*, which resonates with conventional formulations of the responsible neoliberal subject and parent in this case. Thus it could be claimed that there is a preferred and restricted way to present midlife motherhood. The freedom of being either a midlife mother or a grandmother is dependent on being a self-responsible and also both a socially and physically fit subject (Walkerdine, 2003)

Ricki Shaki, in her forties, is a teacher and mother to Hillel, a two-month-old baby. She says that her motherhood came just in time:

> 'I was not ready to be a mother at a younger age, despite the fact that everyone pressured me to have a child. Only recently did I feel ready to be totally devoted to becoming a mother ... I'm at the beginning of the journey, and experiencing joy and happiness alongside great anxiety. All the priorities in my life have changed. Something in the woman's soul changes when she becomes a mother and I don't think that physical fitness and a young appearance is necessarily the right recipe for a better kind of motherhood. (Kadush, 2012)

It could be claimed that Ricki is resisting and confirming to the normative demand for mothers to appear fit and young. However, Ricki's account also taps into what Simpson (2012, 2013, 2015) has termed ageing capital in his study of middle-aged gay men living in Manchester (UK). Simpson argues that ageing capital functions to re-aestheticise and legitimate the midlife or ageing body-self, which could also be accomplished in ways that mark its desirability and creativity.

According to Simpson (2013), some of the men he interviewed have used ageing capital in response to age-related norms and in this way they have distinguished themselves from younger and peer-aged gay men. Simpson further claims that they perceive themselves as free from the discursive pressures of gay consumer-oriented cultures, and draw on their ageing capital in an attempt to increase their social capital. Similar patterns emerge from most of the Israeli and Danish accounts, in which their age provides them with significant resources, such as self-acceptance, social and economic capital and emotional strength.

Kristine Marie Foss, a 42-year-old Danish mother, also believes that midlife is a better time to be a mother. She said she was happy that her daughter didn't have her as mother when she was 30 years old. Now, she sees herself as a more 'balanced' person and therefore a much better and more relaxed mother (Brændgård, 2011). As we can see, both Ricki and Kristine distinguish between their younger and midlife selves. Being a mother at midlife is preferable, as now they are more prepared, relaxed and balanced. Their age provides them with a more agentic and competent maternal self.

Likewise, Helena Mary, quoted earlier, says that she is a better mother because of her age and life experience, while on the other hand, Karina says that her energy as a young grandmother enables her to take part fully in the life of her grandson, for instance by staying up with him at night (Greve, 2016). The grandmother, Karina Faxholm, quoted in the Danish magazine LIV, states that there are many advantages from being a 'young' grandmother, while Helena Mary shares the advantages from becoming a mature mother in her midlife age. Thus age is interpreted as capital in different ways. Age is an advantage both for being a young grandmother, as well as being a more mature and responsible midlife mother.

Kristine even argues that her "dating potential" is higher now, "because I am much happier and because I know that I am fertile. It gives me a tremendous peace of mind that I didn't have before" (Brændgård, 2011). Here, Kristine emphasises how at this stage of her life, motherhood has provided her with tranquillity and has even increased her personal capital on the dating market. In this way, motherhood status and age become a resource for achieving a desired end and in this case they also go along with a heteronormative ideal connoted with couple culture.

Yet, as we can see, both Danish and Israeli women also recognise the disadvantages related to age. For example, when discussing age, Kristine refers to the back problems caused by having to carry her child around, as well as her fear of passing away too early: "It would of course be a pity for her [daughter] if I happen to die while she is still young. So I will have to make an effort to help her to connect to other people" (Brændgård, 2011). Quoted earlier, Rivka says "I am ridden with guilt and pain for him (her child), because he will have to accompany his elderly parents alone to hospitals. I'm not detached from reality, I know how old I will be at his bar mitzvah" (Kadush, 2012).

Rivka, who had her first and only child when she was 50 years old, declares that retrospectively she would have preferred to have a child at the age of 22. When asked why she waited, she answers "I had a delayed emotional development. I had fun, I've travelled all over the world and I believed I could beat biology" (Kadush, 2012). Rivka expresses a more ambivalent account in relation to her age and is aware of both the advantages and disadvantages of midlife motherhood. In contrast, Yael had her first child at the age of 35, the second at the age of 37 and a little girl about six months ago (aged 40) and she admits that in hindsight she would have acted the same way. "I would not have children before age 35, the slow pace suited me ... today I have more patience, I understand the needs of the baby and how it is integrated in my life," she explains (Kadush, 2012).

Yael emphasises her self-determination and justifies her life choices. For her, being slow or late carries substantial advantages, as she now has more patience and more wisdom. This is an example of how age becomes ageing capital and in this case carries moral undertones. Continuing this line of analysis, we suggest that the ageing capital of midlife mothers plays a significant part in their *moral self-presentation as good mothers*. Their age enables them to be more dedicated and patient, in order to provide their children the best possible childhood. For example, 43-year-old Helena didn't feel ready in her twenties, but after turning 40 she gave birth to her son and describes the experience as "huge": "Much bigger than I had imagined." She devotes herself entirely to giving her son the best possible childhood. "Being a mother is the meaning of life for me at the moment and he is never in my way" (Greve, 2016: 33).

In May's (2003) work on mothers in Finland, she analysed how her respondents attempted to create space for themselves within the normative narratives on family and womanhood, and also present themselves as moral actors. A similar attempt could be discerned in the Danish and Israeli accounts. The mothers actively navigate between the definitions of intensive motherhood ideals. In this vein, they actively negotiate the meanings of reproductive schedules and the timing of their motherhood. Following May's observations, we suggest that, in their accounts, midlife mothers claim a viable moral identity in which they perform intensive mothering. Hence, this moral identity is bound up with the cultural ideal of intensive mothering, which is rarely disputed. As noted before, according to Hays, the model of the new 'momism' assumes that mothers are expected to meet their children's needs and desires selflessly, constantly and cheerfully. Moreover, women are expected to bear full responsibility for their child's well-being and their children are assumed to take priority over all other relationships, (Rich, 1995 [1976]; Ruddick, 1980; Hays,1996).

For instance, when Orna Peshach, a single woman who became a mother at 46, was asked if age has an effect on motherhood, she answered:

> 'I became a mother in the right timing for me. My priorities have changed course since Lya was born. I work full time … but at 16:00 I pick up Lya from the kindergarten. Women my age reach managerial positions which involve responsibility, and I still provide results even at work. However, to make things easier I moved from Tel Aviv to a suburb to live near my extended family.' (Kadush, 2012)

Danish Helena negotiates her ideals by pointing out the advantages of her age and current life situation. She has used her life experience to step out of the dream of being part of a nuclear family and focus on the privileges she can give her son: now he has her full attention and she doesn't have to divide it between several children, or use her energy on a bad relationship. He is "top stimulated". She ascribes her patience to her age and the fact that she always has time for him "because there is nothing else in my life that I am in a hurry for" (Greve, 2016: 33).

Thus, midlife motherhood and making the right decision at the right time enables the pursuit of good and intensive motherhood, in which the children come first. Most of the women demonstrated their choices as *timely* and *responsible* ones. By stressing this point, we suggest they also demonstrate their temporal agency by highlighting the control they have on their own reproductive schedules. However, many also present a morally reflective agency by acknowledging that their child's well-being might be put at risk due to their age.

However, Helena also adds worries connected to her age: "I know that I am the best of mothers for him now, however I have had terrible thoughts on what it means to him that I was over 40 when he was born" (Greve, 2016: 33). These thoughts refer to the fear of dying too soon, the sorrow of her son being an only child and the struggles in letting go of the ideal of the 'real family'. She highlights the issue of dealing with the ideal image of the nuclear family as the biggest problem of being a midlife mother:

> 'I grew up in a family with a mother and a father and four siblings, but I am divorced and on my own with an only child. Somehow I feel that a family should resemble the one I had during my own childhood and that dream is shattered.' (Greve, 2016: 33)

Thus, the accounts of midlife mothers are not simplified and, while acknowledging their age as capital, they are also aware of the less positive consequences their children may endure. Yet this form of flexibility is connected to the moral principle of putting the interests of the children first. The children first and foremost serve as moral reference points, according to which the mothers evaluate themselves and their set of priorities.

Conclusion

This chapter has demonstrated how midlife motherhood is an age-coded practice and a gendered and morally charged category. We have explored how age norms construct and categorise moral motherhood and vice versa. Our initial starting point was that the case study of midlife motherhood in both countries shows that age does not merely signify chronological age, but also marks a transgression of societal and moral boundaries. In this vein, the mere terms of 'late motherhood', 'old/older mothers' and 'younger mothers' reflect the transgression of these boundaries. Being 'too young' or being 'too old' represents defying age norms and therefore potentially being morally transgressive. Our textual analysis reveals that midlife mothers are very much aware of potential age-based stigmas and their consequences. We suggest that this motivates them to turn their age skilfully into age capital (Simpson, 2012, 2013, 2015; Lahad and Hvidtfeldt, 2016), which also follows the dictum of active ageing, for which we propose the term *midlife active ageing*, that provides them with the required extra competencies for motherhood; for example, they have more patience, focus, and emotional and economical resources. All of these qualities granted by their midlife phase assist in their self-presentation of being good mothers, who put their children's needs first. It is significant to note that to a large extent and in a way similar to the active ageing regime, a great emphasis is placed on the assumption that age does not 'age' them. They emphasise their vitality and being fit in accordance with the prevalent regime of being self-sufficient, responsible parents.

We therefore suggest that age capital could be seen as a discursive resource, which positions them as moral agents and allows them to claim and demonstrate their duty and responsibility for all of their children's needs. By using their age capital, they convey a twofold message: they express agency and control of their life trajectories, yet also present a moral presentation of their selves and their competent motherhood. By incorporating the ideals of respected, maternal femininity, they abide with the prevailing gendered moralities, heteronormative expectations and women's 'imaginative life schedules' (Halberstam, 2005: 1). This kind of moral work leads to cultural acceptability and respectability, using Skeggs' (1997) terms. Age capital is a means to become a respectable mother and be immersed in the new momism culture (Hays, 1996). As we can see, motherhood and good motherhood are organised through temporal markers, as well as gendered and heteronormative moralities. Thus the accounts by midlife mothers can be seen as moral tales (McCarthy et al., 2000), which often involve comparisons to younger versions of the self.

Our contribution to the studies on gendered moralities is made by bringing the parameters of age and 'bad timing' to this literature. While notions of class (Skeggs, 1997) and race (Skeggs, 1997; Nayak, 2003) have been analysed in relation to respectability, the idea of age has yet to be explored. By extending Skeggs' analysis, we explore how age and the intersecting parameters of the heteronormative and intensive motherhood paradigm creates differential access to the mechanisms for generating, resisting and displaying gendered respectability. Indeed, in the online accounts by midlife mothers, age plays a significant role in crafting their gendered moralities and respectability. Their accounts negotiate age and ageing in moral terms and, as we suggest, provide them with a sense of moral integrity and agency. The pro-natal regimes in Denmark and Israel are influenced by different ideologies, Denmark by the welfare state tradition and Israel by its fear of physical and cultural extinction, but we suggest that the ideology of intensive mothering and new momism prevails in both countries and discursively deconstructs age, motherhood and public morality.

References

Ahmed, S. (2010) *The Promise of Happiness*, Durham, NC: Duke University Press.

Bauman, Z. (2001) *Community: Seeking Safety in an Insecure World, Themes for the 21st Century*. Cambridge: Polity.

Beck, U. and Beck-Gernsheim E. (2002) *Individualization*, London: Sage Publications.

Berkovitch, N. (1997) 'Motherhood as a national mission: the construction of womanhood in the legal discourse in Israel', *Women's Studies International Forum*, 20(5–6): 605–19.

Brændgård, T. (2011) 'Er du (stadig) klar til babygråd og bleskift? [Are you (still) ready for crying babies and diaper changing?]' *Magasinet Liv*, November 2011, Oslo: Benjamin publications.

Calasanti, T.M. and Slevin, K.F. (2006) 'Introduction', in T.M. Calasanti and K.F. Slevin (eds) *Age Matters: Realigning Feminist Thinking*, New York: Routledge: 1–17.

Crittenden, A. (2001) *The Price of Motherhood: Why the Most Important Job in the World is Still the Least Valued*, New York: Metropolitan Books.

Fairclough, N. (2013) *Critical Discourse Analysis: The Critical Study of Language*, London/New York: Routledge.

Fiske, J. (1996) *Media Matters: Race and Gender in US Politics*. Minneapolis: University of Minnesota Press.

Fogiel-Bijaoui, S. (1999) 'Families in Israel: between familism and post modernism', in A. Friedman (eds) *Sex, Gender, Politics: Women in Israel*, Tel Aviv: Hakibbutz Hameuchad [Hebrew].

Giddens, A. (1993) *The Transformation of Intimacy: Sexuality, Love and Eroticism in Modern Societies*, Stanford: Stanford University Press.

Giese, S. (2004) *Moderskab [Motherhood]*, Copenhagen: Tiderne Skifter.

Greve, K. (2016) 'Vi er begge 43 år, men ... [We are both 43 years old, however ...]', *Magasinet Liv*, August, Oslo: Bonnier: 30–5.

Gundelach P. (ed) (2002) *Danskernes værdier 1981–1999 [The Dane's Values]* Copenhagen: Hans Reitzels Forlag.

Hacker, D. (2001) 'Single and married women in the law of Israel: A feminist perspective', *Feminist Legal Studies*, 9(1): 29–56.

Halberstam, J. (2005) *In a Queer Time and Place: Transgender Bodies, Subcultural Lives*, New York/London: New York University Press.

Hays, S. (1996) *The Cultural Contradictions of Motherhood*, New Haven: Yale University Press.

Hoerl, K. and Casey, R.K. (2010) 'The post-nuclear family and the depoliticization of unplanned pregnancy in knocked up, juno, and waitress', *Communication and Critical/Cultural Studies*, 7(4): 360–380.

Huckin, T. (2002) 'Critical discourse analysis and the discourse of condescension', in E. Barton and G. Stygall (eds) *Discourse Studies in Composition*, New York: Hampton Press: 55–176.

Jamieson, L. (1998) *Intimacy*, Cambridge: Polity.

Kadush, R. (2012) 'Not a grandmother, a mother! On motherhood at a late age' *nrg www.nrg.co.il/online/17/ART2/395/829.html*

Katz, S. (1996) *Disciplining Old Age: The Formation of Gerontological Knowledge*, Charlottesville VA: University Press of Virginia.

Katz, S. and Calasanti, T. (2014) 'Critical perspectives on successful aging: Does it "appeal more than it illuminates?"', *The Gerontologist*, 55(1): 26–33.

Lahad, K. (2012) 'Singlehood, waiting, and the sociology of time', *Sociological Forum*, 27(1): 163–86.

Lahad, K. (2013) '"Am I asking for too much?" The selective single woman as a new social problem', *Women's Studies International Forum*, 40(5): 23–32.

Lahad, K. (2014) 'The single woman's choice as a zero-sum game', *Cultural Studies*, 28(2): 240–66.

Lahad, K. (2017) *A Table for One: Re-Scheduling Singlehood, Gender and Time*, Manchester: Manchester University Press.

Lahad, K. and Hvidtfeldt Madsen, K. (2016) '"Like having new batteries installed!" Problematizing the category of the "40+ mother" in contemporary Danish media', *NORA – Nordic Journal of Feminist and Gender Research*, 24(3): 181–95.

May, V. (2003) 'Lone motherhood past and present: the life stories of Finnish lone mothers,' *Nora: Nordic Journal of Women's Studies*, 11(1): 27–39.

May, V. (2004) 'Narrative identity and the re-conceptualization of lone motherhood', *Narrative Inquiry*, 14(1): 169–89.

McCarthy, J.M., Edwards, R. and Gillies, V. (2000) 'Moral tales of the child and the adult: narratives of contemporary family lives under changing circumstances', *Sociology*, 34(4): 785–803.

Nayak, A. (2003) *Race, Place and Globalization: Youth Cultures in a Changing World*, London: Bloomsbury Publishing.

Press, A. and Livingstone, S. (2006) 'Taking audience research into the age of new media: old problems and new challenges', in M. White & J. Schwoch (eds) *The Question of Method in Cultural Studies*. Oxford: Blackwell: 175–200

Rich, A. (1995 [1976]) *Of Woman Born: Motherhood as Experience and Institution*, London: Virago.

Rose, N. (1998) *Inventing Our Selves: Psychology, Power and Personhood*, Cambridge: Cambridge University Press.

Rose, N. (1999a) *Governing the Soul: The Shaping of the Private Self* (2nd edn), London and New York: Routledge.

Rose, N. (1999b) *Powers of Freedom*. Cambridge: Cambridge University Press.

Ruddick, S. (1980) 'Maternal thinking', *Feminist Studies*, 6(2): 342–67.

Simpson, P. (2012) 'Perils, precariousness and pleasures: middle-aged gay men negotiating urban "heterospaces"', *Sociological Research Online*, 17(3): 1–10.

Simpson, P. (2013) Alienation, ambivalence, agency: middle-aged gay men and ageism in Manchester's gay village, *Sexualities*, 16(3–4): 283–99.

Simpson, P. (2015) *Middle-Aged Gay Men, Ageing and Ageism: Over the Rainbow?*, London: Palgrave Macmillan.

Skeggs, B. (1997) *Formations of Class and Gender: Becoming Respectable*, London: Sage Publications.

Tures, E. (2012) 'Sex and the city: the gynecologists will raid the bars', nrg, 4 September, www.makorrishon.co.il/nrg/online/54/ART2/399/821.html?hp=54&cat=870

Van Dijk, T.A. (1993) 'Principles of critical discourse analysis', *Discourse & Society*, 4(2): 249–83.

Vint, S. (2007) 'The new backlash: popular culture's marriage with feminism, or love is all you need', *Journal of Popular Film and Television*, 34: 160–69.

Walkerdine, V. (2003) 'Reclassifying upward mobility: femininity and the neo-liberal subject', *Gender and Education*, 15(3): 237–8.

Young, M.D. and Schuller, T. (1991) *Life after Work: The Arrival of the Ageless Society*. London: HarperCollins Publishers.

Part 3
Dis/empowerments

Part 3: introduction

This section, containing four chapters, explores the dynamics of power relationships concerning ageing, gender and sexualities within and across different contexts. The chapters consider how our different positionings and the intersections of different aspects of our identities can affect experiences and perceptions of dis/empowerment.

The first two chapters both draw on Bourdieu's concept of habitus. In Chapter Eight, 'All change, please: education, mobility and habitus dislocation' Jill Wilkens explores opportunities and practices presented through the education system in the 1940s, which held potential to transform the classed habitus of her respondents: lesbians and bisexual women born between 1940 and 1958. Wilkens draws on the Bourdieu's concept of habitus dislocation to expose the difficulties and 'cost' of social mobility. She argues that while social mobility can be aspirational and empowering, there are also costs associated with habitus dislocation which intersect with her respondents' age, gender and sexual orientation. For some participants, the associated feelings of dislocation and 'unbelonging' have accompanied them all their lives and continue to shadow their later years.

In Chapter Nine, 'Insider or outsider? Issues of power and habitus during life history interviews with menopausal Iranian women', Elham Amini investigates the shifting power dynamics involved in conducting interviews with older women in Iran. Amini considers the tensions that arise from being both an insider and outsider. This resonates with Wilken's argument about positionings where one is caught between a number of social fields – creating multiple misalignments of dispositions and practices and a resulting sense of disequilibrium. Amini also highlights further fluidity in relation to different capitals and habitus, examining power shifts between interviewer and interviewee at different points in the interview.

The following two chapters address the rights of older lesbian, gay, bisexual and trans (LGBT) people in different contexts and settings. Chapter Ten, 'Sexual expression and sexual practices in long-term residential facilities for older people', by Feliciano Villar, explores the intersections between sexual expression and sexual practices alongside aging, gender and sexual diversity. Villar identifies how the sexual rights of older citizens might be curtailed in institutional care settings, deeply influenced by staff and institutional practices. The chapter then considers how sexual expression might be especially challenging among specific populations of older adults living in institutions, with particular attention being paid to people with dementia and LGBT residents. Last, some practical implications as regards sexual expression and sexual rights of older people living in long-term care settings are considered.

In the final chapter in this section (Chapter Eleven), Finn Reygan and Jamil Khan adopt a social justice-oriented lens to address the intricate interplay of race, class, urban/rural realities and the apartheid legacy as they intersect with the lives of lesbian, gay, bisexual, transgender and intersex (LGBTI) elders in South Africa. South Africa has one of the most progressive constitutions in the world in terms of its focus on inclusion and tolerance. However, Reygan and Khan argue that this does not necessarily translate into substantive equality on the ground, particularly in addressing race, sexual orientation and class in old age. While there is still a paucity of research, existing evidence indicates that discrimination against LGBTI people is prevalent in the provision of healthcare and much work is required to create the conditions which could empower LGBTI elders in being able to access and exercise their rights more freely.

Thus all four chapters shed light on intersections of ageing, gender and sexualities in differing contexts and the ways in which multiple positionings are shaped by power, privilege and oppression. This section illustrates different manifestations of dis/empowerment through the complexities of social mobility via education; the play and shifts of power in research interview settings; how some older people's sexual citizenship may be silenced in institutional settings and how normativity related to ageing, gender and sexualities functions to empower some people and to oppress others.

EIGHT

All change please: education, mobility and habitus dislocation

Jill Wilkens

Introduction

This chapter highlights the central importance of social class and mobility, looking particularly at changes in the education system in the 1940s which gave rise to schooling opportunities and practices that transformed the classed lives of the majority of my participants: lesbians and bisexual women born between 1940 and 1958. Participants' mobility, their 'transgressions' of the boundaries of class, gender and sexual identity, intersected to position them as 'different' or out of place across their life course; in Bourdieusian terms creating within them a disjuncture or 'cleft habitus' (Bourdieu, 2004; Friedman, 2016). Here I explain how my participants' understanding and subjective experiences of their own class, gender and sexual identity changed as they were transformed by movement across fields against a backdrop of rapid social and cultural transformation in the UK. Rather than adopting Bourdieu's description of the habitus as 'cleft', with its suggestion of a division, split or rupture, I use the term *habitus dislocation* to signal the weight and enduring consequences of displacement created by multiple mobilities; the pain of being out of place in *so many* fields, for such a long time. This phrase, literally meaning 'placed apart', reminds us that when something is dislocated, although it may *appear* the same, it is always a little bit weaker and more vulnerable. This chapter deploys the concept of habitus dislocation to expose the difficulties and 'cost' of social mobility and as a way of understanding how multiple mobilities and repositionings in different fields render individuals 'fish out of water'. My research suggests that the habitus dislocation that results from movement through such diverse fields of origin and destination is so powerful and so toxic it has motivated participants to seek and create affinity groups where the anxiety and isolation associated with habitus dislocation – the hidden, but persistent, injuries (Sennett and Cobb,

1977) of class, gender and sexual identity transgression – are alleviated through social interaction with other, similarly placed individuals.

Methodology

The study recruited 35 participants from London and the South East, Yorkshire and Lancashire. The participants, who all identified as white, attended a range of social groups. The average age was 64, with only two participants aged over 70. Twenty-five participants (71%) were single. The majority of women identified as lesbian with only two women identifying as bi/queer. No trans women participated.

To tease out some of the inconsistencies created by asking participants to self-identify their social class, I also employed a more objective typology. Drawing on McDermott's (2010) framework, I adapted the category of 'working-class educated' to make it more relevant to the educational opportunities open to this generational cohort. Extending the category to include college *or* the acquisition of professional qualifications as well as university attendance, reveals an extraordinary level of social mobility. Five participants lacked any further or higher education or professional qualifications, and can thus be identified as working-class. Four participants would be classified as middle-class, with the remaining 26 out of 35 (74%) participants located in the category 'working-class educated'. This figure is a testament to the widening of educational opportunities in the 1960s and 1970s. However, it is also an indicator of a potential site of habitus dislocation; many working-class educated participants lacked the economic, cultural and social dispositions to guide them through this new field, leaving some disappointed and others feeling trapped between two worlds, never comfortably fitting in either.

I used qualitative in-depth interviews which lasted between one and two hours. Interviews were recorded and transcribed verbatim and the scripts returned to the women for checking and amendment. The data, which is anonymised to preserve the identity of the women and the groups they attended, was thematically analysed. Initially, my aim was to investigate the significance of the social and support groups attended by participants; asking about loneliness, group composition, benefits conferred and class differentials in experience. The majority of my participants were socialised at a time when homosexuality was seen as deviant or disordered behaviour and the 'heterosexual assumption' (Weeks 2015: 54) prevailed. Many participants lived lives of full or partial self-concealment, socialising with other 'like-minded' individuals in same-sex, same-sexuality groups and venues. However, while the interviews *did* reveal the benefits derived from groups, the participants' preference for exclusively lesbian or mixed company, they also generated conversations about ageing, gender, sexual identity, education, social class and mobility and, most significantly, the intersection of these diverse, multi-layered and complex aspects of human experience. Ultimately, my research turned out to be less about groups and more about the life-course experiences that led these older lesbian and bisexual women to seek friendships and social interaction predicated on shared age and sexual identity.

Education, education, education

While much previous work on cleft habitus has explored the cultural and social schism experienced by working-class students entering *higher education*, this study shows that the contrast between working-class origins and *secondary education* within the elite grammar school system of the 1950s provided an equally fertile site for habitus dislocation. Many participants were schooled in a rapidly changing post-war education system; the provision of free grammar school places, as part of the government's commitment to a universal system of secondary education, profoundly changed the course of several participants' educational trajectories when they became the first in their families to go to a grammar school, leaving them conflicted and caught between two worlds: 'neither here nor there'. Regardless of the vehicle or timing of their mobility, I suggest that the fact that at least three-quarters of participants have been socially mobile, mostly through education, has resulted in habitus disruption with consequences that have lasted into older age. Many of the women interviewed referred to streaming and other classed practices of secondary school as diminishing their confidence and eroding their parents' joy in their daughters' achievements. For some, social mobility became a 'family project'; the girls were pioneers bearing the success of their family, even their school, while the financial and social pressures incurred by their opportunity limited the chances of other family members. Kate recalls the pressure of being a working-class grammar school entrant:

> '[T]he ideology and the life-style and the worry about money were *all* about *class*. We *didn't* have enough money. … That was childhood. It *never leaves you*. … The children were all what they classically called "first and onlys". The *first* child in a mining family or the *only* child in a mining family … there were *eight* of us at the top of the grammar

school vying for the first place.' (Kate, born 1946, retired author and teacher)

Their difference and the privilege of grammar school was made apparent to working-class girls in many ways, as Clary's narrative shows:

'I enjoyed being *clever* but when I went to grammar school and I was amongst a lot of other clever girls, it was a different story. ... They were *a lot* more sophisticated than I was. I was still reading Enid Blyton and they were reading Jane Austen ... *One* teacher said, "Oh girls who come from [name of place] can't speak with a good French accent," so there was quite a lot of stuff, ... about my accent and being working-class and *seen* as being *poor*.' (Clary, born 1951, retired counsellor)

Stahl's (2015: 22) research highlights how education challenges certain dispositions in the habitus of working-class students and is 'fraught with potential risks and embarrassments'. Grammar school proved to be a site of social embarrassment and disappointment for many participants. With insufficient economic and cultural resources to ease their passage into the new field, their awareness of unaffordable opportunities also generated dissatisfaction with their home circumstances. Nell grew up in a Lancashire mill town. Here she describes the shadow cast over her grammar school years by her family's economic situation:

'It made me more irritable, more sort of, "Why hasn't me dad got a better job?" ... I went to grammar school, it was *lovely*, but I was *disappointed* when my best friend, well one of my good friends, who was a bit older than me and bigger, disappointed when I got her last year's frock, last year's school uniform dresses and things like that.' (Nell, born 1942, retired senior bank worker)

Far from being a 'social leveller', school uniform embodied social and economic inequalities in visceral ways; the pain of the memory was often evident in the recounting of the experience:

'I *tried* to fit in. I had a little group of friends ... when we got to the third year we were allowed not to wear gymslips and we could wear skirts. You had to wear a navy blue

A-line skirt and I, *I* had a Girl Guide skirt and *they* had skirts they'd got from Barrie's. ... And so they used to say "Oh, the wind's blowing up our school skirts and up Clary's *Guide* skirt ...". (Clary, born 1951, retired counsellor)

Feminist writers including Reay (1997) and Skeggs (1997) draw on their own experiences alongside empirical research to examine the gendered aspect of mobility, finding it to be particularly problematic for girls, creating feelings of disloyalty and dislocation (Reay, 1997). Rosie's lack of the 'right' cultural capital was painfully memorable. Her parentage, Eastern European Jewish mother and Dutch father, already made her feel different as a child but school set her even further apart:

> 'We went to grammar school but even in primary school we used to have my cousins' cast-offs so that was *difficult*, you know, cardboard in your shoes and things. ... I felt *different* 'cause there were a *lot* of middle-class kids at grammar school so – although I'm grateful to have been there because it gave me my *future* – so I didn't fit in *there*.' (Rosie, born 1949, retired teacher)

Ivy found grammar school 'hard', having come from what she described as a 'really disadvantaged primary school'. Her sense of pain and the embarrassment created by her dislocation was palpable:

> 'I didn't feel as though I *knew the rules*. I didn't quite *get* how to be like the other girls. I didn't quite *get* how to dress or where to shop for clothes ... It all felt like a bit of a foreign language. ... Getting friends' parents to drop me off not too close to home and things like that, so that they didn't see where I lived. ... Going to birthday parties and taking a book token and when you get there realising that *nobody took a book token* to a birthday part... You took *make-up* and things like that but my mum had bought me a book token to take.' (Ivy, born 1955, had been made redundant from her job with a charity shortly before the interview)

Fifteen of the participants went to university or college straight from school and another 15 obtained degrees or professional qualifications as adults. Aspirant but uneducated parents often lacked the dispositions to support their daughters' progression in the way that more middle-class families took for granted. Ivy's career aspirations foundered at the intersection of her gender and class:

> '[W]hen it came to choosing careers, girls were channelled into ... at the grammar school it was nursing, teaching or academia if you were *very* bright ... I picked up all the stuff about horticulture and I really thought I wanted to go into horticulture but it had all the fees on the back cover and my parents said, "Oh we can't afford that." Never realised that we could have got a grant.' (Ivy)

Some women ended up in jobs they hated, while a few benefited from having enlightened and supportive teachers:

> 'Me saving grace was me art teacher who was wonderful and I went to art college from that, thanks to him.' (Brenda, born 1950, retired policewoman and charity worker)

> 'My mother's idea of aspiring was that I should become a secretary. And I should have left school at 16 and done shorthand typing. But the Head teacher persuaded them to let me stay on in the sixth form and from there to university.' (Jacqueline, born 1944, retired teacher and therapist)

Despite having attended grammar school, Nell's future choices were limited by a lack of knowledge about what was 'out there' and the absence of female role models. She didn't go to university, opting for a job in the bank instead:

> '[Y]ou'd no expectations beyond Lancashire working class; you hadn't been much beyond Manchester. ... I was good at chemistry and physics, maths and things like that. And I didn't really know what to *do* to go into the sixth form. I said to my brother "How many women are there at the Manchester School of Technology?" ... He said "None, none." So ... I didn't particularly want to be the only woman.' (Nell, born 1942, retired senior bank worker)

University proved to be another field where the tension of navigating between working-class community of origin and elite institution often resulted in what Bourdieu (2004) describes as a 'double distance' whereby individuals are detached from both the fields of origin and arrival; literally, positioned 'out of class'. Although she went on to higher education and eventually became a teacher and author, Kate dropped out of medical school at the end of the first year, alienated by the privilege and entitlement of her peers: "I couldn't join the *sailing club* – I couldn't afford a *drink.*" Kate's interview, resonated with what Lawler (1999: 11) describes as 'two (related) sets of anxieties'; the fear of returning to working-class poverty set against her sense of being an imposter in her new world. This tension, the sense of being caught between two worlds was not uncommon. Reay (1997: 24) speaks of her own move away from her origins in 'militant working class culture' rendering her a misfit 'out of place and out of time'. Pamela experienced similar feelings dating back to her teenage years. She referred frequently to her subjective sense of difference, ascribing it to her own "eccentricity":

'I never went to university – 'cause it was so hard in '63 – hardly anyone went. And I just knew there was a big difference ... I've never been particularly *socially fluent*, right?' (Pamela, born 1945, semi-retired psychotherapist)

Reay (2015: 13) suggests that when habitus is over-extended by movement across fields, the end result is not the smooth adaptation implicit in the notion of the chameleon habitus but 'struggle and conflict' resulting in 'heavy psychic cost'. For three of the 15 women who went to university straight from school, the experience was devastating and they experienced serious mental health issues in their first year. Clary was sent to a psychiatric hospital after her first term at university; the feelings of difference and inadequacy she had previously experienced at grammar school returned to haunt her:

'Maybe some of it was because I felt, amongst people at university, that I had to work twice as hard to do as well and I spent a lot of time when I'd been to lectures typing up notes afterwards ... The feeling I had at grammar school ... was more *intense* at university.' (Clary, born 1951, retired counsellor)

Class differences were not the only elements of struggle and conflict encountered by socially mobile participants. Catherine came from a strong religious, working-class family. When she 'escaped' her family's surveillance at the age of 20, she fell in love with a female student.

She attributed her mental ill-health directly to the suppression of her same-sex desires:

> 'I went to college in 1970 and … I just had this absolutely massive … breakdown. Which was because I'd had these feelings from the age of 11, probably earlier, for like different girls and then when this happened at college the whole lot sort of caved in.' (Catherine, born 1950, retired teacher and sexual health worker)

A material world: intersections of gender and class in employment

In addition to the emotional and psychological pain of habitus dislocation, class mobility (and immobility) creates material differences, which accumulate across the life course resulting in economic disparities in older age. Some participants were acutely aware of how their working-class origins had affected their middle-class careers. As a teacher and author Kate was conscious of the kudos her working-class lesbian identity carried:

> 'I was *kind of* the working-class token […] I served the *lesbian slot* and the *working-class slot* so they were *sorted.*' (Kate, born 1946, retired author and teacher)

In the 1980s Kate published several books to great acclaim. However, despite her success as an author she wasn't confident operating in a middle-class world, her working-class habitus and sense of being an imposter still holding her back:

> 'I didn't know enough … about getting agents or competition to *handle* that world and it comes back to class. There's the feeling of "they won't let you in". And my mum used to say that, "I'd like to be middle-class but they won't let you in."' (Kate, born 1946, retired author and teacher)

Several participants left school at the age of 15 often with disastrous consequences for their employment prospects and far-reaching impacts on their chances of accruing a living pension. It was evident that while many of the 'educated working-class' participants still experience the conflict and tensions inherent in the divided habitus and retain *feelings* of insecurity about their classed positions, in reality many of them have had access to more permanent employment and better pensions than those participants whose class location has not changed, resulting in greater financial security across their lifetimes and in their older age.

Michelle just missed out on the extension of the school leaving age, but gained a degree as an adult. Now in her late fifties, and in recovery from cancer, she is still doing a variety of quite physical jobs including DIY, decorating, joinery and gardening:

> 'I left school at 15 and I had no qualifications at all so I started out in an office job. I've worked in factories, I've worked on the buses, I've worked for Royal Mail, I worked in a cash-and-carry, in the butcher department … I've filled washing up bottles and bleach bottles. I've worked on production lines, … I've done all sorts.' (Michelle, born 1956, makes and sells pens)

Susan's interview had a fatalistic quality; education had no transformative influence on her life. She grew up in (and still lives in) a small Yorkshire town, left school at 15 and saw her factory job, marriage and children as inevitable for someone of her class and gender:

> 'I liked school; it were all right. But we only went to 15 so there were no chance of taking any O-levels. […] We just went into local factory, like sewing. 'Cause it were good money, so, that were it. There were no … wanting to *get on*, it was just in them days … just thinking oh well, you'll probably get married and that'll be it. Have kids, that's how it were.' (Susan, born 1947, retired factory worker)

This section has illustrated some of the ways participants' social class was either transformed or held unchanged by the beliefs and practices of the 1950s education system, leading to occupational differences which in turn have had economic implications across the life course. I now turn to an understanding of class as a lived experience, looking at the meaning these (im)mobilities held for my participants.

Theorising class identity: 'upward' mobility and habitus dislocation

In the interviews I asked participants to describe their social class and talk about how and why they self-defined in that way. In addition,

I asked separate questions about family background, education, occupation and lifestyle. I am drawing on an understanding of class as a lived experience and significant axis of inequality; a view conceptualised by Reay (1998a: 259) as 'a complicated mixture of the material, the discursive, psychological predispositions and sociological dispositions'.

Robin grew up in a working-class family where she felt ostracised because she loved music, poetry and reading, in an environment where these pursuits were not valued. Robin's self-definition as working class bears none of the shame or stigma suggested in other accounts of working-class women (Skeggs, 1997; Reay, 1998b). Living now in a small rented flat, her sense of class allegiance and pride were uncomplicated:

'Well *now* it signifies a *great pride* for me because it's... apparently *there is no working class anymore*, which I find *astonishing*. It's like when they say post-wave feminism – it's like almost *what the fuck* is post-wave feminism? I'm *in it* I'm *working at it*. ... So this working-class thing that's becoming a myth is... well it's not a myth for *me* and it's not a myth for *lots* of people that I know. And it's *always* been a *pride*; I've *never* been *ashamed* of it.' (Robin, born 1949, retired women's charity worker)

Brenda grew up in the North of England in the 1950s. She went to a Catholic grammar school and then art college. For her, class identification was easily calculated. She still saw herself as working class and traced her class identification back to family and school:

'We lived on a council estate and then I passed my 11 plus and it was oooh... [Jill: 'What was it like?'] Then you get to *school* and they *tell* you you're working-class.' (Brenda, born 1950, retired policewoman and charity worker)

Heaphy (2012) found sexual identities to be stronger than class ones for his lesbian and gay participants although he observes the diverse ways in which they articulated, constructed and lived their class identities. Many of my participants offered similarly complex narratives that acknowledged their social mobility and embraced both their past and present classed identities rather than being based purely on 'objective' class. While I accept and honour these subjective definitions, they can be misleading and conceal vast material differences and power imbalances between participants. Here Annie acknowledges some of these contradictions:

> 'I would say that I'm *working class*. I don't think that I'd be *perceived* as working class; I think I'd be perceived as middle class. And I think that's partly to do with my *education* and the *kind* of work that I've done and quite often people I've mixed with. But, for *me*, I would say I am working class.' (Annie, born 1951, retired social worker and children's advocate)

An analysis of participants' self-definitions, stories of journeys travelled, ambiguous descriptors and sense of allegiance to the working-classes (irrespective of education and occupation) reveals that just under half either self-identified as working class or referenced their working-class roots and history. These narratives were offered in response to my questions about childhood and parental occupation. Participants traced their trajectories through a variety of routes including education, feminism and meeting middle-class lesbians in social groups, and frequently used these stories as a way of positioning themselves. Some of these stories were deeply rooted in emotion and awareness of the classed and gendered limitations for the previous generation.

Traditional studies of 'upward' mobility often portray it as a positive, indeed desired state, where the socially mobile easily bridge class boundaries by becoming culturally omnivorous (Goldthorpe et al., 1980). Friedman (2014, 2016) draws attention to mobility's potential to create habitus separation, suggesting that 'the emotional pull of class loyalties can entangle subjects in the affinities of the past' (2016: 1). Some of my participants' narratives speak to those internal contradictions and conflicts; while acknowledging their now middle-class status and lifestyle they also recognised the social and emotional costs of the painful transition away from working-class origins, often alluding to feelings of attachment or allegiance to their early childhood class and culture:

> 'Well I still feel *incredibly* working class, that's the education I *had* or the *lack* of it, never been to university, so I *feel* very working class. But I *live* a very middle-class lifestyle. But I don't think the two things just come together and *merge* and make you middle class; I *won't* have that.' (Joyce, born 1946, retired housing manager)

The fact that Joyce retains such a strong sense of her working-class self despite her middle-class lifestyle implies that, as Lawler (1999) suggests, for many people, rather than being attached to external markers – indicators such as employment, housing and the accumulation of material goods – class is in fact inscribed as part of the self. Gina's movement through the class structure renders her middle-class identity as tenuous and uncertain but she doesn't feel she 'fits' in a working-class milieu; a position she attributes to growing up feeling 'out of place'. Gina saw herself as middle class *now*:

> '[L]ook at where I *live*. Obviously I'm middle-class, right. I've got two Master's degrees; of course I'm middle class. *But historically* absolutely not. I always feel *really* intimidated by people with posh accents.' (Gina, born 1952, full-time hospice counsellor/social worker)

Gina is not alone in her sense of being an imposter in a 'middle-class world'. Many other women made reference to similar feelings of dislocation, having developed their abilities, skills, attitudes and dispositions under very different social arrangements to the ones they find themselves in as adults. Lawler's research with socially mobile white British women born into working-class families reveals similar findings. She uses Bourdieu's concepts of habitus and cultural capital to understand their expressions of anxiety around class about which she concludes:

> Although these women have acquired a measure of symbolic and cultural capital, they have not inherited these capitals but 'bought' them within systems of education and training, or through the relationship of their adult lives. They cannot fully occupy what Bourdieu calls the 'habitus' ... of the middle classes. (Lawler, 1999: 13)

Annie and Kate's descriptions of their positioning as working-class women moving in predominantly middle-class circles exemplify Lawler's notion that class distinctions are inscribed to the self and cannot just be taken up or left behind. These women acknowledge the disjuncture between their working-class origins and the adult middle-class lifestyles they have acquired through their education, relationships, careers and the subsequent assimilation of the 'dispositions' of the middle class. In many cases, they have been professionals operating at a senior level in careers including education, housing and social work. However, not only do they refuse to identify as middle class but, unlike participants such as Ivy and Gina, their interviews did not resonate with the pain of estrangement that has been associated with aspirational mobility (Lawler, 1999). What they do reveal is a resistance to assume an inauthentic identity, deeply entrenched in a working-class 'loyalty to self' narrative similar to the one identified by Stahl (2015):

> 'The opportunity may start a journey that takes you away from your roots but it doesn't change the *roots*, it changes the *label*, and I … I won't change the label. I am who I am … I am Annie and I identify as working class.' (Annie, born 1951, retired social worker and children's advocate)

The fact that discussions of class were often accompanied by some kind of contextualising story whereby several participants still claimed a working-class identity while acknowledging their middle-class lifestyles would seem to indicate that a working-class identity remains a source of pride; an important and esteemed category for many of the participants, echoing the work of Savage et al.'s (2001: 885) assertion of inverted working-class pride in their study in the Northwest which concluded that '"working classness" is not entirely a stigmatized identity'. Two participants identified as 'educated working class' (Gina and Jacqueline) and 11 women offered fairly straightforward middle-class/comfortable definitions.

While some studies of education and mobility propose a transformation of the habitus – a movement away from the field of origin and the acquisition of new ways of being – Abrahams and Ingram's (2013) study of local students entering university suggests that many people who are socially mobile create a 'third space' whereby a 'chameleon' habitus is possible, adaptable to both the field of 'departure' and the field of 'arrival'. This concept *could* work to explain Annie and Joyce's apparent closeness to their milieu of origin and stated ease in moving between working-class and middle-class fields. However, many other participants, including Ivy and Rosie, linked their mobility to fragile class identities, feeling that they were positioned as 'out of class' and experiencing a sense of hybridity akin to that discussed in accounts of queer and diasporic unbelonging:

> '[M]y *roots* are working class and I would *like* to say I'm working class but I know full well my economic situation means I'm *not*. *But*, but it means you don't *fit* and *there's* an

element of loneliness. Because you're not one or the other.'
(Rosie, born 1949, retired teacher)

Jacqueline's social mobility means that she feels most secure not in the new middle-class world or back in the working-class world of her birth but somewhere halfway between the two:

> 'I call myself the "*educated* class" 'cause I think that's what we are. There's a certain group of friends I have that I feel the most confident with; the *first* ones to go to university, the different backgrounds... so I call us the educated class and for whom education has *continued* to be important.'
> (Jacqueline, born 1944, retired teacher and therapist)

My research reveals the sense of difference that emerges through the contradictions of participants' various positionings as socially mobile, sexual and gender non-conforming adults at a time of rigid and conservative societal norms. Some participants expressed feelings of difference related to their rejection of the prevailing social norms with regard to female roles and appearance, others experienced a profound sense of sexual difference as teenagers and young women; for many their choice to live a lesbian life fractured relationships with parents and siblings and, when shrouded in secrecy and fear, made establishing intimate adult relationships more difficult. For some, social mobility was an early life event; they were propelled via scholarships from working-class family life and primary education into grammar schools with a middle-class milieu. Others encountered middle-class culture through feminist and lesbian groups across the course of their lifetimes. Stories of upward social mobility were threaded through many discussions of family history, suggesting historical and emotional associations as well as a certain precarity in several participants' class of origin. Class disjunctures leading to misalignments between habitus and field run through the life course of many participants.

I suggest these feelings of displacement can be best understood as another example of habitus dislocation. Bourdieu (1999) recognised its occurrence in cases of long-range mobility when the habitus was unable to adjust to the economic, social or cultural conditions of the new. The habitus of participants such as Rosie, Jacqueline and Gina was extended from its working-class roots, through grammar school, university and middle-class occupations. Not only had they never fully adapted to the new circumstances, but also they were unable to return comfortably to the field of origin, habitus dislocation rendering these participants emotionally, socially and culturally alienated. Others have experienced similar habitus disruption through their social encounters with middle-class lesbians exposing them to a new, cultural milieu. Bourdieu suggests that these disruptions are not easily resolved, creating:

> [A] habitus divided against itself, in constant negotiation with itself and with its ambivalence, and therefore doomed to a kind of duplication, to a double perception of self, to successive allegiances and multiple identities. (Bourdieu, 1999: 511)

Conclusion

This chapter has traced the participants' journeys through the life course looking particularly at how social class and social mobility has affected their lives. For a few, lack of educational opportunity served to 'fix' their lives, rendering them socially immobile and creating economic challenges that continue to accumulate in older age. Participants such as Susan have retained their original class identity but traversed gender and sexuality norms, rendering them 'different' from their families of origin, school friends and work colleagues. Others experienced social mobility often as a consequence of access to grammar school and then higher education or via meeting middle-class lesbians in social spaces. Some of these women, for example, Pamela, Ivy and Gina, feel that their class of origin still marks them as being 'out of place'. Several participants, including Kate, have crossed class borders but claim to retain a sense of being authentically working class despite the social and cultural dispositions of their lives today. I believe that this movement across fields, whether it be socially or through educational or occupational opportunities, has created internal conflict in many participants; their habitus stretched between different fields is not fully adapted to either, leaving them 'out of place', neither feeling to belong in their communities and families of origin nor in their new middle-class environments.

While the narratives of aspiration, social class mobility and change offered by my participants are important ones, indicating the social, educational and cultural origins of this generation of elders, they reveal just one aspect of the 'difference' that has positioned many of my participants as 'other' – both socially and materially – and continues to do so in their older age. Whereas recent discussion of cleft habitus is located in the *single* field of social mobility (Ingram, 2011; Abrahams and Ingram, 2013; Friedman, 2016), I suggest that the concept can also be used to understand *multiple* misalignments of dispositions and practices; through their rejection of traditional gender norms and straight sexual identity many of my participants were caught between a number of social fields and have never shaken off the resulting sense of disequilibrium.

Although there is insufficient space to discuss them here, my participants' experiences of transgressing gender role and sexual identity expectations in the mid-20th century also contribute to their habitus dislocation. These contemporary mobilities, which have intersected with the participants' experiences of social class transgression, placed participants into lives where their existing dispositions were inadequate to guide them, where they had no moral or social 'code' to follow, leaving them with feelings of dislocation and 'unbelonging' that have stayed with some participants all their lives and continue to shadow their later years.

References

Abrahams, J. and Ingram, N. (2013) 'The chameleon habitus: exploring local students' negotiations of multiple fields', *Sociological Research Online*, 18(4), www.socresonline.org.uk/18/4/21.html.

Bourdieu, P. (1999) 'A life lost', in Bourdieu, P. et al. *The Weight of the World: Social Suffering in Contemporary Society*, Cambridge: Polit: 507–13.

Bourdieu, P. (2004) *Science of Science and Reflexivity*, Cambridge: Polity.

Friedman, S. (2014) 'The price of the ticket: rethinking the price of social mobility', *Sociology*, 48(2): 352–68.

Friedman, S. (2016) 'Habitus clivé and the emotional imprint of social mobility', *The Sociological Review*, 64(1): 129–47.

Goldthorpe, J.H., Llewellyn, C. and Payne, C. (1980) *Social Mobility and Class Structure in Modern Britain*, Oxford: Clarendon Press.

Heaphy, B. (2012) 'Situating lesbian and gay cultures of class identification', *Cultural Sociology*, 7(3): 303–19.

Ingram, N. (2011) 'Within school and beyond the gate: the complexities of being educationally successful and working class', *Sociology*, 45(2): 287–302.

Lawler, S. (1999) 'Getting out and getting away: women's narratives of class mobility', *Feminist Review*, 63(3): 3–24.

McDermott, E. (2010) '"I wanted to be totally true to myself": class and the making of the sexual self', in Y. Taylor (ed) *Classed Intersections: Spaces, Selves, Knowledges*, Surrey: Ashgate Publishing, 199–216.

Reay, D. (1997) 'The double-bind of the 'working-class' feminist academic: the failure of success or the success of failure?' in P. Mahoney and C. Zmroczek (eds) *Class Matters: 'Working Class' Women's Perspectives on Social Class*. London: Taylor and Francis: 19–30.

Reay, D. (1998a) 'Rethinking social class: qualitative perspectives on gender and social class', *Sociology*, 32(2): 259–75.

Reay, D. (1998b) *Class Work. Mothers' Involvement in their Children's Primary Schooling*. London: UCL Press.

Reay, D. (2015) 'Habitus and the psychosocial: Bourdieu with feelings', *Cambridge Journal of Education*, 45(1): 9–23.

Savage, M., Bagnall, G. and Longhurst, B. (2001) 'Ordinary, ambivalent and defensive: class identities in the Northwest of England', *Sociology*, 35(4): 875–92.

Sennett, R., and Cobb, J. (1977) *The Hidden Injuries of Class*. Cambridge: Cambridge University Press.

Skeggs, B. (1997) *Formations of Class and Gender: Becoming Respectable*, London: Sage Publications.

Stahl, G. (2015) 'Egalitarian habitus: narratives of reconstruction in discourses of aspiration and change', in C. Costa and M. Murphy (eds) *Bourdieu, Habitus and Social Research*, Basingstoke: Palgrave Macmillan, 21–38.

Weeks, J. (2015) 'Gay liberation and its legacies', in D. Paternotte and M. Tremblay (eds) *The Ashgate Companion to Lesbian and Gay Activism*, Surrey: Ashgate Publishing; 45–58.

NINE

Insider or outsider? Issues of power and habitus during life history interviews with menopausal Iranian women

Elham Amini

Introduction

This chapter explores issues concerning the sexuality of Iranian Muslim menopausal women, but focuses on how power was negotiated between me, as an interviewer, and the interviewees throughout the life history interviews I conducted with them. As an Iranian woman conducting interviews with Iranian Muslim menopausal women who practise the Shia Islam faith, I found, in addition to my biography and personal characteristics (such as gender, race, and sexual orientation), what Bourdieu calls the *habitus* (how I spoke, sat and what I wore) had a significant influence in how I negotiated my status with participants. Thus, I argue for the need to go beyond a focus on intersectional categories per se, and to look at the broader social landscape of power and its process. I do this by employing a Bourdieusian perspective, which considers the symbolic and cognitive elements by emphasising the social practice.

This issue of positionality speaks to debates about being an 'insider' or an 'outsider'. From one perspective, since my gender, nationality, language and sexual orientation were apparently the same as the participants, I entered the research field as an insider, giving me a lived familiarity with my research participants (Griffith, 1988: 361). Yet, I found that simultaneously I was an outsider (not an actual member of the specific group under study) because of my different social status and lived experience as a doctoral student at a British (that is, Western) university. Thus, I had a different set of *capitals*, from Bourdieu's (1984, 1990) perspective, which raises the question of my position in this biographical life history research. To understand the effect of these on the power relationship and research process, I employ the Bourdieusian approach, as embedded in a specific time and place, rather than intersectionality theory.

I begin this chapter with a brief review of the methodology of my study and some concerns pertaining to power and reflexivity in order to explain how my biographical research approach led me to be conscious of the power relations between myself and the participants. I then clarify how my social location as a researcher affected my research about Iranian Muslim menopausal women, how I consider insider/outsider status when conducting research on the participants and the intersectional nature of these issues in the Bourdieusian conceptual framework. Following this, I outline the significance of Bourdieu's theory of practice and apply key aspects of this to my research.

Biographical research and methodology

The central aim of my research was to understand the process by which individual menopausal women's sexual biographies are shaped by cultural, social and religious (Shia Islam) structures, and the ways that women's individual agency responds, in turn, to these social structures. I employed a biographical approach, which aims to enable participants to narrate their own stories from their own perspectives.

The biographical approach provides a reflexive space within interviews for the researcher to understand the women's lived experiences, and so relate their individual biographies to their sociocultural structures (O'Neill, 2010). As such, this gave my participants a voice, to construct knowledge in their own way and provide a space for this normally silent group of women to be heard. It places the participants' realities at its centre, focusing on their subjective interpretations and perspectives instead of identifying them as objective facts (O'Neill, 2010).

Furthermore, as the biographical research approach is based on individuals' narrations and the meaning that they give to their everyday lives, it is very dependent on the agency of storytellers to create their unique stories by adjusting narrative types, which sociocultural structures make accessible (Frank, 1995; Plummer 1995). While biographical research is about individuals' experiences, they live within wider sociocultural structures and their stories are narrated through an interaction with these structures, which have considerable impacts on them. Thus, an individual's life story is not just a self-production; it is shaped by the influence of cultural, ideological and historical contexts (Denzin, 1989: 73).

In addition, biographical research can develop a space for dialogue between the researcher and participants, one that inculcates creative listening and understanding (O'Neill, 2015). The style of biographical research approach I conducted was informed by my social justice principles, emphasising non-exploitative, non-hierarchical approaches to participants; thus, exploring my relationship with the participants formed an essential part of my study.

I conducted 30 individual in-depth life history, biographical interviews. To obtain my sample, I attended religious classes in Tehran and Karaj and recruited research participants from the women who attended these classes regularly. To make initial contact, I spoke with my religious friends who attended these classes and, before attending myself, I was introduced to the teachers of the classes and obtained their permission. Indeed, to meet the women regularly, I attended all of these sessions, every week, for four months.

At the first session before the classes were started the teacher introduced me to the other women and then at the end of that session I spoke about myself and my research with the women themselves. I introduced myself as a midwife who has been continuing her studies in the sociology of health and gender. I invited them to join the research by giving me their telephone numbers, or taking mine, in order to have contact with each other and to arrange a date and a time which was suitable for them and at a location of their choice.

Each interview commenced with a brief explanation about myself and an outline of the research. Although I had an interview guide, I let the discussion flow quite freely. However, if a participant diverged from the subject quite a lot, I led the discussion back to the research by asking a question from the interview guide. Hence the interviews were semi-structured and in-depth, which gave the participants significant power to control the process (Corbin and Morse, 2003: 335). The length of the interviews ranged from one to two hours.

Researcher's social status: reflexivity and power, Bourdieusian perspective and intersectionality

Given the importance of understanding my role as a researcher in this study, reflexivity is a crucial issue. Reflexivity is a way to engage with the mutual effects of the researcher (her values, behaviours, and even gender) on the research process and, in turn, how the research process influences the writing up of the research. It is also about the power relationship between the researcher and the participants, and the researcher's consciousness about this interaction (Mays and Pope, 2000).

Bourdieu (1999: 607–8) highlights that although the researcher might be unconscious about how she affects participants during an interview, it is crucial to analyse the potential for these effects to minimise them. The distinction between the positivist researcher and others is between a science which does not acknowledge these effects and dreams of a *perfect innocent science* and the science which is aware of these effects and endeavours to explore them as much as possible, since these effects are inevitable. Bourdieu (1999: 608) clarifies that this reflexivity is 'based on a craft, on a sociological feel or eye, allows one to perceive and monitor on the spot, as the interview is actually taking place, the effect of the social structure within which it is occurring. Similarly, O'Neill (2015) underlines that the conditions and structures in which qualitative interviews occur have considerable influence on the social interaction between researcher and the participants. As an Iranian woman, educated in a Western country, conducting my fieldwork among religious menopausal women in Iran, the issue of my position as the researcher in this biographical research is important.

All the participants were menopausal women and were more than 45 years of age at the time of interview, which means they were older than me. As such, they had a level of power and respect by virtue of their age: Iranian culture treats its elders with great respect and gives them high priority within the family; for instance, if an older person enters a room the younger people have to rise to show their respect. Thus, interviewing women who were older than me was the first challenge of my study, as they might hesitate to narrate their sexual lives for a younger person in order to protect their respected status. In addition, due to belonging to the same culture, it was very difficult for me to ask the older women very sensitive questions about their sexual relationships, since I was worried I would be regarded as a 'rude' person who does not heed 'cultural values'. This made my age very crucial, both with regard to the research process and the power relations between interviewer and participants.

These issues of age cohere with religion. The participants were religious women who practised Islam and I had gained access to them through attending their religious classes, yet I am a young woman who has been educated in a western country (the UK) and lived there alone. It is possible, even likely, that participants would presume that I have been affected by 'Western culture' – an issue that intersects, and may be exacerbated by, my age, given the cultural suspicion with which many older Iranians view the younger generation.

It seems that intersectionality theory, which emphasises the intersection of identities, could be appropriate to address the power relationship within the interviews, especially regarding the age differences. However, in the particular context in which the power is embedded, the social practices of people may be different from the ways in which they have been categorised (Anthias, 2013). The key point here is the way that the categories of intersectionality appear within the interviews as a social practice. I explain later how it can be different, notably when, from the Bourdieusian perspective, it is related to symbolic representations or symbolic capital. Thus the complexity arises when I refer to other dimensions of power relations such as capitals and habitus.

Additionally, intersectional categories are not fixed and unchangeable. Rather, they are emergent through the interactions among the researcher and interviewees. They are shaped through these interactions in a social practice (the interview) and as a part of the exercise of power within the interviews and in relation to capitals and habitus that are brought to bear on them. Hence, interviews need to be viewed as socially located, bodily practices in which embodied agents mediate and negotiate power. In other words, the interviews, as social practices, are shaped through the interplay between the researcher's and interviewees' experiences, shared knowledge and their sociocultural structures (in this case Iranian Muslim Shia).

In this way, by employing a Bourdieusian perspective, I go beyond intersectionality theory, and address the 'doing' of practice itself and its fundamental outcomes, through meaning-making and mediating power. The use of Bourdieu's practice theory, by conceptualising capitals and habitus, can develop individual categories to include cognitive diversity in such a way as to acknowledge the capitals in producing power relation in specific times and places. Habitus can also point out the engagement of the actors (the researcher and interviewees) with structure through practice (interviews). Therefore, I argue that Bourdieu's (1990) theory of practice is an important theoretical framework as it can clarify the interrelation between embodied agents and society in a particular social practice (the interviews) and explores the interview as both a social practice and an aspect of interaction.

Applying Bourdieu's practice theory

By drawing on Bourdieu's practice theory, I aim to explain the process that shaped the data collection according to my position in this biographical research within the Iranian Muslim sociocultural structure. Key defining features of this theoretical framework (capitals, field and habitus), including its explicit attention to power, are illustrated to explore the ways in which this approach can inform a more nuanced understanding of power relation within the interviews.

Bourdieu's practice theory identifies a central interplay between the body and the society. He articulates that habitus is a 'system of durable, transposable, dispositions, structured structures predisposed to function as structuring structures, that is, as principles which generate and organise practices and representations' (Bourdieu, 1990: 53).

Habitus is the position of the individuals in the society according to their understanding from the sociocultural structure. Crossley (2001: 94) argues that habitus functions like an underlying 'grammar' which determines the framework for social practice, but also allows innovation to be created by the users. Similarly, Painter (2000: 242) clarifies that habitus is the 'mediating link' between sociocultural structures (social determination) and individual's agency or in other words it is the internalised component of the individual's history and social norms. In order to situate habitus, Bourdieu develops the concept of *field*, which is the social structure and is in mutual relationship with habitus or the practice of actors: 'a field is a distinct social space, consisting of interrelated and vertically differentiated positions, a "network, or configuration, of objective relations between positions"' (Bourdieu and Wacquant, 1992: 97).

Bourdieu (1984: 101) formulates the relationship between these concepts in the following way: *[(habitus) (capital)] + field = practice*. Capital from Bourdieu's perspective is all of the resources which can have exchange value in various fields (Crossley, 2001: 96), the set of artefacts and actions that maintain some form of worth within the specific social context. *Cultural capital* is an embodied state of non-financial assets that can promote social mobility; *symbolic capital* can explain one's prestige in a social group; and *social capital* refers to the cultural resources a person has based on their networks and group membership (McCormack, 2014).

Cultural capital

Thinking about my capitals in this research, my professional background is in midwifery, and I had been a health professional in Iran for more than six years. Cultural capital defines, in Bourdieu's (1984) view, qualifications and education. In this case, for me, being a midwife is a form of cultural capital. Trusting a health professional, especially a female midwife, makes it relatively easy for women to talk about their sexuality and therefore my cultural capital allowed me to build a trustful relationship with the participants and made it easier for them to narrate their sexual biographies.

However, the participants' educational level varied greatly, from being illiterate to being medical specialist. This shaped the power relationships between me and the participants in various ways. When the participant's educational level was lower than mine (especially when they did not have a university degree), they hesitated to narrate their life stories as they considered their stories 'worthless'. On these occasions, I reminded them of the crucial role of their stories in my research and emphasised that their narratives were central to my study and that it would be weakened without their willingness to participate in the interviews. This indicates that narratives and stories have the power to cross intersectional differences, such as educational level, and thereby potential class differences. For instance, Zohreh[1] who was 47 years old and had high school degree started her interview by asking me:

> ZOHREH: 'I don't have a good education, so I don't think that I can help you; I don't know how I, an uneducated woman, can be helpful for you and your academic research. I can only tell you about my life, is this enough for you?'
>
> ELHAM: 'Oh, yes, I would definitely like to know your life story. My research is about your life story, so it's very important for me to know it. Without your life story, I can't do my research, so, to tell the truth, I am dependent on your story [smiles].'

Thus, although I entered in this particular interview with a certain degree of power, particularly around education and social class, I endeavoured to shift power by explaining the significant role of Zohreh's biography to my study. I also reminded her of my eagerness to learn from her, and that, although I am educated, her lived experiences were important in order to move my understanding from an abstraction to Zohreh's lived realities. This gave Zohreh a more equal power during the interview and made me more of an insider.

In contrast, my interview with Sarah, 57 years old and a paediatrician, started with her mentioning her higher educational level in comparison with my own, arguably as assertion of her power:

---

[1] All the participants names have been changed to preserve anonymity.

SARAH: 'You know, I'm a paediatrician and I know all about the menopause and its consequences.'

ELHAM: 'Yes, and I really appreciate your participation in my research, but now I want to know about your lived experiences and not about what has been written in the text books.'

In this interview, unlike Zohreh's, Sarah entered the interview with a certain degree of power, due to her cultural capital. Although I chose Sarah for interview and I had control over the process of the interview itself, by asking specific questions, Sarah's cultural capital gave her considerable power in our relationship. By pointing out that the goal of the interview was about Sarah's lived experiences, not her professional knowledge, I aimed to rebalance the power between myself and Sarah. On this basis, cultural capital was one of the essential elements in negotiating power during the interviews and the shifting dynamics of power in interview relationships and shows how intersectional differences can be shifted through such practices.

Symbolic capital

Bourdieu (2011) explains that symbolic capital is status, or recognition. Although, the participants and I were female, studying in a Western country (the UK) was a form of symbolic capital for me, which did not have a positive effect on the process of building a trustful space. All the participants were religious practising women who believed in maintaining their traditional, religious culture, which they believed is contrary to 'Western culture', especially in relation to sexuality.

I carefully negotiated my symbolic status, gaining each participant's trust when conducting the interviews. For example, one of the participants, Zahra, 51-years-old, challenged me by claiming that I should be doing my fieldwork in the UK. Although I had been away from Iran (my home country) for only two years before conducting the fieldwork, Zahra believed that as my role as student in a 'Western country' meant that I could not (or perhaps should not) do my research in my own country (as an 'Eastern country'). As a result, the first 10 minutes of the interview were devoted to explaining to her my reasons for choosing the research topic and Iran as the place for the fieldwork:

ZAHRA: 'Isn't there any problem with doing your research about women here?'

ELHAM: 'No, my subject is Iranian women. It's my home country and I like to do my research about Iranian women. Also, I know Iranian women better than English women, so I can do better research about them.'

ZAHRA: 'Don't you need to research in that environment? About the women over there? I mean, you studied there and the women who live there are totally different from us. Don't you need to do your research in the place of your study?'

ELHAM: 'No, not at all. My supervisor has approved it. But in which way do you think they are different?'

ZAHRA: 'Everything, but ... all right.'

ELHAM: 'Do you think I'm different as well?'

ZAHRA: 'Uhum ... willy nilly you studied there too.'

In this case, reflection started when Zahra stated her concern about the 'problematic subject' of the project by questioning my capability of doing the research. Her claim was based on the location of my university, a Western country. From her point of view, studying in a Western country made me one of the 'women there' (the UK) and not one of the 'women here' (Iranian Muslim woman), despite my nationality (Iranian) and conducting the interviews in Farsi. Consequently, I was not sufficiently insider enough to do the interview with her as I was more outsider. This extract reflected the dynamic power relations between Zahra and me throughout the interview, in which she intermittently highlighted my position as an outsider. This example can elaborate that the interviewee (Zahra) as well as interviewer can display their interrelationship through the process of mediating the power in the course of the interview situation. Thus, although Zahra could be categorised as a person with less power in terms of being the interviewee, her symbolic capital as an insider (and mine, classified by her as an outsider) can be used to resist that power dynamic.

My other symbolic capital related to my marital status. I got divorced 10 years ago. Marriage has symbolic importance and meaning in Iranian culture. Moaddel and Azadarmaki (2002) point out that significant value is attached to the institution of marriage in Iran and it is embedded with the meaning of sanctity. Accordingly, divorce or marital dissolution is a distinct cultural stigma. Hojat et al. (2000) assert that Iranian people believe that divorce is a calamity (بلا) and an unfortunate fate (بدبختی). Although divorce is allowed under Islam, it is strongly condemned and viewed as a disaster due to the considerable symbolic importance placed on family and marriage. On this basis, divorce carries a stigma – a negative symbolic capital – especially for women. Indeed, as one of my research participants, Fatemeh, who is a 53 years old, explained, paraphrasing an expression that is very well known in the Farsi language: "My father always told us that women should go to her husband's house with a white dress [a bride's dress] and return [to the family home to be buried] in a white dress." In Islamic tradition, the corpse is typically wrapped in a simple, plain white cloth and buried. Thus, according to this expression, a woman cannot/ should not divorce; she can leave her marriage status just on one condition, which is death.

During the interviews, all of the participants asked about my marital status. Due to the stigma attached to divorce, I felt that it was inappropriate to disclose this information. I believed that they would not answer my questions and would refuse to participate in the interviews. I therefore hid my negative symbolic capital and told them I was single. Consequently, the next question concerned the reasons for me 'still' being single and also involved encouraging me to get married, reminding me that soon it would be 'too late'. Even the women who were unhappily married were vocal in encouraging others, including me, to get married. This illustrates well the value that Iranian Muslim women may place on the social institution of marriage as symbolic capital.

Hiding my marital status could be seen as deception and therefore an ethical dilemma for my study. Nevertheless, according to Bryman (2004: 514) 'Deception occurs when researchers represent their research as something other than what it is.' Since my marital status was not related to the research, it was not considered to be deception; rather it was a strategic element of non-disclosure that facilitated the richest data possible. Yet, it was a symbolic capital with the potential for a negative impact on the process of power during the interview, which shaped my positionality during the interaction.

Social capital

Social capital relates to the power and usefulness of social networks. To access the participants, I gained help of my friends who are themselves religious women. They introduced me to the religious classes that they regularly attended. As the participants knew my friends well and had friendly relationships with them, they accepted me easily. Most of them started their interviews by mentioning that my friends 'said good things' about me to them, so they decided to participate in the research. Thus, my social capital had a positive effect on building a trustful space in order to collect my data. Additionally, my social capital had a positive impact on my positionality, making me more of an insider for the participants due to their relationships with my friends.

Field

The field is a social structure that has mutual relationship with social practice (Bourdieu and Wacquant, 1992). I consider the places where I conducted the interviews as the field for two reasons: first, the locations could shape the positionality of both the participants and myself. Second, they had a notable influence on the power dynamic between the participants and myself (social practice). The location of an interview is not just a physical space; rather, it embodies various relations and symbolic meanings for both the participant and the researcher and can be considered as part of a social structure.

After making contact with the participants, it was necessary to arrange a time and place for each interview. I encouraged my participants to choose locations where they would feel as comfortable as possible. The interviews took place in a variety of agreed settings. Most of the time they were held in the location of the religious classes, at others in participants' houses. In these cases not only were the participants familiar with their chosen places, but there was the symbolic meaning of the places belonging to them, which was not the case for myself. On one occasion it was in my car, in the street in which the participant's house was located, as the participant told me her house was small and her daughter was in the house so she was not comfortable to talk in her company.

It was always the participants' decision to select the location and I had limited power in this regard. The participants took advantage of the opportunity to choose a place which was familiar for them and unfamiliar for me. Depending on their choice, I experienced a different power dynamic. It was their familiar territory; in all locations I was a guest with less power. For instance, one of the interviewees, Maryam, 50 years old who has a BSc degree, asked me to conduct the interview in her house. When I entered, I found Maryam's husband in the same room that she had chosen for doing the interview. As the house was very big and modern I asked Maryam if it was possible to go to another room and conduct the interview in a more private place. However, Maryam answered that her husband liked to be with us in the same room during the interview, and as she wanted to do the interview she accepted her husband's condition. So, the interview was held while Maryam's husband sat at a distance of six metres from us, although with his back to us. He did not utter a word, not even a greeting. Throughout the interview, my feeling was one of fear, and when the interview was finished, I rushed out of their house. I had respected Maryam's decision about the location that she had chosen for interview and the conditions under which it was conducted. However, during the transcription process I realised that she had spoken throughout in a faint voice, so it was difficult to decipher the words.

In this interview, two different power relationships were created by Maryam (interviewee), her husband and I (researcher), based on the location of interview (field). First, the place of interview or the field is inscribed in the gendered social structures that shape the power hierarchy between two women (Maryam and me) and a man (Maryam's husband). The patriarchal power imposed by Maryam's husband's surveillance of the interview, and its pattern of practice authorises men's dominancy over women, which made us to keep our voice down. However, we (Maryam and I) negotiated power and demonstrated our agency by insisting on our desire to continue the interview. Maryam's agency is revealed by her success in doing the interview and selecting her choice from the existing possibilities and constraints. We did not have total freedom of choice, but we actively chose from the possibilities (doing the interview despite the presence of Maryam's husband or abandoning it) and constraints that we had, highlighting our agency.

Second, the other power relationship was shaped between Maryam, as an interviewee, and me, as an interviewer who accepted the conditions of the field. Whereas Maryam was empowered by her familiarity with her own home and knowing about the presence of her husband beforehand, I was disarmed by the discomfort of being in an unfamiliar place with the existence of another person whom I had not expected to be there and its consequence, which was feeling fear. In this case, the process of power relationship according to the chosen field had started before the actual interviewing began, with the negotiation of power based on gender order (between Maryam and her husband) and continued throughout the interview (between Maryam and me, and both of us with her husband). This reveals the importance of the field, of its structured rules of social (and indeed physical) locations, in understanding the dynamics of power relationships during research, and shows the significance of embodied practices to one's positionality.

Habitus

I consider my habitus as my embodied position (how I speak, sit and what I wear) in the field according to my understanding from the sociocultural structure of the field. It was another important factor in the power relationship with the participants and determining my positionality as an insider/outsider, which emphasises the interviews as socially located bodily practices. All the participants wore a hijab in their religious classes, although there were no men there. Moreover, when they wanted to leave the class they wore a chador, a full-body-length fabric, without any hand openings, which covers a woman's body from head to toe over the top of her clothes. Thus, to be an insider, I changed my habitus in a way to show them that I respected their wearing of a complete hijab. So, I too wore a very long and black one, covered my hair completely by a black veil and, in addition, I gave them some small gifts such as arm bands to show my respect for their hijab.

In spite of all these efforts, sometimes I was seen as more of an outsider, as the participants endeavoured to change my view towards their family members, the true insiders, and tried to keep up a gendered appearance. For example, in one of the interviews when Nahid, 51 years old and a midwife, wanted to explain how she recognised her gender, she said:

> 'I found, whenever we wanted to go out, one of my brothers would accompany us. Even if it was a birthday of our friends, we had to go with one of them. If our friend's family didn't let the boys to join in the party, then we had not to go. … But, never think that we weren't free. No, we were free; my parents are educated, intelligent and modern Muslims.'

In this example, Nahid's parents are insider, and the researcher is an outsider who intruded into her family matters and even might judge the insiders. Thus, Nahid tried to not allow me to criticise her family for not giving her freedom. Similarly, Farideh, 57 years old and a teacher, emphasised that telling her story to me was like talking behind her relatives' backs and she did not like to wash her dirty linen in public (in Farsi it is literally 'spit on your own face'); consequently she felt 'bad' about it. After reassuring her that I would not judge her or her relatives, she started her story.

Both of these participants considered me an outsider, certainly compared with their relatives, but not a total outsider as they accepted the invitation to be interviewed and trusted me to narrate their hidden stories. Thus, at first they hesitated to narrate their stories in order to prevent me from judging their insiders. In the above interviews, I was not a total outsider and, simultaneously, not a total insider; my positionality was that of a distanced insider who endeavours to shift to being more of an insider.

Nevertheless, being conscious of the power dynamic between myself and my interviewees and deploying my capitals and habitus within the field helped me to negotiate an insider/outsider dichotomy. Although my research was completed, I was called by other women, who were the interviewee's classmates, to conduct the interview with them. Hadiseh, 60 years old was one of them: "I was waiting for your call to do the interview with me, but you didn't call me. I am wondering if you can do the interview with me like what you did with my friend ..."

This, first of all, indicates that the participants talked about the interviews with their classmates (insiders) and then decided to accept me (the researcher) as someone who they could narrate their hidden part of their life for me. Second, it reveals how needful they were, in wanting to be heard and how they would accept an outsider to give voice to their concerns.

Conclusion

This chapter set out to reflect on the shifting power dynamics in life history interviews that I conducted with menopausal Iranian women. In this chapter I have demonstrated how I sought to make sense of these shifts using Bourdieu's theory of practice (1984, 1990) and its attendant concepts of capitals, field and habitus. I adopted this Bourdieusian approach, rather than an intersectional analysis, to show how dynamic power can be in interviews of this kind. I have therefore sought to demonstrate that rather than categories such as age, gender and sexuality fixing people into locations, a range of embodied practices in those situations are important as well.

In my study I argued that the social practices of the women in the interviews were different from the ways in which they have been categorised. For instance, Zahra has been categorised as a person with less power due to her lower educational level, but she questioned my appropriateness of doing the research due to my symbolic capital. This also reveals my positionality was various even during the course of one interview. In this case, I entered the interview as an outsider but gradually my status shifted to that of an insider whom Zahra trusted to tell her story. Accordingly, categories are not fixed; rather they are shaped through interactions, which themselves are mediated by power. I explained how the power of narrations could shift power within the interviews. In this way, a participant could assert power by choosing not to reveal certain aspects of her story, to stop the interview whenever she wished or not to participate at all. For example, Zohreh's case has been categorised with less power and Sarah's case has been categorised with more power.

Additionally, I have highlighted the importance of specific locations or fields in power relationships. Habitus also indicates the key element of bodily practice in negotiating power as the position of the women and me in the interviews. Simultaneously, I as a researcher by employing my capitals endeavoured to negotiate power in order to gain rich data.

Finally, it is important to remember the shifting dynamics of being an insider/outsider and the ways that intersections are used in that process. I was not a complete outsider (due to our similarities in gender, nationality, language), but neither was I a complete insider (due to our differences in capital and habitus). Thus, the power dynamic within the interviews could not be explained only by identity categories and how they intersected, but also needed to include how the actors deployed them in social practice, that is, in the interview situation. So, rather than consider the status of the researcher to be static, and bounded dichotomously (either as an insider or outsider), instead I experienced a complex, dynamic status as both insider and outsider, during even a single interview, based on the capitals, habitus and the field from Bourdieu's perspective.

Acknowledgement

I would like to express my special thanks of gratitude to Professor Mark McCormack for his comments on an earlier draft of this chapter.

References

Anthias, F. (2013) 'Intersectional what? Social divisions, intersectionality and levels of analysis', *Ethnicities*, 13(1): 3–19.

Bourdieu, P. (1984) *Distinction: A Social Critique of the Judgement of Taste*, Harvard: Harvard University Press.

Bourdieu, P. (1990) *The Logic of Practice*, Cambridge: Polity.

Bourdieu, P. (1999) 'Understanding', in P, Bourdieu (ed) *The Weight of the World: Social Suffering in Contemporary Society*, Cambridge: Polity, 607–29.

Bourdieu, P. (2011) 'The forms of capital' (1986), in I. Szeman and T. Kaposy, *Cultural Theory: An Anthology*, Oxford: Wiley-Blackwell, 81–93

Bourdieu, P. and Wacquant, L.J.D (1992) *An Invitation to Reflexive Sociology*, Cambridge: Polity.

Bryman, A. (2004) *Social Research Methods*, 2nd edn, Oxford: Oxford University Press.

Corbin, J. and Morse, J.M. (2003) 'The unstructured interactive interview: issues of reciprocity and risks when dealing with sensitive topics', *Qualitative Inquiry*, 9(3): 335–54.

Crossley, N. (2001) *The Social Body: Habit, Identity and Desire*, London: Sage Publications.

Denzin, N.K. (1989) *Interpretive Biography*, London: Sage Publications.

Frank, A.W. (1995) *The Wounded Storyteller: Body, Illness, and Ethics*, Chicago: University of Chicago Press.

Griffith, A.I (1998) 'Insider/outsider: epistemological privilege and mothering work', *Human Studies*, 21(4): 361–76.

Hojat, M., Shapurian, R., Foroughi, D., Nayerahmadi, H., Farzaneh, M., Shafieyan, M., and Parsi, M. (2000) 'Gender differences in traditional attitudes toward marriage and the family', *Journal of Family Issues*, 21(4): 419–34.

Mays, N. and Pope, C. (2000) 'Assessing quality in qualitative research', *British Medical Journal*, 320(7226): 50–2.

McCormack, M. (2014) 'The intersection of youth masculinities, decreasing homophobia and class: an ethnography', *The British Journal of Sociology*, 65(1): 130–49.

Moaddel, M. and Azadarmaki, T. (2002) 'The worldviews of Islamic publics: the cases of Egypt, Iran, and Jordan', *Comparative Sociology*, 1(3): 299–19.

O'Neill, M. (2010) *Asylum, Migration and Community*, Bristol: Policy Press.

O'Neill, M. (2015) 'Biographical research: past, present, future', in M. O'Neill, B. Roberts, A. Sparkes (eds) *Advances in Biographical Methods: Creative Applications*, London: Routledge: 73–89.

Painter, J. (2000) 'Pierre Bourdieu', in M. Crang, and N. Thrift (eds) *Thinking Space*, London: Routledge: 239–60.

Plummer, K. (1995) *Telling Sexual Stories: Power, Change and Social Worlds*, London: Routledge.

TEN

Sexual expression and sexual practices in long-term residential facilities for older people

Feliciano Villar

Introduction

This chapter deals with how sexual issues are dealt with, both by residents and professionals, in long-term facilities for older people. Sexuality is a valuable dimension of humanity that may be maintained until a very advanced age (Lindau et al., 2007), and even in the presence of severe illness and dependency at least some older adults continue to be interested and involved in sexual behaviours (Benbow and Beeston, 2012).

A particularly challenging situation in this regard is when a person enters a long-term care (LTC) facility, an event marking a turning point in the older person's life. Although it is true that for some older people living in LTC facilities sex does not hold (or no longer holds) an important place in their life, and they simply do not miss it at all (Villar et al., 2014a), other residents see themselves as sexual beings who still experience sexual needs (Bauer et al., 2013), and consequently issues regarding sexual activities can occur in this setting (Lester et al., 2016).

In this chapter, we outline the study in Box 1. We then first identify the barriers that institutionalised older people might face with regard to the expression of sexual interests. We will explore barriers related to the profile of older people living in those contexts, to the attitudes of residents and staff, to the culture of care held in LTC facilities. Second, we will examine how sexual expression might be especially challenging among specific populations of older adults living in institutions, with particular attention being paid to people with dementia and LGBT (lesbian, gay, bisexual, transgender) residents. Finally, some practical implications as regards sexual expression and sexual rights of older people living in LTC settings will be considered.

In the exposition, the intersection between those topics and ageing, gender and sexual diversity issues will be emphasised. These factors are by themselves systems of inequalities, as they have material consequences and influence life chances (Veenstra, 2011; Calasanti and King, 2015). In our view, their effect in a closed context such as a LTC facility, in which living options are limited and deeply influenced by staff and institutional practices, might intensify inequalities and increase the risk to curtail sexual rights of certain collectives.

Throughout the chapter, I will illustrate certain ideas with some of the results and examples extracted from qualitative research on these issues conducted by Montserrat Celdrán, Rodrigo Serrat, Josep Fabà and myself. This forms part of a project that has been carried out in LTC facilities in Spain by interviewing both staff and residents (see Box 1). The case of Spain is particularly interesting in relation to sexuality in older age for at least two reasons. First, despite secularism being dominant among younger generations, traditionally Spain has been a deeply Catholic country. As is well known, Catholicism is particularly conservative with respect to sexual issues (Curran, 1992). Second, older people now living in LTC facilities in Spain belong to the post-Spanish Civil War generation. They grew up and spend their youth in Franco's dictatorship, a regime which severely axed civil liberties and rights, including sexual ones. Formal sexual education did not exist and open expressions of sexuality, particularly for women, were deemed dirty and sinful (Pérez, 1994). So, we should take into account such cultural and generational particularities when reading older people's responses coming from our research.

Sexual expression in LTC institutions

The sexual dimension of older residents is often ignored in LTC facilities and, when it appears, is considered more a problem or a potential source of conflict than the expression of a natural human need and a question of rights (Tarzia et al., 2012; Villar et al., 2014a). The reasons for this are diverse and interrelated, but three areas of difficulty which hamper older residents from maintaining intimate and sexual relationships in LTC facilities can be distinguished: those related to the social profile and health status of residents, those derived from social attitudes towards sexuality in older age, and those linked to the organisational culture and models of care that are prevalent in LTC facilities.

Box 1: The study

In 2012 a research team based on the University of Barcelona and composed by Feliciano Villar, Montserrat Celdrán, Rodrigo Serrat and Josep Fabà, designed a research project aimed at exploring the attitudes towards sexuality in Spanish LTC facilities. The project, initially funded by the Spanish Institute for Older People and Social Services (IMSERSO) has two stages:

Stage 1
We interviewed 47 residents and 53 professionals (including technical staff and nursing assistants) belonging to five different LTC facilities located in Barcelona and the surrounding area. The interview consisted of some introductory questions regarding sexuality and ageing, such as barriers to residents' sexual expression (Villar et al., 2014a), and perceived needs in this area (Villar et al., 2017). Subsequently, researchers presented some vignettes in which older people were depicted engaging in different sexual behaviours. Participants had to reflect on the situations, saying what they thought and how they would react themselves in the circumstances. Vignettes included masturbation (Villar et al., 2016a, 2016b), heterosexual sexual relationships (Villar et al., 2015a), people disclosing a non-heterosexual sexual orientation (Villar et al., 2015b, 2015c) and sexual relationships involving residents with dementia (Villar et al., 2014b).

Stage 2
Based on the results of stage 1, the research team (with the inclusion of gerontologist Teresa Martínez) designed a questionnaire in which vignettes presenting sexual situations also included different staff reactions. Participants had to indicate what is normally done in their institution (common practice) and what, in their opinion, should be done (best practice). Reactions included both supportive and restrictive practices. As well as the ones presented in stage 1, the questionnaire also included vignettes regarding same-sex sexual relationships and inappropriate sexual behaviours, such as exhibitionism or a staff member experiencing fondling. We also applied a questionnaire on person-centered care and an inventory on institutional policies regarding sexuality.

The questionnaire was applied to 2,300 staff members, including directors, technical staff and nursing assistants (at this stage people living in LTC facilities did not participate), from 152 different institutions across the country. The design and sample size allowed for determining personal and institutional predictors of staff practices. First results have been published in 2018 (see Celdrán et al., 2018; Villar et al., 2018).

Difficulties in relation to social profile and health status of residents

The profile of older people living in residential settings is clearly one factor that accounts for the lower incidence of sexual practices. For instance, Caffrey et al. (2012) estimated that around 70% of Americans living in long-term institutions are women, most of whom are widowed or single, a situation that makes it difficult to find available sexual partners, at least for heterosexual women. A similar situation is found in other countries, such as the UK (ONS, 2014) or Spain (Tobaruela, 2003), where the percentage or women in LTC facilities is similar, or even greater.

It should also be noted that, even for older people living outside institutional settings, having a partner has a decisive influence on sexual activity, although there are gender differences here: men without a partner reported being sexually active far more frequently than women without a partner (Papaharitou et al., 2008), a result that is also replicated among older Spanish people (Palacios-Ceña et al., 2012).

A further issue is that older people living in institutional settings, at least in Spain (Tobaruela, 2003), present a high prevalence of chronic diseases (including cognitive impairment) and dependency, which could impair their sexual drive and make it particularly difficult to express their sexual interest and needs. As a nurse, aged 38, reported, "Many people here are not independent enough to go to the toilet by themselves ... so they can't get involved in sexual matters; they would even need help to masturbate!" (Villar et al., 2014a: 2523).

It should also be taken into account that the high rate of chronic illnesses goes hand in hand with an extraordinarily high use of medication (Dwyer et al., 2010).

Polymedication in older adults is associated with adverse consequences, some of them in the sexual domain (Hillman, 2008). Unfortunately, these consequences for sexual drive and sexual behaviour are not normally assessed or even taken into account by health professionals. Even when older people in LTC facilities experience health issues that impair (or impede) their ability to have sexual intercourse or to masturbate, they may still experience sexual needs and the desire for some kind of physical intimacy, for example, in the form of touching, hugging or kissing (Ehrenfeld et al., 1999). However, there are other barriers that may make even these forms of sexual expression difficult.

Social attitudes toward sexuality in older age

Societal values and beliefs regarding sexuality, and particularly ageist erotophobia, that is, anxieties concerning older people as sexual beings or denial of their sexual capacities or rights (Simpson et al., 2017), have an impact on – and could be a barrier to – a person's ability to maintain sexual activity once he or she moves to a LTC facility.

In countries such as Spain, most people belonging to older generations have received limited or no information and education at all concerning sexual issues (Vázquez & Moreno, 1996). They have grown up in a political regime that restricted liberties and rights and was heavily influenced by extreme Catholic views. A context in which sex, and particularly sex without a reproductive aim, was condemned, and definitely considered as not appropriate in later life.

Such negative views of sexuality may particularly affect the sexuality of women, in whom virtue in most religious denominations, including Catholicism (Curran, 1992; Davidson et al., 2004), was traditionally associated with a lack of initiative in the sexual domain and lack of involvement in non-procreative sexual activities. Furthermore, when it came to sexuality in later life, and despite new social images of sexually active older women (see, for example, Montemurro and Siefken, 2014), older women were traditionally stereotyped as frigid and asexual. The internalisation of such scripts in older generations could account for the findings of Lindau et al. (2007), who noted that women, far more frequently than men, tended to report that sex in older age is 'not important at all' and to mention lack of interest as a motive for sexual inactivity.

Therefore, it comes as no surprise that older adults themselves might be a source of barriers to their peers' sexuality, or that this effect is particularly intense in the closed setting of LTC facilities, where residents share time, space and activities. As one of the residents interviewed by Villar et al. (2014a: 2522), a woman aged 73, said "Every new thing becomes a public affair and sexuality also becomes public. There are no secrets and sex needs secrecy, so people hold themselves back, because nobody likes to be the target of gossip."

In this context, peers' real or anticipated negative reactions towards sex might act as a form of social control that denies the expression of sexuality among residents, or at least leads to them remaining hidden. For instance, residents and staff (Villar et al., 2015a), were asked to imagine what they would feel and how they would react if they caught a heterosexual couple having sex in their room. We found that residents were much more prone than professionals to judge this situation adversely and to express negative emotions. While staff mainly mentioned emotions associated with regret (in other words, they should not have interrupted), residents' most common emotions were unpleasantness and shame. In some cases, they expressed intense rejection. For instance, a male resident, aged 79, said:

> 'They should be ashamed of doing such things at their age, or outside their own home ... or whatever – publicly, you might say. That's what I'd think. May God forgive them because it wouldn't ... Well, it's not something I would like to come across.' (Villar et al., 2015a: 1058)

However, since in younger generations religion is less important, at least in Spain, and attitudes towards sex are more open and liberal than in previous generations (Rowntree, 2014), attitudes toward sex in later life may change. Once these generations grow older and some of them enter LTC facilities, it is likely that sexual issues will become more central. Some studies show, accordingly, that younger people express concerns about the capacity of aged care institutions to recognise their expectations about sexuality (Jönson and Jönsson, 2015).

Social views regarding sexuality in older age not only influence older people's attitudes but also those of their relatives. Families may find it difficult to accept that their older relative (for example, their father or mother) has sexual needs and is sexually active. This denial, or even rejection, could be particularly strong if the older person is widowed and/or if he or she lives in a LTC facility (Gilmer et al., 2010), where it may act as a barrier and lead staff to discourage (or at least not to support) sexual relationships within the institution for fear of how relatives will react.

Organisational culture and concepts of care

One of the most influential factors that may impede sexual relationships within LTC facilities is the organisational culture of the institution. The key issues here are how the institution and its staff conceive of their task, which philosophy of care is promoted and how it is enacted, what kinds of rights residents are afforded, and the extent to which sexuality is acknowledged to be a need and/or right within the structure of organisational beliefs and practices.

In that respect, the traditional (and dominant) conception of care within LTC institutions is based on the medical model, in which the professional is conceived of as a dispenser of care; as such, it is professionals who decide the type and extent of care required by residents. There is thus a tendency to function in a paternalistic way, with the emphasis on controlling behaviour rather than supporting residents' autonomous choices, and with efficiency being the fundamental criterion for achieving quality. Residents thus become patients with needs that have to be met; they should be protected (sometimes from themselves) and are given little room for deciding about their daily lives and the care they receive (Morgan, 2009).

Within this type of care model there are a number of ways in which residents' sexuality may be dealt with. One is to restrict or punish sexual expressions among residents, treating them as problem behaviours to be eliminated. Such a stance is likely to be adopted if the institutional philosophy is based on certain religious or conservative values. Alternatively, sexuality may simply be ignored, with staff acting as if residents have no sexual interests (Doll, 2012). Thus, most LTC facilities have no formal policy guidelines for dealing with residents' sexual expressions, have no trained staff for managing them, and fail to set aside private spaces in which sexual practices could be engaged in (Shuttleworth et al., 2010).

Staff attitudes

Implicit models of care are also important because they have an impact on staff attitudes about residents' sexuality, a factor that the literature has identified as a key barrier to – or potentially a facilitator of – sexual expressions. Thus, when staff perceive that their institution is restrictive they are more likely to feel uncomfortable dealing with sexual issues and to act in a controlling way (Roach, 2004).

The attitudes of professionals are, however, quite diverse. Many of them show respect towards residents' sexual expression, whether in the form of heterosexual relationships (Villar et al., 2015a), masturbation (Villar et al., 2016a) or homosexual relationships (Villar et al., 2015b), and they try not to interfere in such expressions. Such attitudes may reflect a wider generational change, as reflected in the following comment by a staff member, a woman aged 36, regarding masturbation: "It's the resident's body and he can do as he pleases. Times change, and people of my generation don't see it as a sin, or as something shameful that must be kept hidden" (Villar et al., 2016a: 825).

Nevertheless, negative attitudes are also quite common and take different forms, condescending or paternalistic stances being quite frequent (Bauer, 1999). Thus, particularly in the case of partnered heterosexual sexual expressions, staff tend to romanticise them, as 'cute' or 'amusing'. However, such infantilising attitudes are less likely when demonstrations of sexual arousal and desire are explicit (Ehrenfeld et al., 1999).

Joking, mocking or gossiping with workmates are also frequent reactions among staff. This is not always an overt rejection of residents' sexual expression, as at times it may be a way of reducing the tension, discomfort or embarrassment that is provoked by the situation (Bauer, 1999). As well as being a lack of respect of residents' right to privacy, such reactions could discourage residents to rely on staff as a source of help and advice on sexual issues.

Our own research has shown that, although open restriction (for example, reprimanding) of sexual expression is not the norm in Spanish LTC facilities, support of sexual expression is also uncommon (Villar et al., 2015a, 2016a). This suggests that staff have little awareness of the key role they play in terms of supporting and guaranteeing residents' rights (Gilmer et al., 2010). In addition, the wide range of staff reactions highlights the lack of clear and previously agreed institutional policies (Lester et al., 2016). Sexual issues are thus dealt with in an ad hoc way, thereby promoting uncertainty among both professionals and residents (Cook et al., 2017).

Privacy

In the medical approach to care, many nursing homes emphasise the need to standardise staff work and resident activities in order to ensure the smooth running of the institution, regardless of the impact this may have on residents' expression of sexuality and intimacy. Thus, residents are subjected to schedules that they have not chosen and spend many hours in common spaces and in the company of (although not necessarily interacting with) other residents.

Similarly, LTC facilities are often designed in the manner of hospitals, prioritising control and quick access to residents' rooms over the maintenance of their privacy. In addition, most rooms are shared and in many instances there are no locks on doors, the justification being that professionals need to be able to enter quickly in the event of an emergency and should face no barriers in their regular monitoring of residents' activities (Eckert et al., 2009; Morgan, 2009).

In this context, obtaining the privacy needed for sexual relationships is very difficult. In fact, a lack of privacy is the most frequent barrier mentioned by professionals and residents of the Spanish LTC facilities participating in our studies (Villar et al., 2014a). As one of the staff members, a nurse aged 47, said:

'I think the fact of sharing a room and that rooms have no lock doesn't help ... Even the bathrooms are shared. Your room is supposed to be your private space, but even there you can't be sure that nobody is going to come in ... you don't have a single space you can call your own ... that doesn't exist in a residential home.' (Villar et al., 2014a: 2522)

Such a lack of privacy affects partnered sexual relationships, but it also makes it difficult to engage in other sexual behaviours that do not involve a partner, such as masturbation. In a context where, as argued above, establishing a partnered sexual relationship is extremely difficult, masturbation might be a readily available form of sexual release and a way of compensating for and channelling residents' sexual needs (Villar et al., 2016b). However, the lack of private spaces leaves little room for masturbating without concerns.

Diversity and expression of sexual interests in residential settings

If, as noted above, the expression of sexual needs may be difficult for healthy heterosexual residents living in a LTC facility, then it is even more challenging for some of their peers whose situation is somewhat different. In the next two sections I will briefly examine the case of two groups: older adults with dementia and non-heterosexual older adults.

People with dementia

Sexuality among older residents with dementia is a source of practical and ethical dilemmas among staff (Tarzia et al., 2012). The literature on this topic has highlighted two interrelated issues: (a) the effects that dementia may have on the expression of sexuality and the presence of inappropriate sexual behaviours (ISB); and (b) the effects of dementia on a person's cognitive capacities and personality structure, which could undermine his or her ability to make decisions about sexuality.

Dementia and ISB

Regarding dementia, it is well known that, alongside cognitive impairment, behavioural disturbances are likely to manifest at some stage. These behavioural disturbances sometimes affect the sexual conduct of people with dementia, leading to what has been labelled as inappropriate sexual behaviours (Ward and Manchip, 2013), which includes hypersexuality, sexual aggression, unwanted groping of other people or use of foul language. In the context of LTC facilities, the presence of ISB, although relatively infrequent, is likely to impinge on the rights of staff and other residents, thus residents with ISB need to be monitored and adequately managed.

Beyond the clinical implications, ISB could also be a response to unmet intimacy needs that do not disappear simply because the person has dementia; in this respect, these behaviours may constitute strategies (albeit dysfunctional) for interacting with others (Tune and Rosenberg, 2008). Although behaviours of this kind may result in negative interactions, such an outcome may, for the person with dementia, be preferable to no interaction at all, particularly where little is done to enable interaction among residents, as in certain LTC facilities. Examining the meaning of ISB from the residents' perspectives and considering possible ways of channelling such behaviours in an acceptable manner might be a reasonable response. However, professionals, in line with the medical model of care, often try to avoid risks. This may lead them to consider any manifestation of sexuality among people with dementia, regardless of whether it is appropriate or not, as a symptom of the illness that should be controlled rather than as the expression of a need or the exercise of a right (Ward et al., 2005).

Dementia, abuse and consent

Memory and language impairment, as well as possible changes in personality, make it more difficult for the person with dementia to make decisions and communicate his or her preferences. In the case of sexual expressions involving other people, it may be difficult to determine the extent to which the person with dementia really wants or consents to the relationship, and there is an undeniable risk that they may abuse other residents (or even staff) or be abused by them.

In these situations most institutions and professionals opt to minimise risks and preclude any sexual expression among people with dementia as a way of protecting them from abuse; this has been called the 'extreme cautionary stance' (Villar et al., 2014b). Thus, expressions of sexuality in dementia are, by default, an object of suspicion and are treated as a symptom of disease, as a woman, aged 54, doctor and director of an LTC facility, said when was interviewed by Villar et al. (2014b: 406):

> 'You have to be sure that there's not an abuse of authority. Because people with dementia often have frontal impairments, and then they're sexually disinhibited … they're not aware of what other people are doing with them, and maybe … so, we have to protect the weakest, don't we?'

This kind of paternalistic, restrictive and overprotective attitude may become particularly intense when only one person in a partnered relationship has dementia, and it may also be enhanced by relatives' opinions. Thus, institutions may be afraid of being sued by relatives, should the latter discover that their family member with dementia is having sexual relationships, or simply fear that the family would remove their relative (and the corresponding funds) from the institution.

Although well-meaning, attitudes of this kind deprive people with dementia of the right to make their own decisions on sexual issues, or at least to be involved in those decisions. Importantly, research suggests that people with dementia do retain the capacity to express their own values and preferences consistently, particularly when the stage of dementia is mild or moderate (Mak, 2011). The use of non-verbal cues (for example, body language or facial expressions) is particularly useful in this respect, and such cues may offer a reliable sign of how a person with dementia is experiencing a sexual situation.

Specific issues facing older LGBT people

In addition to the barriers already outlined above, older LGBT people living in LTC facilities have to face specific challenges that do not affect their heterosexual peers and suppose a further challenge to their sexual rights.

One of these springs from the fear of being discriminated against (Westwood, 2015). Most likely due to their lifetime experience of abuse and rejection, older LGBT generations express a recurrent concern that they will be mistreated and discriminated against in healthcare settings, including LTC facilities. Specifically, they fear being neglected, judged or abused by healthcare providers, or being rejected or ostracised by roommates or other residents (Stein et al., 2010; White and Gendron, 2016). This may lead many of them, even if they were open about their sexual identities when living in the community, to 'go back into the closet', denying or hiding their sexualities. As a result, they may experience even stronger feelings of isolation and loss than are commonly felt by older people when entering a LTC setting.

Studies of attitudes among residents in Spanish LTC facilities support these concerns. Faced with a hypothetical situation in which a fellow resident discloses his or her gay or lesbian sexual identity, only a minority of the participants interviewed by Villar et al. (2015b) reacted with support or acceptance. Indeed, most of those interviewed expressed negative attitudes, ranging from extreme rejection (one male resident said: '[I'd think] that he's a disgusting pig who should be kicked out') to simply keeping one's distance, as a woman aged 79 said:

> 'Very, very bad ... I'd try to keep away from her ... I'd try to avoid being with her. [I'd tell her] "I don't like your behaviour and I don't like your attitude." I'd ask her to stay away from me.' (Villar et al., 2015b: 1009)

Although most residents stated that they would have no problem sharing communal areas with gay or lesbian residents, the vast majority said that they would not (or would be reluctant to) share a room. It should be noted, however, that these results might not be replicated in other samples, since acceptance (and legal recognition) of LGBT people varies enormously across cultures, communities and religious perspectives. It is also likely, at least in some countries, that the next generation of older people, who have already lived through the normalisation of non-heterosexual sexual identities, will hold less prejudiced attitudes (Herek and McLemore, 2013).

As for staff approaches to LGBT residents, although some discriminatory practices have been reported among social and health service professionals (Addis et al., 2009; Hinrichs and Vacha-Haase, 2010), other studies that focused on staff working in LTC facilities have found that respect and acceptance are not uncommon (Villar et al., 2015c). However, despite any positive dispositions of staff towards LGBT residents, heteronormative assumptions are widespread, which could lead to reinforce the invisibility of LGBT residents and the failure to recognise their distinctive social and care needs and, consequently, the failure to apply supportive practices. Such a situation might entrench inequality on the grounds of a well-meaning intention of 'treating all the residents in the same way' (Simpson et al., 2016; Willis et al., 2016).

Conclusion and practical implications

The research reviewed in this chapter shows that sexual expression among older adults living in LTC facilities is far from being accepted or even respected. Residents' sexual expressions (and even intimate relationships) are limited or at least monitored by staff who perceive such behaviour as potentially problematic or even pathological.

We have also seen how such difficulties also intersect with variables such as gender or sexual orientation, increasing the difficulties for certain collectives to exert sexual rights. For instance, as older women are thought to be more passive and uninterested in sex than men, their sexual expression in a LTC facility could be seen as particularly problematic for both staff and relatives. Similarly, LGBT older people living in LTC facilities perceive and suffer discrimination by peers, leading many of them to hide their sexual orientation to avoid further segregation.

The literature on this topic has highlighted the importance of developing formal and clear institutional guidelines on sexuality (Lester et al., 2016) and of facilitating staff training on sexual issues (Villar et al., 2017). Initiatives of this kind would help to ensure not only a consistent approach to issues of sexuality in the daily functioning of institutions, but also respect for the rights of all individuals, including those residents who are not interested in sex. The progressive presence of person–centred model of care substituting traditional medical models makes us optimistic in this respect. However, a truly person–centred model of care would need to ensure the application of two fundamental principles in relation to sexuality.

First, residents are bearers of rights, including sexual rights, which should be explicitly supported and guaranteed by staff. Their guiding principle should therefore be beneficence rather than non-malficence. In other words, the ability to exercise sexual rights should be taken for granted until proven otherwise, even among persons with dementia. This position implies certain risks (for example, potential abuse), but then so does the cautionary stance I have discussed earlier (that is, the risk of increased dependency, curtailed – or even violated – citizenship rights and non-justified discrimination).

Second, LTC facilities should be conceived of neither as hospitals nor hotels, but places where people live. They are the residents' homes, and as such all efforts should be made to create a personalised setting in which people's lifestyles, decisions and privacy are respected as far as possible. Those who enter a facility of this kind have had previous lives (including previous sexual lives) that should be known about (to the extent that the individual wants it to be) and respected, thus encouraging a sense of continuity. This means that any decision about residents' sexual practices should ultimately lie with them, or at the very least their views and personal histories should be taken into account.

This does not mean that all older people living in LTC facilities wish to be sexually active, or that staff should be pressuring them to express their sexual desires. What is argued is that sexuality should not be a neglected dimension of residents' lives, but a right and an inextricable part of each person's life, just as it was before he or she entered the LTC facility. In this respect, creating the conditions in which a person can retain his or her sexuality, and supporting it if necessary, makes sense not merely because of the benefits this may bring, but also because it represents an ethical imperative of care.

References

Addis, S., Davies, M., Greene, G., MacBride-Stewart, S. and Shepherd, M. (2009) 'The health, social care and housing needs of lesbian, gay, bisexual and transgender older people: a review of the literature', *Health & Social Care in the Community*, 17(6): 647–58.

Bauer, M. (1999) 'The use of humor in addressing the sexuality of elderly nursing home residents', *Sexuality and Disability*, 17(2): 147–55.

Bauer, M., Featherstonhaugh, D., Tarzia, L., Nay, R., Wellman, D. and Beattie, E. (2013) '"I always look under the bed for a man": needs and barriers to the expression of sexuality in residential aged care. The views of residents with and without dementia', *Psychology and Sexuality*, 4: 296–309.

Benbow, S. and Beeston, D. (2012) 'Sexuality, aging, and dementia', *International Psychogeriatrics*, 24(7): 1026–33.

Caffrey, C., Sengupta, M., Park-Lee, E., Moss, A., Rosenoff, A. and Harris-Kojetin, L. (2012) 'Residents living in residential care facilities: United States 2010', *NCHS Data Brief*, 91, www.cdc.gov/nchs/data/databriefs/db91.pdf

Calasanti, T. and King, N. (2015) 'Intersectionality and age', in J. Twigg and W. Martin (eds) *Handbook of Cultural Gerontology*, London: Routledge: 193–200.

Celdrán, M., Villar, F., Serrat, R., Fabà, J. and Martínez, T. (2018) 'Policies regarding sexual expression in Spanish long-term care facilities for older people', *Journal of the American Geriatrics Society*, 66(5): 1444–5. DOI: 10.1111/jgs.15345

Cook, C., Schouten, V., Henrickson, M. and Mcdonald, S. (2017) 'Ethics, intimacy and sexuality in aged care', *Journal of Advanced Nursing*. DOI: 10.1111/jan.13361.

Curran, C.E. (1992) 'Sexual ethics in the Roman Catholic tradition', in R.M. Green (ed) *Religion and Sexual Health*, New York: Springer: 17–35.

Davidson, J.K. Moore, N.B. and Ullstrup, K.M.(2004) 'Religiosity and sexual responsibility: relationships of choice', *American Journal of Health Behavior*, 28(4): 335–46.

Doll, G.A. (2012) *Sexuality and Long-Term Care: Understanding and Supporting the Needs of Older Adults*, Baltimore: Health Professions Press.

Dwyer, LL., Han, B., Woodwell, D.A. and Rechtsteiner, E.A. (2010) 'Polypharmacy in nursing home residents in the United States: results of the 2004 National Nursing Home Survey', *The American Journal of Geriatric Pharmacotherapy*, 8: 63–72.

Eckert, J.K., Carder, P.C., Morgan, L.A., Frankowski, A.C. and Roth, E.G. (2009) *Inside Assisted Living: The Search for Home*, Baltimore: Johns Hopkins University Press.

Ehrenfeld, M., Bronner, G., Tabak, N., Alpert, R. and Bergman, R. (1999) 'Sexuality among institutionalized elderly patients with dementia', *Nursing Ethics*, 6: 144–9.

Gilmer, M.J., Meyer, A., Davidson, J. and Koziol-McLain, J. (2010) 'Staff beliefs about sexuality in aged residential care', *Nursing Praxis in New Zealand*, 26: 17–24.

Herek, G.M. and McLemore, K.A. (2013) 'Sexual stigma', *Annual Review of Psychology*, 64: 309–33.

Hillman, J. (2008) 'Sexual issues and aging within the context of work with older adult patients', *Professional Psychology: Research and Practice*, 39: 290–7

Hinrichs, K.L. and Vacha-Haase, T. (2010) 'Staff perceptions of same-gender sexual contacts in long-term care facilities', *Journal of Homosexuality*, 57(6): 776–89.

Jönson, H. and Jönsson, A. (2015) 'Baby boomers as future care users: an analysis of expectations in print media', *Journal of Aging Studies*, 34: 82–91.

Lester, P.E., Kohen, I., Stefanacci, R.G. and Feuerman, M. (2016) 'Sex in nursing homes: a survey of nursing home policies governing sexual activity', *Journal of the American Medical Directors Association*, 17: 71–4.

Lindau, S.T., Schumm, L.P., Laumann, E.O., Levinson, W., O'Muircheartaigh, C.A. and Waite, L.J. (2007) 'A study of sexuality and health among older adults in the United States', *The New England Journal of Medicine*, 357: 762–74.

Mak, W. (2011) 'Self-reported goal pursuit and purpose in life among people with dementia', *The Journals of Gerontology Series B: Psychological Sciences and Social Sciences*, 66: 177–84.

Montemurro, B. and Siefken, J.M. (2014) 'Cougars on the prowl? New perceptions of older women's sexuality', *Journal of Aging Studies*, 28: 35–43

Morgan, L.A. (2009) 'Balancing safety and privacy: the case of room locks in assisted living', *Journal of Housing for the Elderly*, 23: 185–203.

Office for National Statistics (ONS) (2014) *Changes in the older residential care home population between 2001 and 2011*, London: ONS.

Palacios-Ceña, D., Carrasco-Garrido. P., Hernández-Barrera, V., Alonso-Blanco, C., Jiménez-García, R. and Fernández-de-las-Peñas, C. (2012) 'Sexual behaviors among older adults in Spain: results from a population-based national sexual health survey', *The Journal of Sexual Medicine*, 9(1): 121–9.

Papaharitou, S., Nakopoulou, E., Kirana, P., Giaglis, G., Moraitou, M. and Hatzichristou, D. (2008) 'Factors associated with sexuality in later life: an exploratory study in a group of Greek married older adults', *Archives of Gerontology and Geriatrics*, 46: 191–201.

Pérez, J. (1994) 'La iniciación sexual de la infancia durante el nacional-catolicismo [The sexual initiation of children in the "National-Catholic" regime]', *Revista de Educación*, 304: 177–96.

Roach, S.M. (2004) 'Sexual behavior of nursing home residents: staff perceptions and response', *Journal of Advanced Nursing*, 48: 371–9.

Rowntree, M.R. (2014) '"Comfortable in my own skin": a new form of sexual freedom for ageing baby boomers', *Journal of Aging Studies*, 31:150–8.

Simpson, P., Almack, K. and Walthery, P. (2016) '"We treat them all the same": the attitudes, knowledge and practices of staff concerning old/er lesbian, gay, bisexual and trans residents in care homes', *Ageing & Society*, 1–31, DOI: 10.1017/S0144686X1600132X.

Simpson, P., Wilson, C.B., Brown, L.J., Dickinson, T. and Horne, M. (2017) '"We've had our sex life way back": older care home residents, sexuality and intimacy', *Ageing & Society*, 1–24, DOI: 10.1017/S0144686X17000101.

Shuttleworth, R., Russell, C., Weerakoon, P. and Dune, T. (2010) 'Sexuality in residential aged care: a survey of perceptions and policies in Australian nursing homes', *Sexuality and Disability*, 28(3): 187–94.

Stein, G.L., Beckerman, N.L. and Sherman, P.A. (2010). 'Lesbian and gay elders and long-term care: identifying the unique psychosocial perspectives and challenges', *Journal of Gerontological Social Work*, 53(5): 421–35.

Tarzia, L., Fetherstonhaugh, D. and Bauer, M. (2012) 'Dementia, sexuality and consent in residential aged care facilities', *Journal of Medical Ethics*, 38: 577–8.

Tobaruela, J.L. (2003) *Residencias: Perfil del usuario e impacto del ingreso* [Nursing homes: User's profile and impact of admission], Universidad Complutense de Madrid, non-published doctoral dissertation. http://eprints.ucm.es/7358.

Tune, L.E. and Rosenberg, J. (2008) 'Nonpharmacological treatment of inappropriate sexual behavior in dementia: the case of the Pink Panther', *The American Journal of Geriatric Psychiatry*, 16(7): 612–3.

Vázquez, F. and Moreno, A. (1996) 'Genealogía de la educación sexual en España. De la pedagogía ilustrada a la crisis del Estado del Bienestar' ['Genealogy of sexual education in Spain. From illustrated pedagogy to the Welfare State crisis'], *Revista de Educación*, 309: 67–94.

Veenstra, G. (2011) 'Race, gender, class, and sexual orientation: intersecting axes of inequality and self-rated health in Canada', *International Journal for Equity in Health*, 10: 1–11.

Villar, F., Celdrán, M., Fabà, J. and Serrat, R. (2014a) 'Barriers to sexual expression in residential aged care facilities: comparison of staff and residents' views', *Journal of Advanced Nursing*, 70: 2518–27.

Villar, F., Celdrán, M., Fabà, J. and Serrat, R. (2014b) 'Staff attitudes towards sexual relationships among institutionalized people with dementia: does an extreme cautionary stance predominate?', *International Psychogeriatrics*, 26: 406–12.

Villar, F., Fabà, J., Serrat, R. and Celdrán, M. (2015a) 'What happens in their bedrooms stays in their bedrooms: staff and residents' reactions towards male-female sexual intercourse in residential aged care facilities', *Journal of Sex Research*, 52: 1054–63.

Villar, F., Serrat, R., Fabà, J. and Celdrán, M. (2015b) 'As long as they keep away from me: attitudes toward non-heterosexual sexual orientation among residents living in Spanish residential aged care facilities (RACFs)', *The Gerontologist*, 55(6): 1006–14.

Villar, F., Serrat, R., Fabà, J. and Celdrán, M. (2015c) ' Staff reactions toward lesbian, gay, or bisexual (LGB) people living in residential aged care facilities (RACFs) who actively disclose their sexual orientation', *Journal of Homosexuality*, 62: 1126–43.

Villar, F., Serrat, R., Celdrán, M. and Fabà, J. (2016a) 'Staff attitudes and reactions towards residents' masturbation in Spanish long-term care facilities', *Journal of Clinical Nursing*, 25: 819–28.

Villar, F., Serrat, R., Celdrán, M. and Fabà, J. (2016b) 'Attitudes toward masturbation among residents of Spanish residential aged care facilities', *Sexuality Research and Social Policy*, 13(2): 182–91.

Villar, F., Celdrán, M., Fabà, J. and Serrat, R. (2017) 'Staff members' perceived training needs regarding sexuality in residential aged care facilities', *Gerontology and Geriatrics Education*, DOI: 10.1080/02701960.2015.1127811.

Villar, F., Celdrán, M., Serrat, R., Fabà, J. and Martínez, T. (2018) 'Staff's reactions toward partnered sexual expressions involving people with dementia living in long-term care facilities', *Journal of Advanced Nursing*, 74: 1189–98. DOI: 10.1111/jan.13518

Ward, R.F. and Manchip, S. (2013) '"Inappropriate" sexual behaviours in dementia', *Reviews in Clinical Gerontology*, 23(1): 75–87.

Ward, R., Vass, A.A., Aggarwal, N., Garfield, C. and Cybyk, B. (2005) 'A kiss is still a kiss? The construction of sexuality in dementia care', *Dementia*, 4: 49–73.

Westwood, S. (2015) '"We see it as being heterosexualised, being put into a care home": gender, sexuality and housing/care preferences among older LGB individuals in the UK', *Health and Social Care in the Community*, 24(6): 155–63.

White, J.T. and Gendron, T.L. (2016) 'LGBT elders in nursing homes, long-term care facilities, and residential communities', in D.A. Harley and P.B. Teaster (eds) *Handbook of LGBT Elders*, New York, Springer: 417–37.

Willis, P., Maegusuku-Hewett, T., Raithby, M. and Miles, P. (2016) 'Swimming upstream: the provision of inclusive care to older lesbian, gay and bisexual (LGB) adults in residential and nursing environments in Wales', *Ageing & Society*, 36(2): 282–306.

ELEVEN

Sexual and gender diversity, ageing and elder care in South Africa: voices and realities

Finn Reygan and Jamil Khan

There is an almost complete lack of literature on the needs of – and care services for – lesbian, gay, bisexual, transgender and intersex (LGBTI) elders in South Africa and across the African continent. As a result, with the exception of Henderson and Almack (2016), we present here some of the first writings on this topic in South Africa informed by the literature base that exists in relation to our knowledge of elder populations more generally in the region. Taking a social justice-oriented and intersectional lens, we approach this study from an African standpoint by engaging African epistemologies and ontologies in relation to old age, death and sexuality. We also engage the intricate interplay of race, class, urban/rural realities and the apartheid legacy as they intersect with the lives of LGBTI elders. We conclude the chapter by proposing an Africa-centred and culturally sensitive model of care for LGBTI elders. We purposefully use the term 'elders' to reference the historic respect given to older people across the African continent and so as to situate this study within the Southern African context.

We begin by providing some relevant contextual information on South African realities before engaging with the research on ageing in South Africa and across the continent before looking at the very limited research and writing to date on the lives of LGBTI elders in South Africa. We then present as a case study an interview we conducted with an older, lesbian married couple about their experiences and perspectives on queer ageing in South Africa. We conclude by proposing an African, community- and home-based model of care for older people, including LGBTI elders, informed by contextual realities and African ontologies.

South African realities

South Africa has one of the most progressive constitutions in the world that is often lauded globally as exemplary in terms of its focus on inclusion and tolerance (Woolman, 2015). The protections afforded by the Bill of Rights include a number of specifically enumerated categories including age, gender and sexual orientation and Section 9 of the Constitution states that neither the state nor anyone may '... unfairly discriminate directly or indirectly against anyone on one or more grounds, including race, gender, sex, pregnancy, marital status, ethnic or social origin, colour, sexual orientation, age, disability, religion, conscience, belief, culture, language and birth' (Bill of Rights, RSA 1996).

Specifically in terms of ageing, the law upholding the rights of older people is the Older Persons Act 13 of 2006 which aims to:

> ... deal effectively with the plight of older persons by establishing a framework aimed at the empowerment and protection of older persons and at the promotion and maintenance of their status, rights, well-being, safety and security; and to provide for matters connected therewith.

In short, as is often the case in South Africa, formal equality is clearly enshrined in both the Constitution and in legislation. However, as is also generally the case in South Africa, this does not necessarily translate into substantive equality on the ground. There are a number of organisations whose work focuses on the lives and needs of older people, including the South African Older Persons Forum, Council for the Care of the Aged, the South African Association for Retired Persons and the Afrikaanse Christelike Vroue Vereeniging (Afrikaans Christian Women's Association). However the inequalities that characterise South African society (outlined later) are also reflected in these organisations that represent and support older people. For example, most of the organisations listed above offer support services that are largely framed in terms of managing elder life with regards to health, finance, technology and leisure. Considering the income disparity and inequality between black and white South Africans, services aimed at these issues would serve mostly white people of retirement age.

Barriers to accessing formal elder care in South Africa include exclusion on the basis of race and class. For example, a survey of 145 old age homes across South Africa found that 77% of residents were white, Afrikaans females (Perold and Muller, 2000). Communication was flagged as an issue in old age homes, in terms of language barriers between staff and residents. According to Perold and Muller (2000), caregivers come to their own conclusions about the needs of residents and often only focus on the obvious physical needs; as a result the holistic needs and preferences of the older person are rarely taken into account. Issues of elder abuse are also a growing concern in care facilities across the country. For example, Bigala and Ayiga (2014) studied the prevalence of elder abuse in Mafikeng in North West province. The main predictors of elder abuse were found to be having no surviving children, having no working children, being single, living in an elder couple family, living in rural areas, having a poor self-perception of health and having a disability. Men were more susceptible to physical abuse, while women were more susceptible to sexual abuse and elder abuse was found to more prevalent in rural areas (Bigala and Ayiga, 2014). The work of elder care organisations is also generally specific to a particular town, city or province such as the Durban Association for the Aged in KwaZulu-Natal province and the Western Cape Older Person's Forum in Western Cape province. For definitional clarity, old age in South Africa is typically defined as the period after retirement, which is 60 years for women and 65 for men (Older Persons Act 13 of 2006). Despite the constitutional provisions and the formal rights related to sexual orientation and gender identity, none of these organisations has a focus on the inclusion of LGBTI people.

Given the presence of private care for older people in South Africa, issues of access and affordability emerge as important questions in a context of great inequality. According to a number of measures (Tregenna and Tsela, 2012), South Africa is one of the most unequal countries in the world and this plays out in terms of access to elder healthcare. For example, medical aid schemes generally provide only modest cover and also do not cover care that is administered outside of registered frail care facilities. This emphasis on registered institutional care also excludes the practice of home-based care which is preferred by many black African families. Given the cost of monthly premiums, the target market for medical aid schemes is clearly classed and creates barriers to elder care for those who are poor and less well off (du Preez, 2015). In general elder LGBTI communities remain invisible and their needs are not mentioned as a concern for medical aid schemes, which seem to operate on the assumption that the needs of heterosexual elders are no different from those of LGBTI elders. Wider evidence indicates that LGBTI people can receive suboptimal care due to assumed heterosexuality and because of a lack of awareness and gaps in the knowledge base (Röndahl et al., 2006). When considering the ways in which institutions of care and support in South Africa still bear resemblance to the raced and classed inequalities created by the apartheid/colonial system, it becomes clear that the challenges facing LGBTI elders goes beyond sexual orientation and gender identity. These marginalised positionalities intersect with multiple axes of difference to bring to light a very specific lived experience on the African continent.

(South) African worldviews and experiences of ageing

South Africa occupies a geopolitical space that places it among both developed and developing countries (Nieman and Fouché, 2016). It is a member of the BRICS (Brazil, Russia, India, China and South Africa) grouping of developing nations and – while the country has some of the severest levels of inequality in the world – is it is also one of the leading economic powerhouse economies on the African continent along with Nigeria. Any understanding of issues of ageing and elder care must be cognisant of these issues and developing world and African ontologies. For example, Makiwane (2011), in exploring the type of family structures that support or hinder the process of growing old well in a South African context, points out that in many developing countries elders often live with their children which may be partially explained by both filial piety and by economic realities. However across the African continent such living arrangements, while beneficial in terms of care and support, also leave elders susceptible to abuse from family members (Bigala and Ayiga, 2104). Within this broader context, the care needs and related concerns of LGBTI elders remain unresearched and undocumented.

Looking at ageing and elder care from an African perspective foregrounds diverse conceptualisations and experiences of ageing across the continent. For example, in a study of the factors predicting mortality in older patients admitted to a medical intensive care unit in Morocco, Belayachi et al. (2012) note an inadequate number of doctors, lack of hospital beds and poorly maintained hospitals, all of which severely restricts access to quality healthcare services. In South Africa, Kalula (2011) explored the quality of healthcare for older people and found that overcrowding, lack of transport, inefficient appointment systems, inadequate public health education, understaffing, inadequate skills and a shortage of medication impeded their access to high-calibre healthcare.

In the global North, the evidence indicates that LGBTI people in old age may be more likely to live alone and less likely to have adult children or other kin to provide support. As a result they may be more likely to need formal care services but at the same time are fearful of approaching such services based on previous experiences of stigma and discrimination (Brotmanet al., 2003; Bristowe et al., 2018). There is as yet a paucity of research on this issue in South Africa and Southern Africa contexts although existing evidence indicates that discrimination against LGBTI people is prevalent in the provision of healthcare (Gillespie and Reygan, 2017).

Mamba and Ntuli (2014) highlight the key role of home-based care in their study of the experiences of home-based carers in Soweto in Gauteng province, South Africa. They found that home-based carers were generally involved in nursing care, household chores, and in counselling patients and their families among other activities. However challenges such as lack of resources, lack of training and support, lack of remuneration, the stigmatisation of patients by families, and patients not disclosing their diagnoses to significant others were reported as concerns by participants. Importantly, Mamba and Ntuli (2014) note that the inadequacies of the frail-health system impede the proper functioning of the home-based carer model and recommend a much greater focus on determining and supporting the needs of home-based carers who are a key resource in (South) African contexts in terms of delivery of care to older people.

In the city of Tshwane in Gauteng province, Bohman et al. (2010) found that older African people's experiences of old age were framed in a number of specific ways. For example, older people felt that the burden of care for elders was shared by those in the community regardless of family ties and that care was generally community based. Consequently, the resources for elder care came primarily from other community members, most of whom mostly rely on state support and state pensions (Bohman et al., 2010). Here also, shifting definitions of when old age starts reveal important insights into the political and social contexts in which people age in South Africa. For example, Bohman et al. (2010) found that old age was considered to begin on the date of receiving the old age pension from the state, which contrasts with the findings of Ramakeula et al. (2014) who found that old age was conceptualised among women in rural Vhembe, Limpopo province, as beginning on the cessation of menstruation. Overall, it is clear that the rapid urbanisation and changing cultural contexts of (South) African societies require much deeper engagement with understandings of ageing, old age and elder care needs (King, 2008).

A key lens in deepening the understanding of ageing, old age and elder care needs in the (South) African context is the concept of ubuntu and the role of the ancestors. The philosophy of ubuntu is encapsulated in the isiZulu expression *umuntu ngumuntu ngabantu* which roughly translated into English means 'a person is a person because of other people' or more figuratively 'I am because you are'. Ubuntu points to the fundamentally African philosophy of the interconnectedness of life and to the value of interdependence. The philosophy of ubuntu is closely linked to past generations, the ancestors and to the unseen forces of daily life. In this worldview older people are seen as mediators and interpreters of messages from the ancestors and also from the living to the ancestors. This role is seen as unifying and one that proves the elders are still influential in the family (Bohman et al., 2010), which arguably has a profound influence on conceptualisations of ageing, both at personal and community levels, as well as of personal experiences and expectations around growing older. In summary, the authors highlight a need for support of home-based care and the protection of older people outside of structures which are able to enforce the law. This is, again, even more pertinent in the case of LGBTI elders who could face additional marginalisation based on sexual orientation. The need to redefine the category of 'old', as informed by subjective and cultural norms, is also an important consideration when determining who should be eligible for support and care under this banner. When considering the hierarchical role of older people as influential links to the ancestors – which would be accorded a certain level of respect and prestige – it could be important to consider prejudice against LGBTI elders as a factor in negating such respect and creating a negative experience of ageing. This reveals yet another case for community-based care interventions that enforce the law outside of formal structures.

South Africa has the highest HIV/AIDS prevalence in the world and has the largest per capita anti-retroviral public health programme in the world (Hontelez et al., 2016). HIV/AIDS has affected all areas of society, including older populations, socially, economically and psychologically (Lekalakala-Mokgele, 2011). High HIV/AIDS prevalence places a heavy burden of care on older people who have to care for their children and grandchildren, and the elders become primary caregivers despite requiring care themselves. With shorter life spans (Nyirenda et al., 2012) in part resulting from the HIV/AIDS epidemic, the definition of what is considered old age in South Africa differs from elsewhere, especially from countries in the global North. In such a context, poverty combined with the lack of adequate and efficient healthcare makes the likelihood of institutionalised, private elder care an unreality for the majority of South Africans. These complexities and challenges related to ageing and elder care both in South Africa and across the continent are further nuanced when engaging with issues related to sexual orientation and gender identity.

LGBTI ageing in South Africa

The literature cited in this chapter has highlighted that ageing in (South) Africa can have various meanings and take on different forms. Important for understanding this conceptualisation of ageing is an intersectional lens. Race, class, gender, age, sexuality and gender identity are experienced differently depending on how each of these axes of difference are co-constructed and co-constituted by each other. Because constellations of oppression and privilege crystallise differently in a given situation, an intersectional lens is important for engaging the nuances and complexities that are bound to characterise any analysis of elder LGBTI lived experiences of care and support.

South Africa is one of the most unequal societies in the world and the distribution of wealth, resources and land ownership continues to substantially favour white South Africans with white, cis gender, heterosexual males at the top of a raced, classed and gendered hierarchy (Commey 2014; Akala and Divala 2016). This legacy is one of the most obvious remnants of white minority rule and the apartheid era, which continues in determining of the life courses of many. Therefore, many LGBTI people find themselves caught at the intersection of racism, classism and homophobia. Although embedded within the Bill of Rights, the Older Persons Act 13 of 2006 makes no explicit reference to best practice guidelines for the care of older members of the LGBTI community (Henderson and Almack, 2016). The limited research to date indicates that older people often do not follow up on their rights regarding end-of-life care (Henderson and Almack, 2016). Opportunistic infections still receive the bulk of focus in healthcare, with little attention given to LGBTI persons with ageing and other healthcare concerns. South Africa's public healthcare system is also under-resourced, which compromises the extent of services that can be offered, further compounded by a lack of competent staff and decisive leadership. Social work intervention in dealing with older LGBTI clients or older clients in general is also an area in need of focus. Retirement options for LGBTI persons is another aspect that is 'superseded by a lack of retirement options for the broader population' (Henderson and Almack, 2016: 275).

Although the constitution provides protection for minorities, many LGBTI persons still feel restricted in accessing their rights (Osche, 2011). As a white, middle-class lesbian participant over the age of 30 from Pretoria, South Africa, in Osche (2011: 7) pointed out:

> 'I think the constitution is amazing, but, like I have said to other people too, the reality is that legal protection does not necessarily translate into social acceptance because you sit with people's perception, their stereotypes, all of that that people have grown up with from political, religious and cultural perspectives.'

Another lesbian participant in Osche (2011: 7) stated "My take on it is the constitution is fantastic ... [but] in terms of the reality of implementation, in terms of how society behaves regardless of the constitution, is another problem."

An article by Hayward (2016) published in *Exit*, a South African online LGBTI newspaper, also highlights the raced and classed nature of LGBTI elder care. Speaking to issues of judgement, freedom of expression, exclusivity, leisure, childlessness, maintenance of large suburban homes, emigration and access to land, the concerns of the white, male and middle-class readership of this gay magazine speak to a limited view of the needs of the majority of LGBTI people in South Africa who do not have access to the resources required for such an investment (Hayward, 2016).

The literature and research on ageing in African contexts is almost completely silent in relation to sexual and gender minorities. Although the literature, highlighted previously, speaks to issues of class, gender and race there is no mention of the ways in which these intersect with sexual and gender identities. The work in promoting the rights of older persons has been mostly done by the Department of Social Development and the South African Human Rights Commission, but again there is no focus on sexual- and gender-minority ageing. There is also no link currently being made between Section 9 of the Constitution, the Older Persons Act 13 of 2006 and the Civil Unions Acts of 2006, which would be necessary in terms of the rights of married or civil partnered, same-sex couples to elder institutionalised care. Exploring the extent to which older LGBTI people access their rights and what social justice institutions in South Africa are doing to provide this information could also be useful in understanding the factors affecting the well-being of older queer people.

Conversations on LGBTI ageing and care

As part of a research project on LGBT ageing and care in two provinces in South Africa funded by the University of the Western Cape, we held a workshop in July 2016 to start conversations on the topic of LGBTI ageing and care. The session was attended by various representatives and activists of the LGBTI community and allies of the community. What emerged from the dialogue paints a first-hand account of how the issues of LGBTI ageing are lived in South Africa and the types of action required to promote the rights and care needs of LGBTI elders. The group supported the idea of framing the issue of elder LGBTI care in South Africa as a social justice issue along with a clear acknowledgement of the intersectional realities of the people who make up this group, thereby recognising various constituencies and vulnerabilities along multiple axes of oppression. Questions were raised concerning what needs to be done in order to create the conditions in which LGBTI elders may access and exercise their rights more freely. A second important theme was the need to foreground stories and experiences of older LGBTI people themselves so as to deepen our awareness and understanding of LGBTI ageing within an African context. Embedded within these narratives are the implications of culture, norms, socioeconomic status, quality of healthcare and subjective experiences of ageing for LGBTI Africans.

We also conducted an interview with an older lesbian couple (we use the pseudonyms 'Patricia' and 'Carmen' in quotes given below), who are both political and feminist activists, on their experiences of ageing and care. Falling into the 50–65 age group and being mixed race, the couple represent a particular constellation of privilege and marginalisation. The interview highlighted the intersectional issues of age, race, language, gender, sexuality and class among others and a number of key themes emerged. It is important to acknowledge that factors cited as protective were being middle-class, looking white, speaking a foreign language and living in a suburb with a family. The biggest vulnerability cited for both participants was being a woman. Although they do not form part of the most vulnerable demographics, what this reifies is that race, age, class, sexuality and gender do indeed play major roles in determining the life chances and shaping the lived experiences of people.

Among these was the loss of respect for older people which found expression in the ways in which older people, including older LGBTI people, are perceived and treated in South Africa. In general, the worth of women, especially older women, is gauged by the levels of care work they provide:

> 'The economic situation in the world makes it more difficult to have help for new families, then they start to be the responsibility of the old women. Old women need to look after their grandchildren, after the sick people – even if you are one of them it doesn't matter. That is good in one way, because you've got some place in the society but it's bad because you are doing the caregiving but not receiving it.' (Patricia)

When looking at the intersection of age and sexuality, both participants expressed that there is an erasure at play. The perception that older people are not sexual is held generally and even from within the LGBTI community there are views that LGBTI people are not supposed to age. This unrealistic expectation adds to the pressure on LGBTI people to present in a certain way, while still facing erasure and a loss of status in old age. In particular, it is the erasure of a sexual identity that is imposed on older people:

> 'LGBT is sexuality: it is sex, and old people and sex don't go together! When you have a very narrow way to see sexuality, or sexual orientations, or sexual identities you can do this kind of reading. This is not your identity: it's your sexual actions and when you're old you don't have sexual actions! I don't think it's something that is verbalised but it is entrenched in how to read these things. If I kiss Carmen, I am sweet. If you kiss your boyfriend, you are hot! Even if we are doing exactly the same thing.' (Patricia)

The issues of medical assistance and of recognition were also important ones. In a heterosexist society, same-sex partnership is often not considered to be legitimate, even if it is a legal union as is the case in South Africa where marriage equality was introduced in 2006. Despite same-sex marriage being legal in South Africa, Patricia and Carmen felt that in case of a medical emergency, they would not be believed to be each other's legal spouse and expected the administration to be unfairly challenging:

> 'If I have an event [that needs] medical intervention immediately then I need my partner to sign. With us it's

different, because it's a legal thing but even if it is a legal thing, the problem is being believed and proving that we're a couple.' (Patricia)

Both participants felt that healthcare provision for older people is generally grim in South Africa due to the fact that older people are not considered valuable to society once they reach older age. This loss of value makes them less likely to be the recipients of efforts to protect their health, and when this loss of value is coupled with the prejudice and stigma still directed towards LGBTI people the prospects of fair and equal treatment are even further reduced. As a result the potential for abuse at the hands of caregivers becomes a reality:

'Old people have less value so people don't care much because you are down on the scale but when you are an LGBT person you're even further down on the scale. The amount of care that you receive is less because your value is less and you are attacking the religion and tradition of society and they can feel that they – caregivers – have the right to make you suffer for that.' (Patricia)

Both participants felt that a general lack of understanding of the needs of LGBTI people generally, and of LGBTI elders in particulars, is evident in South Africa and needs to be addressed if older LGBTI people are to have access to care facilities that respect their rights to dignity:

'I think of the clinics that are very proud of all the LGBT messaging that they have on the walls and none of that has an old person in it. There isn't a picture with an old person in it, not even a middle-aged person: there are only young people. So the health facilities say "Yes, we're here for everyone!" but there would be a necessity for older LGBT people to feature in that. I think of trans issues and then what people think a body must look like, or can look like. If you think of nurses in care facilities who encounter patients who are male, for example, but still have a vagina, they're not going to want to have anything to do with that person. So what it means to the person is one thing but that nurse is totally unprepared.' (Carmen)

When considering care in the future, both Patricia and Carmen agreed that financial constraints would prevent them from accessing top quality care and that home-based care would be a more viable option. Even so, hired help would be difficult to fund, leaving them with the option of caring for each other or soliciting assistance from their children. If institutionalised care were to be explored, Patricia and Carmen feared that they would be separated and not acknowledged as a couple.

Conclusion

Much is yet to be known about the life experiences and care needs of older queer people in both South Africa and across the continent. Even in contexts such as South Africa where formal equality is guaranteed in the Constitution and in legislation, this has yet to translate into substantive equality, especially for more vulnerable and marginalised constituencies in sexual and gender communities. We highlighted some of the key issues related to elder care in some African contexts as a way to delineate the ways in which ageing and elder care needs are conceptualised and culturally embedded in the region. A combination of a philosophy of interdependence as manifest in ubuntu creates tensions in community contexts where the ravages of HIV/AIDS have left grandparents as the sole providers of care to their grandchildren. In South Africa, the colonial and apartheid legacy that perpetuates white privilege has also created a situation in which both medical insurance and many of the elder care facilities cater primarily for the needs of older white South Africans. The idea that children will look after their parents is a commonly accepted as a norm in the African context, but in such settings research has shown that older people can become susceptible to multiple forms of abuse when disempowered by an unequal care dynamic. However there is also a long history of agency among elders, evident in many communities across the continent, where elders hold influence as bearers of wisdom.

We therefore recommend, cognisant of deep, ongoing and seemingly intractable and worsening inequalities on the grounds of class and race, that a community-based model of elder care, including care for LGBTI elders, be further researched and supported by stakeholders, policy makers and government departments. We caution against a model of separate care for LGBTI communities as this would further perpetuate the race and class privilege already so prevalent in South Africa with such services being tailored to the needs of affluent, white gay men and, perhaps, lesbian women. Rather we advocate for a more inclusive and socially just project of elder care in South Africa that speaks to the needs of all communities, regardless of class, that is grounded in African conceptualisations and understandings of ageing and elder care. In a time of global, reactive backlash against sexual and gender minority rights, as evident at the time of writing in the Trump administration in the US and in the introduction of homophobic legislation in a number of African states, it becomes all the more important to guard against already vulnerable cohorts within sexual and gender minority communities being further stigmatised. In resource-constrained and developing economy contexts, as is the case in South Africa, programmes and interventions must necessarily consider locally grounded, culturally relevant and effective approaches that engage with the lived realities and their understandings of ageing, elder care and of sexual and gender diversity, particularly from African perspectives.

References

Akala, B. and Divala, J. (2016) 'Gender equity tensions in South Africa's post-apartheid higher education: in defence of differentiation', *South African Journal of Higher Education*, 30(1): 1–16.

Belayachi, J., El khayari, M., Dendane, T., Madani, N., Abidi, K., Abouqal, R., Zeggwagh, A.A. (2012) 'Factors predicting mortality in elderly patients admitted to a Moroccan medical intensive care unit', *Southern African Journal of Critical Care*, 28(1): 22–7.

Bigala, P. and Ayiga, N. (2014) 'Prevalence and predictors of elder abuse in Mafikeng Local Municipality in South Africa', *African Population Studies*, 28(1): 463–74.

Bohman, D.M., van Wyk, N.C. and Ekman, S-L. (2011) 'South Africans' experiences of being old and of care and caring in a transitional period', *International Journal of Older People Nursing*, 6(3): 187–95.

Bristowe, K., Hodson, M., Wee, B., Almack, K., Johnson, K., Daveson, B.A., Koffman, J., McEnhill, L. and Harding, R. (2018) 'Recommendations to reduce inequalities for LGBT people facing advanced illness: ACCESSCare national qualitative interview study', *Palliative Medicine*, 32(1): 23–35.

Brotman S., Ryan B. and Cormier, R. (2003) 'The health and social services needs of gay and lesbian elders and their families in Canada', *The Gerontologist*, 43(2):192–202.

Commey, P. (2014) 'South Africa's landless blacks: Why does the impasse continue?', *New African*, https://newafricanmagazine.com/news-analysis/long-reads/south-africas-landless-blacks-impasse-continues/2/.

du Preez, L. (2015) 'Frail care: what you should know', *IOL News*, www.iol.co.za/business/personal-finance/frail-care-what-you-should-know-1860431.

Gillespie, N. and Reygan, F. (2017) 'Enhancing healthcare services for sexual and gender minorities in Africa: more inclusive policies needed', *HSRC Review*, 15(3): 25–6.

Hayward, G. (2016) 'The Family Farm – a better way to grow old gay', *Exit*, quoted in Mason, C.L. (ed) (2018) *Routledge Handbook of Queer Development Studies*, London: Routledge.

Henderson, N. and Almack, K. (2016) 'Lesbian, gay, bisexual, transgender ageing and care', *Social Work/Maatskaplike Werk*, 52(2): 267–79.

Hontelez, J.C., Tanser, F.C., Naidu, K.K., Pillay, D. and Bärnighausen, T. (2016) 'Health care utilization in rural South Africa: a population-based cohort study', *Plos ONE*, 11(7): 1–15.

Kalula, S.Z. (2011) 'The quality of health care for older persons in South Africa. Is there quality care?', *ESR Review*, 11: 22–5

King S.V. (2008) 'Introduction to the journal of cross-cultural gerontology, special issue on aging and social change in Africa', *Journal of Cross Cultural Gerontology*, 23: 107–10

Lekalakala-Mokgele, E. (2011) 'A literature review of the impact of HIV and AIDS on the role of the elderly in the sub-Saharan African community', *Health SA Gesondheid*, 16(1): 1–6.

Makiwane, M. (2011) 'The burden of ageing in South Africa', *ESR Review*, 12(1): 20–1.

Mamba, S.T. and Ntuli, B.E. (2014) 'Activities and challenges in caring for chronically ill patients: experiences of home-based carers in Soweto, South Africa', *African Journal for Physical, Health Education, Recreation and Dance*, 1(2): 409–19.

Nieman, G. and Fouché, K. (2016) 'Developing a regulatory framework for the financial, management performance and social reporting systems for co-operatives in developing countries: a case study of South Africa', *Acta Commercii*, 16(1): 285.

Nyirenda, M., Chatterji, S., Falkingham, J., Mutevedzi, P., Hosegood, V., Evandrou, M. and Newell, M. (2012) 'An investigation of factors associated with the health and well-being of HIV-infected or HIV-affected older people in rural South Africa', *BMC Public Health*, 12(1): 259–72.

Ochse, A. (2011) '"*Real* women" and " *real* lesbians": discourses of heteronormativity amongst a group of lesbians', *South African Review of Sociology*, 42(1): 3–20.

Perold, A. and Muller, M. (2000) 'The composition of old age homes in South Africa in relation to the residents and nursing personnel', *Curationis*, 23(1): 87–94.

Ramakuela, N.J., Akinsola, H.A., Khoza, L.B., Lebese, R.T. and Tugli, A. (2014) 'Perceptions of menopause and aging in rural villages of Limpopo Province, South Africa', *Health SA Gesondheid*, 19(1): 1–8.

Röndahl, G., Innala, S. and Carlsson, M. (2006) 'Heterosexual assumptions in verbal and non-verbal communication in nursing', *Journal of Advanced Nursing*, 56(4): 373–81.

Tregenna, F. and Tsela, M. (2012) 'Inequality in South Africa: the distribution of income, expenditure and earnings', *Development Southern Africa*, 29(1): 35–61.

Woolman, S. (2015) 'Understanding South Africa's aspirational Constitution as scaffolding', *New York Law School Law Review*, 60(2): 283–95.

Part 4
Health and well-being

Part 4: introduction

There are strong associations, both culturally and sociologically, between ageing, health and well-being. Moreover, multiple research studies have indicated that the health and well-being of older people intersects with gender and sexuality, and that disparities are observed based on majority/minority status and other inequalities. The three chapters in this section all take those issues as a starting point for exploration.

Chapter Twelve, by Mark Hughes, explores the intersection of ageing, gender and sexualities by examining quantitative studies of the health and well-being of older lesbians, gay men and bisexual (LGB) people. Hughes notes that intersectional studies that employ quantitative methods are rare, despite the possibility that quantitative studies have for uncovering, at a broad level, the sorts of structural-level inequalities that intersectionality theory identifies as of central importance. In the chapter, Hughes synthesises data from six large-scale studies, conducted in Australia, the UK and the US, while simultaneously noting that it is important when drawing conclusions from quantitative research to be conscious of methodological limitations. Indeed, Hughes emphasises that much of the research synthesised in the chapter takes identity categories as taken-for-granted variables, although he also makes recommendations that more intra-categorical intersectionality, the differences within and between older LGB people, could be captured.

The following chapters in this section of the book then focus on specific groups of older men. Chapter Thirteen focuses on those with so-called 'erectile dysfunction' and in Chapter Fourteen, gay and bisexual men living with prostate cancer.

In 'Questioning the sexy oldie: masculinity, age and sexuality in the Viagra era', Raffaella Ferrero Camoletto examines shifts in older masculinity, from the 'sexually retired' to the 'sexy oldie', in an era dominated by Viagra and the medicalisation of sexual potency in later life. Ferrero Camoletto uses data from a research project she conducted in Italy, which explored how medical experts, in dealing with their ageing male patients' sexual problems, both adopt and question currently available narratives of ageing, gender and sexualities. As such, the chapter shows how medical experts, including urologists, sexual counsellors and endocrinologists among others, use their authority to create ideas about 'respectable' sexuality in later life for heterosexual men. Hence, the chapter further adds to our understanding about the intersection of power with ageing, gender and sexuality in the construction of older men's sexual health and well-being.

The final chapter in the book, Chapter Fourteen by Julie Fish, examines the experiences of six gay and one bisexual man, aged between 43 and 69 years, who had received diagnoses of prostate cancer. Illustrating the importance of discourses of sexuality with notions of masculinity, particularly hegemonic masculinity, Fish shows how the men understand and renegotiate their sexualities in relation to cancer by drawing on an intra-categorical intersectional approach, which focuses on the fine-grained analysis of differences within social categories by exploring their complexity and nuance. In this respect, Fish's chapter differs from that of Hughes, who examines the broader dynamics of an intersectional approach, but her chapter provides equally important insights into experiences of illness, health and well-being.

TWELVE

Health and well-being of lesbians, gay men and bisexual people in later life: examining the commonalities and differences from quantitative research

Mark Hughes

Introduction

While the complexities and intersections of age, gender and sexualities can be difficult to capture in quantitative studies, findings from quantitative research do relate to majority experiences and general patterns within populations, and hence are important sources of knowledge. However, with the frequent aggregation of people into one LGBT (lesbian, gay, bisexual, transgender and gender diverse) category there is a risk that quantitative research misrepresents the diverse issues and needs of LGBT people.

This chapter argues that careful analysis of quantitative findings is needed to ensure that diversity is respected. Because the focus of much quantitative research is on sexuality, the experiences of transgender, intersex and gender diverse people are not specifically examined here. Instead the chapter centres on the intersection of gender, sexuality and ageing for lesbians, gay men and bisexual (LGB) older people and explores some of the commonalities and differences across these groups in the quantitative findings from international research on health and well-being.

Research on the health and well-being of LGB people

Over the past couple of decades there has been increasing research evidence that LGB people face particular health conditions at an elevated rate compared with the general population. In particular, large probability-based studies and meta-analyses have consistently identified LGB adults as facing an increased risk of most mental health conditions, including depression, anxiety and suicidal ideation (for example, Cochran and Mays, 2009; Lewis, 2009; Chakraborty et al., 2011). Some specific physical health issues are also more prevalent among LGB people. For example, lesbians and bisexual women report higher rates of alcohol and tobacco use (Burgard et al., 2005) and obesity (Simoni et al., 2016) than their heterosexual counterparts. And in all regions of the world, HIV prevalence is substantially higher among men who have sex with men, compared with the general adult male population (Beyrer et al., 2012). Despite these findings there has, until recently, been a major gap in understanding of LGB older people's health and well-being.

Unfortunately, the research on the health disparities faced by LGB people has also been limited by the common treatment of identity categories as unidimensional and independent (Bowleg, 2012). Those calling for an intersectional approach to understanding health disparities have stressed the need to examine social categories as 'multiple, interdependent and mutually constitutive' (Bowleg, 2012: 1268). For Crenshaw (1991) an intersectionality approach involves analysing the structural patterns of inequality that lead some people, because of their membership of multiple social groups, to be more marginalised than others. It also involves examining the political dimensions involved in multiple group membership where one aspect of a social identity (for example, 'race') is perceived to be in conflict with another (for example, gender), as well as representational intersectionality where the intersection of membership of different social groups renders individuals invisible or disparaged culturally.

In a review of literature on LGB ageing, Fredriksen-Goldsen and Muraco (2010: 406) called for research on the intersection of various social categories to 'better understand the variation that exists both between and among individuals in the older LGB populations'. More recently these authors articulated a health equity promotion model that incorporates an understanding of how intersecting membership of different social groups shifts over the life course to present risks to, as well as enable resilience in, individuals' health (Fredriksen-Goldsen et al., 2014). Thus the potential for developing an intersectional understanding of the health disparities faced by older LGB people seems considerable. Nonetheless, there are some challenges to overcome in applying this approach to quantitative research. The next section documents some of these challenges and explains the basis for selecting the studies discussed in the remainder of the chapter.

Intersectionality, LGB older people and quantitative research

It is relatively uncommon to find quantitative research that uses an intersectionality approach to directly inform its research question. Rather, most studies use the approach as an underpinning perspective to help explain multiple group membership (Shields, 2008). Thus, it can be challenging to draw conclusions about the intersections of ageing, gender and sexuality (among other dimensions) for LGB older people where the research questions did not specifically seek to examine these intersectionalities. Bowleg (2008) pointed to the ways both quantitative and qualitative research can assume that identities and experiences of marginalisation are additive rather than intersectional. Despite a grounding in intersectionality, Bowleg noted that even in her own research participants were sometimes led to rank order their identities. Reliance on demographic questions to gain insight into an individual's identities can also be fraught – with little sense gained as to what these identities mean to the person in different contexts.

Despite these challenges, quantitative research – even that conducted outside of an intersectional approach – can inform intersectional understandings. While qualitative research offers unique insights into diverse and intersecting biographies and life experiences (for example, Cronin et al., 2010), it lacks the population-level analysis that is possible via quantitative research, and which is so valuable for policy makers. This speaks to Crenshaw's (1991) identification of the need to examine structural intersectionality, alongside political and representational intersectionality. This population-level analysis can illustrate powerfully the systematic subordination of some people on the basis of multiple and intersecting social categories (such as, in Crenshaw's example, the disproportionate exposure of immigrant women of colour in the US to domestic violence). At the individual, family and community levels these patterns may be obscured – it may not be until the disparities are identified at the population level, through quantitative research, that the structural disadvantage experienced by some people is exposed. For McCall (2005) analysis of patterns of inequalities across categories – while challenging to fully achieve or report on in quantitative research – is a necessary accompaniment to more qualitative intersectional methodologies that scrutinise category boundaries or examine neglected intersections between different identity categories. In this way, analysis of existing quantitative research on comparing the health differences across groups/categories of LGB older people will provide an – albeit incomplete – account of the intersectionalities of health disparities faced by them.

The remainder of this chapter discusses findings on the health disparities faced by LGB older people to shed light on some of the structural intersectionalities affecting them. There is an emerging body of literature on LGB health disparities, but for the purposes of this chapter a relatively small number is focused on to illuminate the issues. The criteria for selecting these studies were that they: 1) employed quantitative methods; 2) compared across LGB (male and female) categories; 3) included an analysis of older age; 4) had a sufficiently large sample (for example, 1,000 and over) to enable meaningful comparison across categories, and 5) were published within the last 10 years (that is, from 2007–17). It is recognised that these criteria have limited the range of studies that can feasibly provide insight into the health disparities faced by LGB older people, but nonetheless the studies selected do provide a basis from which tentative conclusions can be drawn. It is also important to note that what follows is not a systematic review or meta-analysis of these research studies, and that the approach taken does not conform to such review conventions.

Commonalities and differences across intersecting LGB older people categories

Six studies were identified as meeting the above criteria (Table 1): one from Australia (Private Lives 2), one from the UK (Stonewall) and four from the US (CHIS 2001–7, CHIS 2003–7, Caring and Aging with Pride, WA-BRFSS). Three employed, or made use of existing, probability-based samples (CHIS 2001–7, CHIS 2003–7, WA-BRFSS). One comprised a mixed sampling approach combining representative and convenience samples (Stonewall). The remainder drew on non-probability convenience samples that were reliant on distribution of surveys via LGBT media, commercial venues, service providers and community networks. The population-based studies pooled data across multiple years of the delivery of the surveys (CHIS 2001–7, CHIS 2003–7, WA-BRFSS). Some focused solely on those in the upper age groups, typically aged 50 and over (CHIS 2003–7, Caring and Aging with Pride, Stonewall, WA-BRFSS), while others included adults across the life course and compared across age categories (CHIS 2001–7, Private Lives 2).

It is important when drawing conclusions from quantitative research to be conscious of methodological limitations. With respect to the research drawn on here, a key limitation of the CHIS 2001-7 and

Table 1: Studies examined

Study source	Abbreviation	Country	LGB participants	Heterosexual comparison group	Sampling	Variables reported on in chapter	Source document
California Health Interviews Surveys – pooled data 2001, 2003, 2005, 2007	CHIS 2001–7	US	5,548 LGB people aged 18–85: 1,281 lesbians, 1,436 bisexual women, 2,037 gay men, 794 bisexual men	157,673 heterosexual people aged 18–85: 92,379 women, 65,294 men	Stratified random sampling of non-institutionalised population	• Smoking • Drinking • Physical activity	Boehmer et al. (2012)
California Health Interviews Surveys – pooled data 2003, 2005, 2007	CHIS 2003–7	US	1,052 LGB people aged 50–70: further breakdown not available in source document	Number of heterosexual participants aged 50–70 not specified in source document	Stratified random sampling of non-institutionalised population	• Physical health status • Disability • Hypertension • Diabetes • Psychological distress	Wallace et al. (2011)
Caring and Aging with Pride study 2010	Caring and Aging with Pride	US	2,362 LGB people aged 50+: 1,462 gay men, 773 lesbians, 127 bisexual people	No substantive heterosexual comparison group*	Convenience sample based on distribution by 11 agencies across the nation	• General physical health • Disability • Obesity • Depression • Anxiety	Fredriksen-Goldsen et al. (2011) Fredriksen-Goldsen et al. (2015)

(continued)

Table 1: Studies examined (continued)

Study source	Abbreviation	Country	LGB participants	Heterosexual comparison group	Sampling	Variables reported on in chapter	Source document
LGB Later in Life study 2010	Stonewall	UK	1,036 LGB people aged 55+: further breakdown not available in source document	1,050 heterosexual people aged 55+	Partial representative sample based on YouGov panel survey, supplemented by convenience sampling of LGB individuals via Stonewall	• Smoking • Drinking • Physical activity • Depression • Anxiety	Guasp (2011)
Private Lives 2 study 2011	Private Lives 2	Australia	3,245 LGB people aged 16–89: 1,314 lesbians, 1,479 gay men, 324 bisexual women, 128 bisexual men	No substantive heterosexual comparison group*	Convenience sample – distributed via community organisations, events & media	• Psychological distress • Diagnosis of mental health condition • Resilience	Leonard et al. (2015)
Washington State Behavioral Risk Factor Surveillance System study – pooled annual data 2003 to 2010	WA-BRFSS	US	1,531 LGB people aged 50+: 562 lesbians, 291 bisexual women, 463 gay men, 215 bisexual men	94,608 heterosexual people: 57,466 women, 37,142 men	Stratified random sample of non-institutionalised adults	• Disability • Smoking • Drinking • Obesity • Physical activity • Cardiovascular disease • General mental health	Fredriksen-Goldsen et al. (2013)

* Study included a small number of transgender, intersex or gender diverse people who identified as heterosexual, but this group was not used as a basis for comparison with the heterosexual population.

CHIS 2003-7 studies is that the California Health Interviews Surveys did not control for HIV status (Wallace et al., 2011). A further limitation is the lack of longitudinal data and the necessity of multiple studies to pool data across the multiple years (Boehmer et al., 2012). Convenience samples are limited of course by their non-representative nature and concern has been expressed, in particular, about a tendency to under-sample lesbians and bisexual women. The Stonewall study, for example, has been criticised for under-representing women (who comprised about 30% of the sample) and particularly older women (Westwood, 2013). In the studies reported on in this chapter there were also limitations in the reporting of the findings due to small numbers in some categories, even given the relatively large sample sizes. Further, comparison across different studies was limited not only by use of different measures, but also because not all source documents consistently presented data comparing different age groupings (for example, Private Lives 2 did not present obesity data across age groups). Despite these limitations, comparing findings from these studies does provide insight into the emerging trends in quantitative research on the health and well-being of LGB older people, the commonalities and differences in these findings, and the extent to which structural intersectionality across different categories is evident.

General physical health and disability

With respect to general physical health status and disability, a series of differences was identified across gender and sexuality categories. In Caring and Aging with Pride, bisexual men aged 50 and over were significantly more likely to report worse physical health (29%) compared with gay men (22%), lesbians (23%) or bisexual women (22%). CHIS 2003–7 revealed that, among people aged 50 to 70, gay and bisexual men had 1.24 greater odds of reporting fair or poor health status, compared with heterosexual men, while lesbians and bisexual women had 1.26 greater odds than heterosexual women.

Increased odds of disability among LGB older people were evident in both CHIS 2003-7 and WA-BRFSS. In the former, gay and bisexual men aged 50 to 70 reported 1.24 greater odds of disability than heterosexual men, while lesbians and bisexual women in the same age range had 1.32 greater odds of disability than heterosexual women. In WA-BRFSS, lesbians and bisexual women aged 50 and over had an odds ratio of 1.47 of disability (adjusted for age, income and education) compared with heterosexual women, while gay and bisexual men aged 50 and over had an adjusted odds ratio of 1.26 of disability compared with heterosexual men. In *Caring and Aging with Pride*, it appeared that lesbians (53%) and bisexual men (54%) were more at risk of disability than gay men (41%) or bisexual women (41%).

These findings suggest that LGB older people may experience elevated levels of poor physical health and disability compared with their heterosexual counterparts, and that among LGB people there is some indication that bisexual older men may be particularly at risk, in terms of both lower general physical well-being and disability, while lesbians also appear at greater risk of disability.

Health behaviours and related conditions

A series of health behaviours (for example, smoking and alcohol consumption) and related conditions (for example, obesity, diabetes and hypertension) may explain why LGB older people report lower general physical health and higher rates of disability than heterosexual people. With respect to smoking, the Stonewall study reported that 12% of LGB people aged 55 and over were daily smokers, compared with the same proportion of heterosexual people. The rate for those aged 70 and over was slightly higher among LGB people (6%), compared with heterosexual people (4%). These findings contrast with research from the US, which demonstrate substantially higher rates of smoking among LGB older people. For example, in WA-BRFSS, involving people aged 50 and over, the adjusted odds ratio of lesbians and bisexual women of being a current smoker was 1.57 compared with heterosexual women, while for gay and bisexual men it was 1.52 compared with heterosexual men. Broadly similar findings were reported in CHIS 2001–7. But in this study, there was more detail on how smoking patterns appear to vary across categories and in relation to age. For both lesbians and bisexual women, current smoking was reported less among those aged 50 and over than among those in the younger age group. However, for lesbians this remained at a significantly higher rate (45% more) than for heterosexual women, whereas for bisexual women aged 50 and over there was no discernible difference compared with heterosexual women. In contrast, it was bisexual men aged 50 and over who had a greater rate of being a current smoker (59%) compared with heterosexual men. Gay men actually had a slightly lower rate of being a current smoker than heterosexual men in this older cohort. These findings suggest that those at greatest risk of being a current smoker in later life are lesbians and bisexual men.

Mixed findings were apparent in relation to drinking behaviour. In the Stonewall study, more men than women reported that they drank alcohol every day or at least five to six times per week – with more gay and bisexual men reporting this (35%) than heterosexual men (25%). Nineteen per cent of lesbians and bisexual women reported drinking to this degree compared with 15% of heterosexual women. In WA-BRFSS, similar differences between LGB and heterosexual people were also apparent – with gay and bisexual men aged 50 and over 47% more likely (based on an adjusted odds ratio) to drink excessively than heterosexual men; and lesbians and bisexual women aged 50 and over 43% more likely to drink excessively compared with heterosexual women. In comparison, CHIS 2001–7 did not identify any significant differences between men according to sexuality in relation to binge drinking. With respect to having consumed alcohol in the past month, gay men aged under 50 were 70% more likely to have done this than heterosexual men in the same age range, but not more likely if aged 50 and over. Notably, in this study, lesbians' binge drinking was consistently greater than for heterosexual women across both age categories (an adjusted odds ratio of 1.72 for those aged under 50 and 1.74 for those aged 50 and over). For bisexual women aged under 50 the odds ratio was 1.74 but no differences were found between bisexual women and heterosexual women aged 50 and over. In relation to consuming alcohol in the past month the differences between lesbians and bisexual women and heterosexual women were most noticeable for those aged under 50 (odds ratios of 1.72 and 1.74 respectively) than for those aged 50 and over (1.25 and 1.03 respectively). Broadly the findings suggest that more LGB older people may be consuming alcohol than their heterosexual counterparts, but that this is likely to be in fewer numbers than among younger people. The results from CHIS 2001-7 suggest that binge drinking may be a particular concern among lesbians across the life course.

Obesity and physical activity were examined in a range of studies. With respect to obesity, in Caring and Aging with Pride, 34% of lesbians aged 50 and over were classified as obese (according to Body Mass Index), compared with 34% of bisexual women, 19% of gay men and 18% of bisexual men. In WA-BRFSS, lesbians and bisexual women aged 50 and over had increased odds (1.42) of obesity compared with heterosexual women, while gay and bisexual men aged 50 and over had lower odds (0.72) compared with heterosexual men. While WA-BRFSS did not identify any significant differences across the sexuality groups according to physical activity, other studies have pointed to a trend of greater physical activity among lesbian, gay and bisexual people compared with heterosexual people. In CHIS 2001–7 there were increased odds that lesbians had participated in moderate activity (1.41 aged under 50 and 1.11 aged 50 and over) compared with heterosexual women; for bisexual women there were increased odds of muscle strengthening in the younger age group only (1.25). With respect to men, only muscle strengthening activity was found to vary according to sexuality – with increased odds for gay and bisexual men aged under 50 (1.50 and 1.37 respectively) and aged 50 and over (1.17 and 1.48 respectively) compared with their heterosexual counterparts. More broadly, in the UK Stonewall study 35% of LGB people aged 55 and over reported they exercised at least five days per week, compared with 28% of heterosexual people. These findings suggest that while obesity is a particular issue for older lesbians and bisexual women, its negative effects may be mediated by higher rates of physical activity than is found among heterosexual women. And, more positively, there is some indication that older gay and bisexual men may fare better than heterosexual men in relation to both obesity and physical activity.

Other physical health conditions have not been as systematically addressed in the various studies, and the findings that have emerged do not appear to form a consistent pattern. CHIS 2003–7 examined rates of hypertension and diabetes and found that gay and bisexual men aged 50 to 70 had a 1.17 increased odds of hypertension but there were no significant differences among women. Similarly 1.28 greater odds of diabetes were apparent among gay and bisexual men aged 50 to 70 compared with heterosexual men and again no differences among women. Both these findings appear, on face value, to run counter to evidence that gay and bisexual men experience lower rates of obesity and are more physically actively than heterosexual men, although it could be accounted for by higher rates of smoking and alcohol consumption. More consistent with other findings was the report in WA-BRFSS that lesbians and bisexual women aged 50 and over faced increased odds of cardiovascular disease compared with heterosexual women in the same age range, although this was not evident in CHIS 2003–7.

General mental health and resilience

A series of measures has been used to assess the general mental health and psychological well-being of LGB older people, including the Kessler 6 (K6) and Kessler 10 (K10) measures of psychological distress and the SF-8 measure of health-related quality of life. When compared with their heterosexual counterparts, older gay and bisexual men appear to face a greater disparity in terms of general mental health than lesbians and bisexual women. For example, in CHIS 2003-7, involving people aged 50 to 70, gay and bisexual men experienced 1.45 greater odds of psychological distress (on the K6 measure), while lesbians and bisexual women experienced 1.35 greater odds (compared with heterosexual women). Similarly, in WA-BRFSS, lesbians and bisexual women had 1.40 greater odds of having poor mental health than heterosexual women, while gay and bisexual men had 1.77 greater odds than heterosexual men. While these findings suggest older lesbians and bisexual women fare better, the results may not be so clear cut. In most countries women generally report higher levels of psychological distress than men (Drapeau et al., 2012) and so the absolute rates for older lesbians and bisexual women may be comparable to that experienced by older gay and bisexual men.

In the Australian Private Lives 2 study, which included 3,245 LGB people aged 16 to 89, differences according to age were apparent. Across all four groups (lesbians, bisexual women, gay men, bisexual men) the rate of psychological distress was reported to be lower among older people than younger people. For instance, the mean psychological distress (K10) score for lesbians aged 16 to 24 was 23.6 while the mean score for those aged 60 to 89 was 15.2; for bisexual women the mean score for those aged 16 to 24 was 24.6 compared with 20.4 for those aged 45 to 59. Similarly, for men, the mean psychological distress score for gay men aged 16 to 24 was 22.0, while for those aged 60 to 89 it was 15.9. For bisexual men the mean score for those aged 16 to 24 was 23.5 compared with 17.7 for those aged 45 to 59. Unfortunately the results for bisexual people aged 60 to 80 were not reported due to the small number of respondents in these categories. Generally, though, these findings reflect patterns in the general population, which indicate that the prevalence of psychological distress is lower among older than younger sections of the population (Drapeau et al., 2012).

One of the other strengths of Private Lives 2 was its examination of resilience – reflecting Fredriksen-Goldsen et al.'s (2014) call for research that moves beyond deficit models of health and well-being of LGB people. In this Australian study, resilience was measured by the Brief Resilience Scale, which assessed respondents' ability to cope with stressful life events (with mean scores ranging from 1 to 5, with the higher score indicating greater resilience). Reflecting psychological distress patterns, resilience was reported to be greater among the older rather than younger groups – and this was reflected across all categories. For example, the mean resilience score for lesbians aged 16 to 24 was 3.1 compared with 3.7 for lesbians aged 60 to 89; while the mean score for bisexual women aged 16 to 24 was 3.0 compared with 3.2 for those aged 45 to 59. The mean score for gay men aged 16 to 24 was 3.3 compared with 3.6 for those aged 60 to 89; while the mean score for bisexual men aged 16 to 24 was 3.1 compared with 3.7 for 45 to 59 year olds. Thus the research findings appear to be consolidating that general mental well-being and resilience is better for older than young LGB people, even though it does not match that experienced by heterosexual people.

Mental health conditions

As might be expected given the findings on general mental health, LGB older people in the studies examined reported higher rates of specific mental health conditions than are typically found in the general population. In the UK Stonewall study of people aged 55 and over, 40% of lesbians and bisexual women reported ever receiving a diagnosis of depression, compared with 33% of heterosexual women. Similarly 34% of gay and bisexual men reported such a diagnosis compared with 17% of heterosexual men. In the US, Caring and Aging with Pride found depressive symptoms at a clinical level (on the Center for Epidemiological Studies Depression Scale) in 27% of lesbians aged 50 and over, 35% of bisexual women, 29% of gay men and 36% of bisexual men.

Similar findings are evident in relation to diagnoses of anxiety. In the UK Stonewall study, 33% of lesbians and bisexual women aged 55 and over had ever received a diagnosis of anxiety compared with 26% of heterosexual women, 29% of gay and bisexual men, and 13% of heterosexual men. In the US Caring and Aging with Pride study, 22% of lesbians aged 50 and over reported a diagnosis of anxiety compared with 34% of bisexual women, 22% of gay men and 24% of bisexual men. This greater prevalence of anxiety and depression among bisexual women was also reflected in the Australian Private Lives 2 study where the proportion of those diagnosed or treated for a mental health disorder (including depression and anxiety) in the previous three years for lesbians aged 45 to 59 was 34.3% and bisexual women 52.7%. In contrast, the proportion of gay men aged 45 to 59 was 28.9% and bisexual men 20.8%. This study also demonstrated that the rates of mental health diagnosis tend to be higher in younger than older age groups.

Broadly, the findings in relation to mental health suggest that LGB older people, like other LGB adults, experience higher rates of both general psychological distress and specific mental health conditions (such as depression and anxiety) than their heterosexual counterparts. While the disparity between the rates of gay and bisexual men compared with heterosexual men is probably greater, in general it appears that the elevated rates among same-sex attracted women and men are roughly similar. However, of particular concern is the indication in some studies that bisexual women and men experience rates of psychological distress and specific mental health conditions at a higher level than lesbians and gay men. What is also noticeable is that, similar to the findings in the general population, the rates of mental health issues are lower in the older compared with younger age groups. These findings do point to the strengths and resilience evident in the older LGB population.

Implications

For researchers, service providers and policy makers, drawing conclusions about the health disparities faced by LGB people across the lifespan, including in older age, needs to be done judiciously. Nonetheless, some commonalities and differences in the health and well-being of gay, lesbian and bisexual women and men compared with heterosexual people across age categories are apparent. The following appear to be some broad trends in relation to physical health:

1. There is some evidence that LGB older people experience in common lower levels of physical health and greater disability than heterosexual older people.
2. Older lesbians and older bisexual men appear to be more at risk of physical health challenges (including disability and smoking) than not only older heterosexual people, but also older bisexual women and older gay men.
3. It appears that the disparity between LGB people and heterosexual people in relation to alcohol consumption reduces with age, except possibly for older lesbians.
4. Older lesbians and older bisexual women experience in common higher rates of obesity even though there is some evidence that they are more physically active than older heterosexual women.
5. Older gay and older bisexual men in common appear advantaged in relation to obesity and physical activity compared with the rest of the older population.

With respect to mental health:

1. LGB older people appear to experience in common lower levels of mental health than their heterosexual counterparts.
2. There is some indication that mental health is experienced differently across the age cohorts with older cohorts faring better than younger cohorts. LGB people experience this in common with heterosexual people.
3. While the difference in psychological distress is greater between older gay and bisexual men compared with older heterosexual men than it is between older lesbians and bisexual women compared with older heterosexual women, it appears that same-sex attracted men and women experience about the same degree of higher psychological distress.
4. Despite this, there is some indication that older bisexual women and men experience in common specific mental health conditions (such as depression and anxiety) at a higher rate compared with lesbians and gay men.

Finally, while the findings on health differences are important, it is also important to stress that the vast majority of LGB older people do not experience physical or mental illness. Indeed, most people are as well as the rest of the population. And, as evidenced in the Australian Private Lives 2 study, there is substantial resilience among this population.

In each of the studies reported on in this chapter there were difficulties identifying differences and similarities across sexual minority groups (for example, lesbians compared with bisexual women, compared with gay men, compared with bisexual men) simply because the relatively small number of people in some of these groups makes statistical comparison impossible (Bourne et al., 2017). In some studies, same-sex attracted people were grouped together and in others it was not possible to compare across some age groups for each of the categories. The difficulties quantitative researchers have had in generating sufficient numbers of people in each category reduces the power to detect statistically significant findings (Burgard et al., 2005) and has hampered analysis of the heterogeneity of risk and resiliency factors among LGB people (Cochran and Mays, 2009). Lack of longitudinal data has also limited research progress, although a new Aging with Pride longitudinal study has been funded in the US, and the more consistent inclusion of sexuality variables in population-level studies suggests that the scope for longitudinal analysis will increase.

There are also issues in quantitative research with respect to the conceptualisation and operationalisation of key variables. Despite substantial literature on queer theory and more nuanced understandings of gender and sexuality – including recognition that some people view themselves as gender and/or sexually diverse – much quantitative research has relied on predetermined sexuality categories (such as lesbian, gay and bisexual) (Lewis, 2009), and this was the case for most of the studies reported on in this chapter. Concerns have also been expressed that important variables are missing in the analysis of LGB health disparities. For example, Lewis (2009) concluded that most prior research had divorced analysis of mental health outcomes from place-based variables, such as local support for LGB communities, which are increasingly identified as important in scholarship on sexual citizenship, space and health. Further, there remain doubts about the impact of HIV-status on the physical and mental well-being of gay and bisexual men, in particular, as HIV has commonly not been controlled for in population-based studies (Cochran and Mays, 2009).

There is a range of strategies that can be adopted to advance quantitative research on intersectionality and the health and well-being of LGB older people. With respect to quantitative research generally, inclusion of sexuality and gender diversity variables within large-scale population-based studies is critical. Concerns about the sensitivity of these questions and implications for non-response rates appear to be unfounded (Byles et al., 2013; Fredriksen-Goldsen et al., 2015). Longitudinal research is also needed to assess cohort differences over time as well as changes in experience across the lifespan. To enhance analysis of intersectionality, quantitative questions need to be designed to enable respondents to articulate the intersection of their identities, personal characteristics and community affiliations, rather than relying solely on traditional demographic variables. Researchers should also draw on more sophisticated measures that reflect the complexity and multi-dimensional nature of concepts such as gender, age, class and sexuality (Bowleg, 2008). There is a tendency in quantitative research to treat social categories in additive ways that, as Bowleg (2008) acknowledges, is almost impossible to avoid. Thus, quantitative research on intersectionality and the health and well-being of LGB older people will almost always need to be accompanied by detailed qualitative and narrative accounts of the lived experience of structural disadvantage alongside political and representational disadvantages.

Conclusion

The findings from these research studies provide substantial insights into the structural intersectionality that configures to marginalise groups of older LGB people. In this chapter commonalities and differences have been examined in relation to sexuality, gender and age. Other dimensions of identity, personal characteristics and group affiliation – such as ethnicity, geographical location, transgender and intersex background, and class – will intersect with sexuality, gender and age to influence individuals' experience. While additional quantitative research can be employed to examine these intersections in relation to structural intersectionality, qualitative research is also needed to explore the nuances of the range of ways LGB older people's identities, personal characteristics and community affiliations intersect to impact on their health and wellbeing.

References

Beyrer, C., Baral, S.D., van Griensven, F., Goodreau, S.M., Chariyalertsak, S., Wirtz, A.L. and Brookmeyer, R. (2012) 'Global epidemiology of HIV infection in men who have sex with men', *The Lancet*, 380(9839): 367–77.

Boehmer, U., Glickman, M., Milton, J. and Winter, M. (2012) 'Health-related quality of life in breast cancer survivors of different sexual orientations', *Quality of Life Research*, 21(2): 225–36.

Bourne, A., Davey, C., Hickson, F., Reid, D. and Weatherburn, P. (2017) 'Physical health inequalities among gay and bisexual men in England: a large community-based cross-sectional survey', *Journal of Public Health*, 39(2): 290–6.

Bowleg, L. (2008) 'When black + lesbian + woman ≠ black lesbian woman: the methodological challenges of qualitative and quantitative intersectionality research', *Sex Roles*, 59(5–6): 312–25.

Bowleg, L. (2012) 'The problem with the phrase women and minorities: intersectionality – an important theoretical framework for public health', *American Journal of Public Health*, 102(7): 1267–73.

Burgard, S.A., Cochran, S.D. and Mays, V.M. (2005) 'Alcohol and tobacco use patterns among heterosexually and homosexually experienced California women', *Drug and Alcohol Dependence*, 77: 61–70.

Byles, J.E., Forder, P.M., Grulich, A. and Prestage, G. (2013) 'It's okay to ask: inclusion of sexual orientation questions is feasible in population health surveys', *Australian and New Zealand Journal of Public Health*, 37(4): 390–1.

Chakraborty, A., McManus, S., Brugha, T.S., Bebbington, P. and King, M. (2011) 'Mental health of the non-heterosexual population of England', *The British Journal of Psychiatry*, 198(2): 143–8.

Cochran, S.D. and Mays, V.M. (2009) 'Burden of psychiatric morbidity among lesbian, gay, and bisexual individuals in the California quality of life survey', *Journal of Abnormal Psychology*, 118(13): 647–58.

Crenshaw, K. (1991) 'Mapping the margins: intersectionality, identity politics, and violence against women of color', *Stanford Law Review*, 43(6): 1241–99.

Cronin, A., Ward, R., Pugh, S., King, A. and Price, E. (2010) 'Categories and their consequences: understanding and supporting the caring relationships of older lesbian, gay and bisexual people', *International Social Work*, 54(3): 421–35.

Drapeau, A., Marchand, A. and Beaulieu-Prevost, D., (2012) Epidemiology of psychological distress, in L. L'Abate (ed) *Mental Illnesses: Understanding, Prediction and Control*, Rijeka: InTech, 105–34

Fredriksen-Goldsen, K.I. and Kim, H-J. (2015) 'Count me in: response to sexual orientation measures among older adults', *Research on Aging*, 37(5): 464–80.

Fredriksen-Goldsen, K.I. and Muraco, A. (2010) 'Aging and sexual orientation: a 25-year review of the literature', *Research on Aging*, 32(3): 372–413.

Fredriksen-Goldsen, K., Kim, H., Emlet, C., Muraco, A., Erosheva, E., Hoy-Ellis, C., Goldsen, J. and Petry, H., (2011) *The Aging and Health Report: Disparities and Resilience among Lesbian, Gay, Bisexual, and Transgender Older Adults*, Seattle: Institute for Multigenerational Health

Fredriksen-Goldsen, K.I., Kim, H-J., Barkan, S.E., Muraco, A. and Hoy-Ellis, C.P. (2013) 'Health disparities among lesbian, gay, and bisexual older adults: results from a population-based study', *American Journal of Public Health*, 103(10): 1802–9.

Fredriksen-Goldsen, K.I., Simoni, J.M., Kim, H-J., Lehavot, K., Walters, K.L., Yang, J., Hoy-Ellis., C.P. and Muraco, A. (2014) 'The health equity promotion model: reconceptualization of lesbian, gay, bisexual, and transgender (LGBT) health disparities', *American Journal of Orthopsychiatry*, 84(6): 653–63.

Fredriksen-Goldsen, K.I., Kim, H-J., Shiu, C., Goldsen, J. and Emlet, C.A. (2015) 'Successful aging among LGBT older adults: physical and mental health-related quality of life by age group', *The Gerontologist*, 55(1): 154–68.

Guasp, A. (2011) *Lesbian, Gay and Bisexual People in Later Life*, London: Stonewall.

Leonard, W., Lyons, A. and Bariola, E. (2015) *A Closer Look at Private Lives 2: Addressing the Mental Health and Well-Being of Lesbian, Gay, Bisexual and Transgender (LGBT) Australians*, Melbourne: Australian Research Centre in Sex, Health and Society, La Trobe University

Lewis, N.M. (2009) 'Mental health in sexual minorities: recent indicators, trends, and their relationships to place in north America and Europe', *Health & Place*, 15(4): 1029–45.

McCall, L. (2005) 'The complexity of intersectionality', *Signs: Journal of Women in Culture and Society*, 30(3): 1771–800.

Shields, S.A. (2008) 'Gender: an intersectionality perspective', *Sex Roles*, 59(5–6): 301–11.

Simoni, J.M., Smith, L., Oost, K.M., Lehavot, K. and Fredriksen-Goldsen, K. (2016) 'Disparities in physical health conditions among lesbian and bisexual women: a systematic review of population-based studies', *Journal of Homosexuality*, 64(1): 32–44.

Wallace, S., Cochran, S., Durazo, E. and Ford, C. (2011) *Health of aging lesbian, gay and bisexual adults in California*, Los Angeles, CA: UCLA Center for Health Policy Research.

Westwood, S. (2013) 'Researching older lesbians: problems and partial solutions', *Journal of Lesbian Studies*, 17(3–4): 380–92.

THIRTEEN

Questioning the sexy oldie: masculinity, age and sexuality in the Viagra era

Raffaella Ferrero Camoletto

Once one has seen the norms of female ageing reshaped by hormone replacement therapy, or the norms of ageing male sexuality reshaped by Viagra, the 'normal' process of growing old seems only one possibility in a field of choices, at least for those in the wealthy West. (Rose, 2001: 16)

Introduction

This chapter explores the intersections of gender, sexuality and ageing in the Viagra era, by investigating expert medical discourses and the social representations of men's sexual health problems. I will focus on the transformation of the social representation and cultural norms concerning ageing at the intersection of two cultural phenomena, which are analytically distinct but empirically intertwined: the 'positive ageing' imperative and the advent of sexuopharmaceuticals such as Viagra and its competitors. At the crossroads of these two phenomena we find a shift from 'asexual old age' or the 'sexually retired' ideal type to the new 'sexy oldie' (Gott, 2005) or 'sexy senior' ideal (Marshall, 2010).

Drawing on data from a recent mixed-method qualitative research project carried out in Italy, I will analyse how medical experts, dealing with their ageing male patients' sexual problems, both adopt and question currently available narratives of ageing, gender and sexuality. Following Johnson et al. (2016), I adopt the science and technology studies (STS) notion of enrolment, which provides a fruitful analytical tool to reconstruct how different roles are given to various actants involved in discourses defining age-related male sexual dysfunctions and their cures. More specifically, I will investigate how doctors, being called on and woven into a medical and pharmaceutical discursive framework, contribute to define new sexual techno-social subjectivities, like the 'forever functional' ageing man (Marshall and Katz, 2002). Physicians use various discursive strategies to construct a multifaceted profile of 'legitimate' patients by referring to cultural representations of gender and ageing according to their specific medical knowledge and to the marketing discourses about sexuopharmaceuticals. In so doing, the medical experts are embedded in a network that includes other human actors (that is, potential patients and their partners) as well as non-human actants (such as sexuopharmaceuticals). Within a pharmaceutical imagination (Marshall, 2010), medical experts are therefore enrolled in taking up a proactive role, supporting and promoting their ageing male patients in monitoring their own sexual health, but also in an authoritative position of defining the boundaries of legitimate medical problems and solutions. Analysis shows how medical experts thus reproduce, renegotiate and question what they perceive as a 'respectable sexuality' (Bertone and Ferrero Camoletto, 2009) and a 'mature masculinity' (Wentzell, 2013a, b).

'Positive ageing' and the Viagra revolution

In recent decades, gerontologists have critically discussed the notions of 'successful' and 'active' ageing because of the neoliberal focus on productivity and the consumeristic anti-ageing approach, both of which restrict our understanding of the ageing process (for a critical review, see Katz and Calasanti, 2015). However, the connection between the imperative of successful ageing and the myth of an ageless sexuality fostered by the innovation in sexual medicine and pharmacology seems to be a recent issue, due also to the delay in addressing the connection of ageing, sexuality and masculinity. Keeping one's body busy at any age has become a core condition of the new ageing script: to age successfully active resistance to the culturally designated markers of old age is required (Katz and Marshall, 2004; Gross and Blundo, 2005). Within this frame, lifelong sexual function becomes a primary component of healthy and successful ageing (Marshall and Katz, 2002), imposing the new imperative of sex for life (Katz and Marshall, 2003), and envisaging a virility surveillance (Marshall, 2010) by which the floppy penis (Calasanti and King, 2005) in ageing men is seen as a warning signal of a precariously abnormal condition, either current or future, requiring medically assisted restoration (Marshall, 2006, 2008).

So-called 'Viagra studies' have emerged as one of the research streams investigating men's ageing and sexuality within a medicalised frame (Loe 2001, 2004, 2006; Potts et al., 2004; Marshall, 2006, 2008; Wentzell and Salmeron, 2009; Sandberg 2013; Wentzell 2013a,

2013b). The advent of Viagra has triggered a radical transformation in the perception of age-related changes in male sexuality. In the pre-Viagra era a narrative of male sexual decline prevailed, in which ageing was associated with an inevitable reduction of erectile ability. Another marginal narrative was available, the 'progress' narrative, which interpreted the effects of decreased erectile ability as an opportunity to live a sexuality less centered on penetrative potency and to be open to experimentation with different sources and forms of sex (Potts et al., 2006). In the Viagra era both these narratives have largely been replaced by the sexy oldie narrative, which follows a forever-functional imperative that connects healthy ageing with lifelong sexual activity (Marshall and Katz, 2002). Progress is reinterpreted in terms of the restoration of youthful sexual skills or of the enhancement of hitherto never attained sexual performances (Potts et al., 2006).

Nevertheless, research on ageing men shows the persistence of the narrative of decline. A study on Mexican men (Wentzell, 2013b) shows how erectile dysfunction medication can endanger some men's notions of respectable sexuality and of mature and responsible masculinity. Sexual 'difficulties' are therefore redefined as sexual 'changes', thereby rejecting the pathologising label of sexual dysfunction (Wentzell and Salmeron, 2009). Some ageing men, however, do adopt the progress narrative (Potts et al., 2006; Wentzell, 2013b) as an alternative intimacy narrative (Sandberg, 2013), claiming that life-course-related sexual changes may be interpreted as an opportunity to experience different forms of sexual expression.

While providing a multifaceted picture of patients and consumers, Viagra studies often assign to medical experts the role of being part of the transmission chains of a top-down process of the medicalisation of sexuality. Questioning what is sometimes depicted as compliance by the medical profession with the new engine of pharmaceuticalisation, I try to explore the complexities of the medical experts' accounts in order to make space for negotiation and to challenge the medicalised frame *from within* the medical field.

Viagra and other sexuopharmaceuticals provide doctors with a discursive framework which assigns them distinct features, functions and tasks (Johnson and Åsberg, 2012). In this chapter I explore how Italian doctors, in the ways that they account for their practice in dealing with men's sexual problems in the Viagra era, not only construct their own position as experts, but also forge new sexual techno-social subjectivities, thereby reshaping gender and age relations. I will also show how physicians' positioning also enrols ageing male patients within the Viagra-mediated healthy sexual ageing discourse.

Italian context

In recent decades, adult heterosexual men's sexuality in Italy has become much more visible in the public arena, largely in the form of sexual scandals published in the media, the sexual affairs of Italian media tycoon and politician Silvio Berlusconi being an emblematic case. The medicalisation of male sexuality in the public sphere is another means of such visibility, appearing as a scientifically grounded and therefore more socially legitimate new public discourse on masculinity.

Since the beginning of the 21st century, insistent social campaigns – partly due to the banning of direct-to-consumer advertising of prescription drugs in Europe – have started to problematise the plurality of dimensions of male sexual lifestyles and life courses and to endorse adjustment through medical treatments and pharmaceutical devices. These social campaigns, promoted by professional associations of physicians (urologists, andrologists, sexologists and others) and supported, in most cases, both by institutional bodies (including the Ministry of Health in Italy) and pharmaceutical companies, aim both to inform the general population about the diffusion of male sexual dysfunctions and to illustrate available effective medical treatments. In so doing, they contribute to positioning male sexual health as a new public issue, and thus to constructing both the masculinity to be 'fixed' and the new forms of medical expertise legitimised to treat it (for a previous analysis of these campaigns, see Ferrero Camoletto and Bertone, 2012).

Methodology

I have drawn on the following diverse empirical material, collected in a recent mixed-method qualitative research project (2010–15) on the medicalisation of male sexuality in Italy: the main national awareness campaigns on male sexual health websites and videos;[1] websites on male sexual health managed by medical experts;[2] 19 interviews and one roundtable with experts in the field of sexual medicine (urologists, endocrinologists, sexologists, sex counsellors), recruited because of

---

[1] 'Amare senza pensieri' in 2008–9; 'Amico andrologo' since 2009; 'Basta scuse' in 2010; 'Chiedi aiuto' in 2012; 'Uomo e salute' in 2013.

[2] www.pianetauomo.eu, promoted by SIU (Italian Urological Society); www.prevenzioneandrologica.it, promoted by SIA (Italian Society of Andrology); www.lillyuroandrologia.it, promoted by Lilly pharmaceutical company.

their involvement in these campaigns;[3] and interviews with two groups from product development (uro-andrology treatments) and marketing managers, all from leading pharma companies Menarini and Lilly.

For the purpose of the chapter, I will focus on the in-depth interviews and the roundtable with the medical experts. The interviews, lasting from 30–40 minutes to one-and-a-half hours, have been fully transcribed and submitted to open and axial coding procedures with Atlas.ti software. Following a thematic analysis (Braun and Clarke, 2006), I identified how doctors raise the issue of ageing as a core dimension when defining who the 'legitimate patient' is in the medical discourse on pharma-mediated male sexuality. The same thematic analysis and attention to the definition of the legitimate patient was applied when dealing with the roundtable transcription.

Age matters: in search of the legitimate patient

Clinical literature on erectile dysfunction and its treatment identifies a critical point in the expansion of sexuopharmaceuticals for recreational use and without medical prescription (for a review, see Smith and Romanelli, 2005). Doctors have therefore been called on to set the boundaries between the legitimate use of such drugs and their misuse or abuse. As a urologist stated, "we are not suppliers of pharmaceuticals at all costs", and medical experts have reacted by reaffirming their power to define the 'real' patient and therefore the criteria for defining the 'legitimacy of the cure'(Ferrero Camoletto and Bertone, 2017: 204).

In their search for shared and objective criteria to set boundaries for the 'authentic' – and hence legitimate – problem, patient and treatment, the medical profession has relied on cultural definitions of ageing, gender and sexuality. When discussing age-related changes in male sexuality,[4] physicians did not refer to the standard, pre-Viagra narrative of linear sexual decline, but mobilised and combined old and new narratives, depicting multiple profiles of typical patients.

The typical target for erectile dysfunction treatment is the ageing man: "the patient over 70 who, because of physical or physiological factors, is the normal and absolutely natural case, and suffers from erectile deficit due to hormonal deficiency" (George, 65, male

---

[3] The key limitation of the study was the small scale of the sample, which prevented us from taking more into account, for example, the influence of some of the structural dimensions, mainly the gender and age cohorts.

[4] In clinical literature a new pathological label has recently emerged, making reference to age as a key dimension: ARED (age-related erectile deficit).

urologist). Many doctors, welcoming Viagra as a therapeutic revolution, tended to blame the character of the "resigned old man, likely to hang up his boots" who says "my time has arrived, that's it" (Carmen, 55, female urologist). Critically, this patient was reinterpreted as the problematic expression of reluctance to ask for help and denial of the real problem. Such cultural and personal passiveness was seen in contrast to the ideology of positive ageing with its acknowledgment that nowadays it is possible to medically solve the problem.

Expert medical opinion acknowledges the older man's aspiration to retain lifelong sexual functionality. This is the legitimate characteristic of the new sexy senior, an older man "culturally ready to be part of the Viagra generation" (Eric, 54, male endocrinologist and sexologist), positively perceived as a compliant patient who accepts both the medical definition of his problem and the solution proposed.

> 'Old people in good health, they surely need it, so they can take the pill under medical prescription and have their performances ... people on average over 60 who still want ... I mean ... to have their say [about sex].' (Frank, 66, male sexual counsellor)

> '... the 80-year-old man who still wants what is his due, his bit of "how's-your-father" [smiling]. And he is cute [smiling].' (Stephen, 59, male endocrinologist)

The figure of the sexy senior, however, is ambiguous: while portrayed as positive, it can also become excessive and recall the character of the pathetic dirty old man (Walz, 2002), unable to accept age-related changes and chasing an impossible return to ideal youthful sexuality, thereby running the risk of becoming a sugar-daddy and thus to be mocked or condemned.

> 'Taking a step back into the past, a man of a certain age living in his family and accepting the idea of getting older, content with his old wife as a companion ... gradually sinking into old age ... boom! There is an explosion because he can use this drug, giving him the possibility to get back into the game again [laughing]. ... Men become old fools ... When they equate Viagra with "Now I can return to my twenties" ... Then, of course, things begin to fall apart. Why? ... Because ... because ... for many reasons, if nothing else because overall ageing takes place in any case,

so to become a sugar-daddy mocked by young girls who have clear ideas and intentions … This makes everything more painful.' (Andrew, 72, male urologist)

The ambivalent boundary between the positive sexy oldie and the shameful dirty old man opens up a legitimate discursive space for physicians to discuss the controversial aspects of the Viagra culture and the impacts of redefining ageing in between health and respectability. As the following paragraphs illustrate, in their accounts doctors swing between a strictly medical discourse on healthy ageing to one of a social and moral understanding of the ageing process.

Boundary making: between biological and biographical timings

Many of the physicians interviewed expressed concerns about their patients' searches for a pharma-mediated second youth, the 'Peter Pan syndrome' by which old men strive for artificial maintenance of typically youthful sexual skills.

'These drugs – and the campaigns and media too – make it impossible for the patient to get any older. … Therefore it becomes a disease; in the past, without the drug, people came to terms with it … so men cannot give up, therefore they need doping, they need Viagra to maintain these levels of performances. … It's the media's fault that, today, having a long-term relationship with someone you marry and you love is considered out of fashion … . Well, because of this kind of message men must do … must have an affair. Then, if at 50 I base my extramarital relationship only on sex, I will need Viagra – it's inevitable, but this doesn't mean I suffer from ED [erectile dysfunction] … I often have patients who are adolescent till their fifties.' (Jerry, 52, male urologist and sexologist)

Some physicians retrieved the narrative of decline. The imperative of always-and-forever-functional contrasts with natural biological timing, recalling the physiological limits of ageing to be acknowledged and accepted in order to come to terms with getting older. This naturalness of biological timing is linked to a moral timing, attributing a normative dimension to life-course changes and in turn attaining a respectable sexuality and a mature masculinity.

Medical experts then made the distinction between eroticism and legitimate sexual treatment, the latter aiming at re-establishing the 'right' sexuality for the 'right' age.

'We are here to try to make people and couples, first of all, feel better … . We are absolutely not available … for eroticism, that is, if the patient, as it happens, comes to tell me "When I was 20 to 30 my sexual activity was xxx, now that I am 60 it is only double x," I reply "That's it, thank you." I am not here to make a 60-year-old person go back to [being] 20. … You should always interpret the evolution of Mother Earth, ok, and sexuality should be consistent with what should be the right one for each age of life.' (Philip, 68, male urologist)

'Sexual health means normalcy. Then we must clearly explain what is normal, because … at 80 normalcy is something different from at 20, but … if the Heavenly Father gave us a certain hormonal stock there [must be reasons for it].' (Michael, 72, male urologist and geriatrician)

The overlapping of natural and moral timings is reinforced by religious references such as Mother Earth and the Heavenly Father. This religious repertoire is not surprising, since in Italy the most critical stand against the imperative of ageless sexuality has been taken up by Catholic medical groups that are fuelling the bioethical debate on health issues.[5]

The reference to a natural or normative age, however, does not fully solve the problem of clearly defining the boundaries of the legitimate patient and treatment. Since the meaning of ageing remains open to negotiation, medical experts resort to other dimensions to try to construct an undisputed definition to legitimise clinical practice.

Whose ageless sex? The coupledom imperative

In medical accounts, age is seen to intersect with another relevant variable: the type of relationship in which lifelong sexuality is enacted. The pharmaceutical aid is a socially and medically acceptable possibility

---

[5] For example, the first workshop on bioethics and sexual medicine on the theme 'The medicalisation of male sexuality' was held in 2004 at Ateneo Pontificio Regina Apostolorum, Rome, in cooperation with the Italian Society of Andrology.

if sex takes place within long-term heterosexual coupledom: the kind of couple that "has become aware of their sexuality, they want to live it all the way, till… without age limits, without saying 'Well, we are 70, what we have done is enough.'" (Stephen, 59, male endocrinologist)

But when ageing men are searching for sexual performances in order to keep up with the expectations of new and younger partners, in some medical accounts age intersects with a normative understanding of the life course concerning what kind of sexuality is 'appropriate' for every phase of a man's life. In such medical accounts, an adult or older man's respectable sexuality is enacted within a relational context, not within recreational sex, which is regarded as acceptable only for younger men. As with the Mexican older men described by Wentzell (2013a, 2013b), the Italian medical experts referred to a male life-course sexual script entailing a gradual shift from a youthful phase of sexual experimentation to one of mature masculinity in which men are expected to settle down in significant and long-term coupledom and to refocus on respectable or intimate sexuality (see also Bertone and Ferrero Camoletto, 2009; Ferrero Camoletto et al., 2015).

Such moral condemnation recalled two further dimensions: ethnicity and social class. It is the so-called 'caretaker effect', which blames the sex appeal of young Eastern European 'needy' women who seduce older men and trigger 'grey divorces' and 'Viagra widowhood'. "Now we find the care-taker effect – that is, before Viagra a 60 year old could not afford to run away with the young Ukrainian – forgive me the racist expression, a bit rude … now he can do it" (Eric, 54, male endocrinologist and sexologist).

The normative assumption about the relational context of pharma-mediated sexuality is based on the idea of a lifelong sexually active heterosexual couple. In this medical discourse the female partner is called on to undertake a double task: on the one hand, she is expected to keep herself sexually active and therefore to be interested in and available for sexual intercourse; on the other hand, she is required to undertake a supportive role, helping her male partner to cope with his sexual problems in order to restore couple harmony. If the female partner does not comply with this role, she is criticised for being dysfunctional or for being sexually passive or for boycotting sexual intimacy, thus impeding not only the success of the male's treatment but the restoration of their sexual happiness.

> 'Because the wife [says] "It doesn't matter, it's not a problem," so they start [out on the] wrong foot.' (Michael, male urologist and geriatrician, 72)

'She says "Giovanni, listen, we have been together for
40 years – let it go."' (Andrew, 72, male urologist)

Such female profiles are not only stigmatised but are also subject to
further medicalisation. Their lack of sexual interest and 'availability' can
mobilise different therapeutic solutions: a psychological therapy to face
intrapsychic problems, a relational therapy to manage the crisis of the
couple, or, the more common solution, resorting to pharmaceutical
devices to 'fix' the sexual 'problems' created by menopause.

Discussion and conclusion

With regard to the physicians' clinical experiences, we have seen how
they are called on to reproduce the dominant meanings of gender and
sexuality endorsed by medical and pharmaceutical discourses around
the advent of sexuopharmaceuticals (Johnson and Åsberg, 2012).
However, the issue of ageing seems to introduce a more disputed
dimension in the construction of the legitimate patient for sexual
medicine intervention. What emerges is an unresolved dialectic
between the recently advanced ageing script of the 'sexy oldie' and
the conventional script of mature masculinity and respectable sexuality.
This dialectic shows not only that doctors are not wholly enrolled in a
chain of transmission to promote Viagra and the discourse of successful
ageing, but also how they are able to negotiate their positioning and
contribute to shaping plural sexual subjectivities for ageing men.

As we have seen, Viagra and other similar drugs have fostered
the notion of ageless virility in which maintaining sexual potency
(measured according to penetrative capacity) is a signal of good health
and of positive/active/successful ageing. This dominant discourse
assigns doctors the role of supporting their older patients in taking up
the sexy oldie identity, and acknowledging that the new generation
of elders have both the right and expectation to maintain a good level
of sexual activity, thanks to pharmacological devices.

Through the doctors' discussions about their clinical practice with
ageing men we have also seen how room is made for a different
positioning, both for doctors and patients. By refusing to accept a
consumeristic approach to sex with its unrealistic dream of never-
ending sexual youth, physicians can claim to be maintaining their
social role as gatekeepers of sexual health and respectable sexual ageing.
Moreover, doctors also seem to call older men to order by linking
their understanding of a healthy and respectable sexual ageing to the
notion of male self-control. From the sexy oldie perspective, the

point is to (re)gain pharma-mediated control over the body against the 'pathological' ageing process (Katz and Marshall, 2003). Physicians are able to make reference to another discursive resource, the maturing masculinity discourse (Wentzell, 2013a, 2013b), where control means moral self-mastery in men's self-containment of excessive and deviant drives to instead settle down to family life and long-term loving and sexually active relationships.

In the effort to define legitimate patients and treatments, the medical profession seems to fall into the trap of what Jones and Higgs (2010) called a normalisation of ageing through a moralisation of health. In the medical discourse, to escape the 'dark side' of the notion of the sexy oldie ageing men are required to channel their desires and their bodies, in order to live up to the ideal of mature masculinity and respectable sexuality (Wentzell and Salmeron, 2009). Medical accounts, in their ambivalent definition of the 'functional age' at the intersection of biological and biographical trajectories, are emblematic of the 'contradictions of "post-ageist" discourses and practices that promise to liberate bodies from chronological age, while simultaneously re-naturalising gender in sexed bodies' (Marshall and Katz, 2012: 222).

Few medical experts fully challenge the myth of an ageless sexuality by acknowledging that there are contextual variabilities of sexual functioning, and of sexual desire itself (Ferrero Camoletto and Bertone, 2017). Separately from the research on patients we found traces of counter-discourses among physicians, which tended to neutralise suggestions of contextual variability. When, in a dedicated online forum for experts in the field of male sexual health, I submitted the case of a patient who refused the pharmacological treatment for the reason that he had discovered new satisfactory sexual practices, the only feedback I received neutralised such a possible reading by interpreting the patient's position as that of being resistant to the therapy due to misinformation and fears.

Healthy ageing is reconciled with a narrow understanding of 'respectable sexuality' (Wentzell, 2013b): what seems left out in medical accounts is really a progressive narrative of sexual ageing: making room for older men, and their partners, to come to terms with the sexual changes that occur across the life course and to redefine and accommodate more appropriate and satisfying forms of emotional and physical intimacy (Sandberg, 2013).

References

Bertone, C. and Ferrero Camoletto, R. (2009) 'Beyond the sex machine? Sexual practices and masculinity in adult men's heterosexual accounts', *Journal of Gender Studies*, 18(4): 369–86.

Braun, V. and Clarke, V. (2006) 'Using thematic analysis in psychology', *Qualitative Research in Psychology*, 3(2): 77–101.

Calasanti, T. and King, N. (2005) 'Firming the floppy penis: age, class, and gender relations in the lives of old men', *Men and Masculinities*, 8(1): 3–23.

Ferrero Camoletto, R. and Bertone, C. (2012) 'Italians (should) do it better? Medicalisation and the disempowering of intimacy', *Modern Italy*, 17(4): 433–48.

Ferrero Camoletto, R. and Bertone, C. (2017) 'Medicalized virilism under scrutiny: expert knowledge on male sexual health in Italy', in A. King, A.C. Santos and I. Crowhurst (eds) *Sexuality in Theory and Practice: Insights and Critical Debates from Europe and Beyond*, London: Routledge.

Ferrero Camoletto, R., Bertone, C. and Salis, F. (2015) 'Medicalizing male underperformance: expert discourses on male sexual health in Italy', *Salute e Società*, XIV(1): 183–205.

Gott, M. (2005) *Sexuality, Sexual Health and Ageing*, Maidenhead: Open University Press.

Gross, G. and Blundo, R. (2005) 'Viagra: medical technology constructing aging masculinity', *Journal of Sociology & Social Welfare*, 32(1): 85–97.

Johnson, E. and Åsberg, C. (2012) 'Enrolling men, their doctors, and partners: individual and collective responses to erectile dysfunction', *Science & Technology Studies*, 25(2): 46–60.

Johnson, E., Sjögren, E. and Åsberg, C. (2016) *Glocal Pharma: International Brands and the Imagination of Local Masculinity*, London/New York: Routledge.

Jones I.R. and Higgs P.F. (2010) 'The natural, the normal and the normative: contested terrains in ageing and old age' *Social Science & Medicine*, 71(8): 1513–19.

Katz, S. and Marshall, B. (2003) 'New sex for old: lifestyle, consumerism, and the ethics of aging well', *Journal of Aging Studies*, 17(1): 3–16.

Katz S. and Marshall B.L. (2004) 'Is the functional 'normal'? Aging, sexuality and the bio-marking of successful living', *History of the Human Sciences*, 17(1): 53–75.

Katz, S. and Calasanti, T. (2015) 'Critical perspectives on successful aging: does it "appeal more than it illuminates"?', *The Gerontologist*, 55(1): 26–33.

Loe, M. (2001) 'Fixing broken masculinity: Viagra as a technology for the production of gender and sexuality', *Sexuality and Culture*, 5(3): 97–125.

Loe M. (2004) *The rise of Viagra: how the little blue pill changed sex in America*, New York: New York University Press.

Loe, M. (2006) 'The Viagra blues: embracing or resisting the Viagra body', in D. Rosenfeld and C. Faircloth (eds) *Medicalized Masculinities*, Philadelphia: Temple University Press: 21–44.

Marshall, B.L. (2006) 'The new virility: Viagra, male aging and sexual function', *Sexualities*, 9(3): 345–62.

Marshall, B.L (2008) Older men and sexual health: post-Viagra views of changes in function. *Generations*, 32(1): 21–7.

Marshall, B.L. (2010) 'Science, medicine and virility surveillance: 'sexy seniors' in the pharmaceutical imagination', *Sociology of Health & Illness*, 32(2): 211–24.

Marshall, B.L. and Katz S. (2002) 'Forever functional: sexual fitness and the ageing male body', *Body & Society*, 8(4): 43–70.

Marshall, B.L. and Katz S. (2012) 'The embodied life course: post-ageism or the renaturalization of gender?', *Societies*, 2(4): 222–34.

Potts, A., Grace, V. M., Gavey, N. and Vares, T. (2004) 'Viagra stories': challenging 'erectile dysfunction', *Social Science & Medicine*, 59(3): 489–99.

Potts, A., Grace, V. M., Vares, T and Gavey, N. (2006) 'Sex for life'? Men's counter-rhetoric on 'erectile dysfunction', male sexuality and aging', *Sociology of Health & Illness*, 28(3): 306–29.

Sandberg, L. (2013) 'Just feeling a naked body close to you: men, sexuality and intimacy in later life', *Sexualities*, 16(3–4): 261–82.

Smith, K.M. and Romanelli, F. (2005) 'Recreational use and misuse of phosphodiesterase 5 inhibitors', *Journal of the American Pharmacists Association*, 45(1): 63–75.

Walz, T. (2002) 'Crones, dirty old men, sexy seniors: representations of the sexuality of older persons', *Journal of Aging and Identity*, 7(2): 99–112.

Wentzell, E. (2013a) *Maturing Masculinities. Ageing, Chronic Illness and Viagra in Mexico*, Durham NC/London: Duke University Press.

Wentzell, E. (2013b) 'Aging respectably by rejecting medicalization: Mexican men's reasons for not using erectile dysfunction drugs', *Medical Anthropology Quarterly*, 27(1): 3–22.

Wentzell, E. and Salmerón, J. (2009) 'You'll 'get Viagraed': Mexican men's preference for alternative erectile dysfunction treatment', *Social Science & Medicine*, 68(10): 1759–65.

FOURTEEN

Intersecting identities of age, gender and sexual orientation in gay and bisexual men's narratives of prostate cancer

Julie Fish

Intersectionality and health

Intersectionality is emerging as a key theoretical approach in health research, bringing a distinctive lens to understanding nuanced differences in health status, health experiences and health outcomes (Fish, 2008). This chapter draws on McCall's (2005) approach of intra-categorical complexity to examine the cross-cutting identities of age, gender and sexual orientation in the narratives of gay and bisexual (GB) men who took part in a study of their experiences of prostate cancer. Although McCall's (2005) typology of intersectionality has been widely cited (for example, Fish, 2008; Cronin and King, 2010; Monro and Richardson, 2010), I will first offer a brief overview. She identifies three approaches to intersectionality, which she conceptualises as anti-categorical, inter-categorical and intra-categorical intersectionality. In brief, anti-categorical approaches, such as queer theory, seek to dismantle identity categories. The second approach, inter-categorical complexity has constituted the most common analysis of power and subordination across social groups characterised by privilege and penalty. While this approach has usefully identified the differential experiences between the principal categories of race or gender, it is often the case that other marginalised social groups are homogenised. The contingent, temporal and risky nature of GB men's experiences are reflected in the titles of papers: men face the challenge of prostate cancer as they age (Asencio et al., 2009), the threat of sexual disqualification (Ussher et al., 2017), sexual dysfunction (Hartman et al., 2014) and are reported to experience worse health-related quality of life (Hart et al., 2011).

This chapter contributes to the developing field of intersectional approaches to men's health (Griffith, 2012) by drawing on an intra-categorical approach which offers a fine-grained analysis of differences within social categories by exploring their complexity and nuance. Such an approach seeks to complicate and critically engage with identity categories to reveal multiple and often conflicting experiences of power and subordination, and derives meaning 'from the partial crystallization of social relations in the identities of particular groups' (McCall, 2005: 1781).

In the next section of the chapter, I consider the wider social context to enable exploration of how the intersections of age, gender and sexual orientation may affect the lives of GB men and influence their lived reality of prostate cancer.

Age and ageing in the lives of gay and bisexual men

Prostate cancer is a disease which primarily affects men in their sixties or early seventies (Blank et al., 2009). Previous research has revealed that GB men are diagnosed at a younger age than other men (Wasserug et al., 2013), suggesting they may have to cope with the disease through mid-life with potentially longer-term and distinctive impacts on their quality of life. Biomedical approaches define 'successful ageing' in terms of limiting the impact of chronic disease on physical and mental capabilities (Bowling and Dieppe, 2005); a diagnosis of prostate cancer, then, might hinder successful ageing. Men with prostate cancer may undergo a range of treatments including surgery, radiotherapy and hormone therapy; while they are becoming more effective in extending life expectancy, they do have complex sequelae for men's physical, psychological and sexual well-being.

In public perceptions, GB men are sometimes depicted as sad and isolated individuals who are more likely to live alone (Robinson, 2016); moreover, in some GB male spaces they may feel excluded from the youth-oriented scene (Simpson, 2015; King, 2016). Psychosocial theories of successful ageing emphasise the development of psychological resources such as effective strategies in the face of changing circumstances and positive relationships with others. Although GB men did not have the benefit of feminist activism which developed social networks and solidarity among lesbian and bisexual women (Wilkens, 2016), they did mobilise highly effective campaigns in the fight against AIDS (Shilts, 1987). GB men over 50 comprise the cohort most likely to have been affected by the HIV/ AIDS pandemic and whose social networks have been damaged by multiple bereavements (Owen and Catalan, 2012). Moreover, they are the group affected by the penalties of privatised relationships enforced by the 1967 Sexual Offences Act which may have affected their sense of a publicly validated self. A framework informed by intersectionality emphasises both the threats and resilience for GB men in facing a life-threatening disease. Prostate cancer, because of the possibility of sexual 'dysfunction', may pose a singular threat to sexual identities, but GB men may be able to draw on psychological resources developed through their (previous) outsider status and the social relationships forged through activism around HIV/AIDS.

Gender and hegemonic masculinity

Prostate cancer is often assumed to be a couple's disease which those in heterosexual, married or long-term, monogamous relationships go through together (Asencio et al., 2009). The significance of spousal support is implied in titles such as 'getting through' rather than 'going under' (Emslie et al., 2009). The extensive literature on prostate cancer is permeated by discourses of hegemonic masculinity where men work to control their emotions and distance themselves from feelings of vulnerability. Within such hegemonic gender regimes, women perform the role of nurturers and carers, encouraging men to seek a diagnosis, making notes at medical consultations, supporting them to change their lifestyles (such as alcohol consumption), and taking responsibility for their husband's health. In a strategy described as emotional buffering, women colluded in their husband's silence, because interjecting with a question during a medical consultation stirred up men's emotions (Boehmer and Clark, 2001). In these accounts, women played a key role in doing emotional labour with, and on behalf of, men to promote their recovery. Moreover, the treatments for prostate cancer may bring life-altering physical and sexual consequences including urinary incontinence and erectile dysfunction which can affect a man's sense of masculinity. Within discourses of hegemonic masculinity, men deny the effects of these embodied changes on their relationships and are reluctant to discuss their symptoms with other men or seek help from healthcare professionals (Boehmer and Clark, 2001). These experiential and affective responses, shaped by social and cultural expectations of masculinity, can render invisible other experiences of prostate cancer. Speer (2001) argues that hegemonic masculinity constitutes a cultural category which men draw on in contingent, temporal and context-specific ways. In this way, notions of hegemonic masculinity may operate in a distinctive register for GB men. Wall and Kristjanson

(2005) have argued that collateral or subordinated masculinities allow for the expression of other, more nuanced, experiences. They pose the question: would a reframing of the construct of masculinity elicit other knowledge and experiences?

Sexual orientation

The heteronormativity underpinning the social organisation of care provides a structure which at times constrains or limits GB men's access to, or degree of comfort, in healthcare. The agential act of disclosure can enable GB men to reframe health communications, allowing them to bring their whole selves to the health encounter. But their interactions are often underpinned by an awkward choreography wherein GB men talk of fragmented patterns of disclosure (Fish and Williamson, 2016), highlighting the uneasiness during, in addition to the planning which preceded, the consultations with oncologists or other professionals. Structural or multi-systemic factors may influence access to cancer treatment and care including an individual's knowledge of symptoms and health-seeking behaviours, their sources of support from partners and friends, cultural norms including health beliefs and previous health-related experiences, and community factors such as support groups, availability of information and resources (Hutchinson et al., 2006). Previous studies have suggested that GB men experience significantly worse health-related quality of life than heterosexual men. Moreover, the standard tools used to assess quality of life may reflect the concerns of heterosexual prostate cancer patients (Lee et al., 2013).

In the substantial literature on prostate cancer, GB men's experiences have been largely overlooked. According to Wall and Kristjanson (2005), they have been included as participants in mainstream studies but excluded from the presentation and discussion of findings. As a consequence, GB men with prostate cancer have been described by researchers as a 'forgotten' (Latini, 2013); 'invisible' (Blank, 2005) or a 'hidden' population (Filiault et al., 2008).

The study discussed in this chapter has a small sample, as do a number of other studies of prostrate cancer and GB men, for example Filiault et al., (2008) three men, Thomas et al., (2013) 10 men, Hartman et al., (2014) six men. However, the intention of this chapter is to contribute to theory development rather than to make claims to represent the experiences of GB men with prostate cancer.

Methodology

Recruitment

The study was funded as a 12-month project by a local cancer charity; interviews were conducted between July and December 2014 (see Fish and Williamson, 2016). Purposive sampling strategies were adopted that included a range of community-based organisations, diverse media outlets and social media which are well established in qualitative research (Carter and Little, 2007). A project-designed flyer was utilised which summarised the aims of the study; potential participants contacted the researcher by mobile phone, email or social media and an initial discussion took place about the aims and purpose of the study. Participants were sent a participant information sheet, provided informed consent and gave brief demographic information before taking part in the study.

Participants

Seven GB men who had received a diagnosis for prostate cancer within the previous six months to five years were recruited to a larger qualitative study about cancer care (see Table 1). Inclusion criteria were that participants should self-define as gay or bisexual.

Data collection

Semi-structured interviews lasting between one–two hours took place in a location of the participants' choice, mainly their own homes or in university or other private offices; these were digitally recorded and transcribed verbatim. An interview topic schedule, designed in collaboration with a stakeholder group that included a gay man

Table 1: Participant details

Pseudonym	Age	Identity	Relationship status
1. Quentin	56	Gay man	Partnered
2. Karl	59	Gay man	Partnered
3. Noel	69	Gay man	Newly partnered
4. Tim	65	Bisexual man	Partnered (male)
5. Nathan	43	Gay man	Single
6. Craig	65	Gay man	Partnered
7. Norman	52	Gay man	Single

with prostate cancer, included broad, open-ended questions with the intention of facilitating diverse experiences of cancer treatment, care and psycho-social support.

Ethical considerations

Ethical approval was obtained from one of De Montfort University's Faculty Research Ethics Committee in December 2013. The study was conducted in accordance with the British Psychological Society, Code of Research Ethics (BPS, 2010). Participants were provided with full information to enable them to take part, confidentiality and privacy were assured and we obtained informed consent; a distress protocol was implemented and participants had the right to pause, reconvene or terminate the interview. All data was anonymised, participants were allocated a pseudonym and data was securely stored.

Thematic analysis

Initial meanings were generated from the data following immersive readings. A coding frame was devised using concepts relevant to an intersectional framework. The themes were then refined to make sure the 'overall story the analysis tells' reflects the data collected (Braun and Clark, 2006: 87).

Gay and bisexual men's embodied sense of self

Men do not simply have bodies; their bodies mediate their experiences of everyday lives. Embodiment refers to altered corporeality, but also the social and cultural contexts in which men inhabit their bodies in the world. Cancer is often conceived of as a disease affecting somatic health through the identification of risk factors, biomarkers and predisposing genes. Embodiment encapsulates how cancer affects the ways that men think and feel about their bodies. Rather than proposing a mind/body dichotomy, embodiment conceptualises their symbiotic relationship. In this theme, I reflect on men's embodied sense of self following treatment. Tim resists being positioned as an older bisexual man with prostate cancer by 'keeping quiet' about his illness until he has to tell people: "I am now a pensioner and I am probably looked at in a different light. I am an older man with cancer, oh dear, poor old thing. And I don't want to give myself that label" (Tim, bisexual man, aged 65).

Tim says he is looked at in a different light because of his age and possibly his employment status (pensioner), but the additional experience of prostate cancer means that he would be looked at with pity: "oh dear". Moreover, his embodied experience of the illness subtly alters his identity from a man to an object or a "thing". His personhood becomes at stake. He feels that the 'label' of cancer subsumes his other identities. Currently, his illness is being managed and he shows no visible signs of it; because of this, he can choose whether or when to adopt the cancer label.

In the men's narratives, prostate cancer has led them to develop a new sense of their bodies. Their talk is characterised by feelings of an altered body, of being highly sensitised to signs of further changes, they express a sense that they could not trust their bodies and feelings of vulnerability. Karl articulates his sense of physical vulnerability implied by his use of 'major' illness, but he also expresses disbelief in his sense of the surreal:

> 'I feel very vulnerable in comparison to how I used to feel. I've never been ill ill, I've had all the usual ailments but nothing really major, and I think this sort of, it took me by surprise and I think there's a feeling that you can no longer trust your body to do what you expected it to do. ... It still doesn't seem real when I say I've got cancer.' (Karl, gay man, aged 59)

Embodiment encapsulates the integration of the body and the mind in illness experiences. The changes wrought on the body are a constant reminder of illness so that prostate cancer is always an immediate and present experience even after treatment:

> 'It does make me think now ... because I was told if it's going to go anywhere ... it's going to go into my bones ... every time I get ... a twinge in my leg it feels like it's in my bones ... I am conscious of things on my body's inside. Does it [metastases] feel like that? I don't know. So you are permanently conscious about that kind of thing.' (Nathan, gay man, aged 43)

Previous (inter-categorical) research suggests that gay men have a greater fear of cancer recurrence (Hart et al., 2011); in the above data extract, this fear is expressed in intrusive thoughts which may be triggered by 'normal' bodily functions such as muscle spasms. Nathan has become more conscious of the internal workings of the body: "the body's inside" and his thoughts turn to self-care activities which may prevent recurrence of the disease.

Some of the men articulated a sense of bodily acceptance, but managing the side-effects of treatment, such as urinary incontinence, was a concern in daily living:

> 'I don't want to wear pads – I just don't want to do that …
> the bladder and bowel will always be weaker, so I have to
> work around that. So if I'm coming to a meeting … I don't
> eat and I don't drink … it impacts upon you psychologically.'
> (Quentin, gay man, aged 56)

Only one man articulated a sense that being open about identity had contributed to improved outcomes for cancer. His comfort about his identity in healthcare enabled him to cope better with the bodily impact of cancer:

> 'I've only been out probably about 10 years or something
> like that, I'm nearly 70 now, but if I wasn't [out] … if I had
> gone back to the old me, all that added stress I'm sure in
> my own mind it's, […] the outcomes of these treatments
> wouldn't have been so good.' (Noel, gay man, aged 69)

Tim, as the only bisexual man in the study, suggests that being comfortable about one's identity is reflected in a coherent sense of self:

> 'I know a number of bisexual men who are absolutely scared
> stiff of anybody finding out … I don't think they are right
> in their attitude, but because prostate cancer tends to be a
> middle-aged and elderly men's problem, it is a generation
> that is perhaps not comfortable in its own skin.' (Tim,
> bisexual man, aged 65)

In these narratives, men express a sense of vulnerability and heightened awareness of their bodies following prostate cancer treatment. In a previous study (Asencio et al., 2009) of gay men's *perceptions* of prostate cancer, younger men said they would choose treatments more likely to retain sexual functioning; while older men, being more focused on survival, would choose surgery to remove all trace of cancer. In the experiences reported here older men were also concerned by the impacts of treatment on their sexual relationships.

The concept of embodiment draws on notions of the 'sociological body' (Thomas-MacLean, 2005) wherein the body forms the means by which we live our identities in the world. Prostate cancer brings men's bodies into sharper focus: for some the body is consciously present in the mind. For others, strategies of accommodation form part and parcel of everyday life; for example, Quentin sought to prevent urinary incontinence by not eating or drinking before a meeting and taking a change of clothes.

Managing the emotional roller-coaster of prostate cancer diagnosis and treatment

In discursive representations of hegemonic masculinity, heterosexual men are not able to express their emotions, or allow themselves to feel fear, or acknowledge they need help (for example, Cecil et al., 2010). Instead, presumed heterosexual men put emotional distance between themselves and the implications of the diagnosis. In previous studies of spousal support, heterosexual women perform the necessary emotional labour by acting as a buffer between heterosexual men and their illness (Wall and Kristjanson, 2005). Asking for help is a challenge to masculinity as it undermines men's sense of 'mastery'; Norman suggests the lack of ability to ask for help limits his leverage of social support for cancer: "Being a man gets in the way of being a man with prostate cancer. I am not going to stop and ask for directions, I will die before I do that" (Norman, gay man, aged 52).

Norman recognises that, for himself and other men, being a man means that he cannot ask for directions as that would deny a crucial element of power and control invested in hegemonic masculinity, which not only prevents men from seeking support but also curtails the ability to share their emotions. For GB men who are already subordinated by hegemonic ideals, this would pose a further intersectional de-masculinisation of their sense of self. By contrast, Noel made the decision to tell people early in his diagnosis, unlike his sister who had a stiff upper lip (she died of breast cancer); he found reassurance in speaking to an ex-partner of a friend.

Meanwhile, Nathan, as a single gay man, perhaps with a smaller social network, struggles to find social support and a place to express his emotions:

'I think there's probably, the biggest thing is to me is that where do you go, who do you talk to? ... I looked round ... and there's nothing, you don't feel confident enough to go

> into places to ask … But there's nothing that's specifically said anything about cancer … if I hadn't seen on Facebook that there was a support group in [northern city] I probably would have been sat here thinking well who do I talk to? Is there somebody?' (Nathan, gay man, aged 43)

Nathan articulates a strong sense of being alone with the illness. Others have suggested that there are no sources of information for GB men with prostate cancer (Duncan et al., 2011). GB men without cancer, who were asked about sources of support for cancer, said that they would attend a mainstream support group believing that men undergoing treatment for prostate cancer would be welcoming of any man in the same situation (Blank et al., 2009). In many of the accounts here, the men said that the heteronormative environment of such groups militated against their engagement in them. They said they would not be able to express their feelings or seek support in such a group. This is partly because some heterosexual men struggle to express their emotions and do not talk to other men without their wives being present. But also discussing the implications of prostate cancer treatment in relation to anal sex was difficult in heteronormative environments.

In the early stages of the disease, not talking seemed to be a strategy where men in a coupled relationship were able to circumvent the biographical disruption posed by cancer to resume life as usual following the diagnosis (Bury, 1982). Quentin and his partner carried on as if nothing had happened, but he describes the period as a "very dark" and "scary" place. A number of men talked about the use of meditation or mindfulness as strategies in coping with their cancer, while others had drawn on learning through personal growth to be expressive of emotions rather than try to problem-solve:

> 'And heart circle is all about how do I feel, what do I want, no story, and nobody tries to fix me, even I don't try and fix myself I just say it the way that it is. And I found that so powerful and we were really good at it. And sometimes I would cry for three or four minutes and cry like a hundred yards in my heart not just in my head and in my eyeballs, like an elephant [roars].' (Norman, gay man, aged 52)

In this extract, Norman is able to articulate his profound emotional response to the disease and challenge his previous conceptions of his own sense of masculinity. The men in this study re-evaluated their lives and relationships, which brought a new focus on the things that matter. For Nathan, cancer meant that he no longer defers things and has found a "bigger drive in my life". Wall and Kristjanson (2005: 95) provide a critique of the tendency of previous studies to present hegemonic masculinity as unproblematised in prostate cancer narratives arguing that it has enabled the researchers to present their findings in a 'less complex form (men, after all, are just men)'.

Intimate and sexual relationships following prostate cancer

In the literature, prostate cancer is said to pose particular problems for GB men's sexuality and sexual behaviours due to the diversity of their 'sexual practices and sexual roles' (Asencio et al., 2009: 45). While this does foreground GB men's sexual needs as equally important to those of heterosexual men, it also perhaps tends to reinscribe historic assumptions of GB men as having an over-sexualised identity. The impact of treatment on men's sexuality and sexual behaviours featured in most of the narratives.

Erectile functioning can have different meanings for GB men due to the need for an erect penis in some forms of sex between men. Karl expresses his frustration at the lack of understanding by oncology professionals about the impact of treatment on his sexual relationships. He felt that professionals presented a picture of the treatment effects as "over sanitised", "over simplified" and "far too optimistic". He was told that he would feel poorly for two months, but that any erectile problems could be treated with Viagra. For GB men, the advice that you can resume sexual activity takes no account of men's sexual preferences and practices. While this may be an effective treatment in heterosexual relationships, where men can have insertive sex with a softer penis, anal sex requires a firmer erection. He turned to a public blog to counter the assumption that a 'soft orgasm' gives equal pleasure:

> 'I remember it was the Macmillan nurse who said to me about these soft orgasms, you know, they can be as good as everything you've experienced up until now. Well I've told her since they're crap. I actually wrote it in a blog and she read the blog before I'd told her and she said I remember that was me that said that to you. She said "I never realised." I think she and probably the doctor were being as honest as they could but I don't think they really understood.' (Karl, gay man, aged 59)

The absence of ejaculation, which the nurse had euphemistically described as "dry orgasms", may have a different impact on men's intimate relationships because of the intimacy associated with the exchange of semen during sex between men:

> '... amongst gay men there's this big thing about the actual show of cum. You can't do that anymore so that's gone as well.' (Karl, gay man, aged 59)

The notion of sexual disqualification did feature in some men's accounts of their feelings about sex and sexual performance. For Karl, previously, his sex life was 10 out of 10; now it's probably 2 out of 10.

Another man discussed how he and his partner had renegotiated sexual intimacy within their relationship:

> 'To start with the erectile thing wasn't too much of a problem, you modify things as you go along ... we have been together now for 22 years and to live with and love someone and share your life for that length of time and still be best friends you know life moves on, life has all sorts of twists and changes and turn arounds, and in both our lives quite a lot has changed. I think it would be a bit naïve to assume that things would stand still. And you take the ups and downs and make your modifications as you go along.' (Craig, gay man, aged 65)

For some GB men, open relationships present a way of addressing differing sex needs. By setting mutually agreed boundaries a partner can have sex with another man outside of the couple relationship; other men may choose to have multiple sexual relationships. Noel and his partner have come to a negotiated agreement about meeting sexual needs:

> 'There's been some testing times because with the treatments, although my libido is still there it's much, much reduced. In all honesty, I don't know if part of that is just because of my age anyway. And he's a younger guy but I recognise that he's got needs and we come more or less to an agreement. Well I am not going to be following his every move or anything like that, if he gets his needs met elsewhere, as long as he respects my point of view as well and up to yet that's working. Again I'm not saying that's

[pause], it's one of these things, things change with age and stuff like that.' (Noel, gay man, aged 69)

Norman is able to achieve sexual satisfaction through a change in his sexual behaviour and in how he thinks about sex:

'When my libido got switched off I thought that was the end of the world ... I thought I was in charge, my dick was in charge ... I don't think men realise how we are designed until it got switched off and I discovered sensuality, it's like shit I can have better sex without my cock getting in the way, I have never experienced that before.' (Norman, gay man, aged 52)

The changes following treatment may have different impacts on men's sexuality because of the importance of the prostate as an erogenous zone in sex for GB men; moreover the presence of an erect phallus and the exchange of semen are both intimate and erotic for many GB men. Alongside the sense of loss that Karl expresses, some men find resourceful ways of achieving sexual satisfaction by other forms of sensuality, as Norman has been able to do through his commitment to personal growth. For other men, accommodating these changes through open relationships or intimacy may take different forms in longer-term relationships.

Discussion

Intersectional approaches pay attention to 'privilege and penalty' (Bowleg, 2013) in the lives of GB men with prostate cancer. This data allows us also to understand men's strategies of resistance in coping with adversity. They are not privileged by heterosexual gender relations, but their narratives here suggest they draw on discourses of hegemonic masculinity in contingent and temporal ways. Norman had set up a support group for prostate cancer, but ('being a man') found that he was unable to ask for support for his own needs. Subsequently, by drawing on strategies for personal growth he was able to build resilience in coping with cancer in distinct ways. GB men in this small sample, did look to each other for emotional support.

The data presented in this chapter suggests that GB men's gender is problematised by other cross-cutting identities such as age and sexual orientation. The interaction of their multiple identities suggests that they 'do' gender (Butler, 1990) in subtly different ways and in the absence of gender relations wherein women perform the role of maintaining heterosexual men's health. GB men do not merely occupy the spaces left by hegemonic masculinity, but when they deploy hegemonic masculinity they do it differently from heterosexual men.

There were perhaps greater penalties expressed in the accounts of men who were single; Nathan articulated a sense of isolation in finding someone to talk to. There are wider implications for this data; there are only three cancer support groups in the UK which provide a vital function in GB men's recovery, but these are sustained by men who face a life-threatening illness in a voluntary capacity.

References

Asencio, M., Blank, T., Descartes, L. and Crawford, A. (2009) 'The prospect of prostate cancer: a challenge for gay men's sexualities as they age', *Sexuality Research and Social Policy*, 6(4): 38–51.

Blank, T. (2005) 'Gay men and prostate cancer: invisible diversity', *Journal of Clinical Oncology*, 23(12): 2593–6.

Blank, T.O., Asencio, M., Descartes, L. and Griggs, J. (2009) 'Intersection of older GLBT health issues: aging, health, and GLBTQ family and community life', *Journal of GLBT Family Studies*, 5(1–2): 9–34.

Boehmer, U. and Clark, J.A. (2001) 'Married couples' perspectives on prostate cancer diagnosis and treatment decision-making', *Psycho-Oncology*, 10: 147–55.

Bowleg, L. (2013) '"Once you've blended the cake, you can't take the parts back to the main ingredients": black gay and bisexual men's descriptions and experiences of intersectionality', *Sex Roles*, 68(11–12): 754–67.

Bowling, A. and Dieppe, P. (2005) 'What is successful ageing and who should define it?', *British Medical Journal*, 331: 1548–51.

BPS (British Psychological Society) (2010) Code of human research ethics, www.bps.org.uk/sites/default/files/documents/code_of_human_research_ethics.pdf

Braun, V. and Clarke, V. (2006) 'Using thematic analysis in psychology', *Qualitative Research in Psychology*, 3(2): 77–110.

Butler, J. (1990) *Gender Trouble: Feminism and the Subversion of Identity*. New York: Routledge.

Bury, M. (1982) 'Chronic illness as biographical disruption', *Sociology of Health & Illness*, 4(2): 167–82.

Carter, S.M and Little, M. (2007) 'Justifying knowledge, justifying method, taking action: epistemologies, methodologies and methods in qualitative research', *Qualitative Health Research*, 17(10): 1316–28.

Cecil, R., McCaughan, E. and Parahoo, K. (2010) "'It's hard to take because I am a man's man": an ethnographic exploration of cancer and masculinity', *European Journal of Cancer Care*, 19(4): 501–9.

Cronin, A. and King, A. (2010) 'Power, inequality and identification: exploring diversity and intersectionality amongst older LGB adults', *Sociology*, 44(5): 876–92.

Duncan, D., Watson, J., Westle, A., Mitchell, A., Dowsett, G. (2011) *Gay Men and Prostate Cancer: Report on an Audit of Existing Resources and Websites Providing Information to Men Living with Prostate Cancer in Australia, 2011*, Melbourne: Australian Research Centre in Sex, Health and Society, La Trobe University.

Emslie, C., Browne, S., Macleod, U., Rozmovits, L., Mitchell, E. and Ziebland, S. (2009) "'Getting through" not "going under": a qualitative study of gender and spousal support after diagnosis with colorectal cancer', *Social Science & Medicine*, 68(6): 1169–75.

Filiault, S.M., Drummond, M.J.N. and Smith, J.A. (2008) 'Gay men and prostate cancer: voicing the concerns of a hidden population', *Journal of Men's Health*, 5(4): 327–32.

Fish, J. (2008) 'Navigating queer street: researching the intersections of LGBT health', *Sociological Research Online*, 13(1), www.socresonline.org.uk/13/1/12.html

Fish, J. and Williamson, I. (2016) 'Exploring lesbian, gay and bisexual patients' accounts of their experiences of cancer care in the UK', *European Journal of Cancer Care*, 27(1): 1–13.

Griffith, D.M. (2012) 'An intersectional approach to men's health', *Journal of Men's Health*, 9(2): 106–12.

Hart, S., Coon, D., Kowalski, M. and Latini, D. (2011) 'Gay men with prostate cancer report significantly worse HRQOL than heterosexual men', *Journal of Urology*, 18: 68–9.

Hartman, M., Irvine, J., Currie, K.L., Ritvo, P., Trachtenberg, L., Louis A., Trachtenberg, J., Jamnicky, L., Matthew, A.G. (2014) 'Exploring gay couples' experience with sexual dysfunction after radical prostatectomy: a qualitative study', *Journal of Sex & Marital Therapy*, 40(3). 233–53.

Hutchinson, M.K., Thompson, A.C. and Cederbaum, J.A., (2006) 'Multisystem factors contributing to disparities in preventive health care among lesbian women', *Journal of Obstetric, Gynecologic & Neonatal Nursing*, 35(3): 393–402.

King, A. (2016) *Older Lesbian, Gay and Bisexual Adults: Identities, Intersections and Institutions*, London: Routledge.

Latini, D. (2013) 'Forgotten subgroups: prostate cancer in gay men', *Asia-Pacific Journal of Clinical Oncology*, 9:(Suppl. 1): 34 [abstract], https://onlinelibrary.wiley.com/doi/pdf/10.1111/ajco.12098_3.

Lee, T.K., Breau, R.H. and Eapen, L. (2013) 'Pilot study on quality of life and sexual function in men-who-have-sex-with-men treated for prostate cancer', *Journal of Sexual Medicine*, 10(8): 2094–100.

McCall, L. (2005) 'The complexity of intersectionality', *Signs: Journal of Women in Culture & Society*, 30: 1771–800

Monro, S. and Richardson, D. (2010) 'Intersectionality and sexuality: the case of sexuality and transgender equalities work in UK local government', in Y. Taylor, S. Hines and M. Casey (eds) *Theorizing Intersectionality and Sexuality*, Basingstoke: Palgrave Macmillan: 115–35.

Owen, G. and Catalan, J. (2012) '"We never expected this to happen": narratives of ageing with HIV among gay men living in London, UK', *Culture, Health & Sexuality*, 14(1): 59–72.

Robinson, P. (2016) 'Ageing fears and concerns of gay men aged 60 and over', *Quality Ageing Older Adults*, 17(1): 6–15.

Shilts, R. (1987) *And the Band Played on: Politics, People and the AIDS Epidemic*, London: Penguin.

Simpson, P. (2015) *Middle-Aged Gay Men, Ageing and Ageism: Over the Rainbow?*, Basingstoke: Palgrave Macmillan.

Speer, S.A. (2001) 'Reconsidering the concept of hegemonic masculinity: discursive psychology, conversation analysis and participants' orientations', *Feminism & Psychology*, 11(1): 107–35.

Thomas, C., Wootten, A. and Robinson, P. (2013) 'The experiences of gay and bisexual men diagnosed with prostate cancer: results from an online focus group', *European Journal of Cancer Care*, 22(4): 522–9.

Thomas-Maclean, R. (2005) 'Beyond dichotomies of health and illness: life after breast cancer', *Nursing Inquiry*, 12(3): 200–9.

Ussher, J.M., Perz, J., Rose, D., Dowsett, G.W., Chambers, S., Williams, S., Davis, I., Latini, D. (2017) 'Threat of sexual disqualification: the consequences of erectile dysfunction and other sexual changes for gay and bisexual men with prostate cancer', *Archives of Sexual Behavior*, 46(7): 2043–57.

Wall, D. and Kristjanson, L. (2005) 'Men, culture and hegemonic masculinity: understanding the experience of prostate cancer', *Nursing Inquiry*, 12(2): 87–97.

Wassersug, R.J., Lyons, A., Duncan, D., Dowsett, G.W. and Pitts, M. (2013) 'Diagnostic and outcome differences between heterosexual and non-heterosexual men treated for prostate cancer', *Urology*, 82(3): 565–71.

Wilkens, J. (2016) 'The significance of affinity groups and safe spaces for older lesbians and bisexual women: creating support networks and resisting heteronormativity in older age', *Quality Ageing Older Adults*, 17(1): 26–35.

Index

Note: Page numbers for tables appear in *italics*